"The American national story is a myth, built on a series of myths that Richard Hughes reveals in this critical book. *Myths America Lives By* is a book we all need in order to understand ourselves, to understand our nation, to understand White supremacy."

—**Ibram X. Kendi,** National Book Award-winning author of *Stamped from the Beginning: The Definitive History of Racist Ideas in America*

"Richard Hughes's *Myths America Lives By* was already required reading when it was released back in the pre-Trump era. With this update of his lacerating critique of the sordidness of American civil religion and other destructive myths, Hughes now indicts white supremacy as the foundational myth providing the most accelerant to those other myths that have burned through our history. Richard Hughes thinks hard and listens even harder to the historians, the scholars and, most of all, the prophets who understood the malignancy of white supremacy long before he did. The result is *Myths America Lives By: White Supremacy and the Stories that Gives Us Meaning*. Once again, Hughes' willingness to tell the truth about the myths we live by has put us all in his debt."

—**Tony Norman,** columnist, *Pittsburgh Post-Gazette*

"I have been under the tutelage of Dr. Richard Hughes since I was mentored by him in graduate school. He never ceases to challenge my easy assumptions, invoke history I do not know, and lift my vision to more elevated realms. Agree with him on every matter or not, I am better for having contended with him. How much we need voices such as his today."

—**Stephen Mansfield,** *New York Times* bestselling author of *The Faith of Barack Obama*

"It takes a whole lot of courage for white theologians and scholars to speak the truth about race. If we had more white theologians and religion scholars like Hughes who would break their silence about white supremacy and face it for what it is, we—together—could make a better world."

—**James H. Cone,** author of *The Cross and the Lynching Tree*

"In this provocative and prescient argument, Richard Hughes challenges us to re-think the fundamental framework around which we view our country, our leaders, our neighbors, and ourselves. Meticulously researched, this book represents not only extraordinary scholarship, but a powerful and timely call to have the courage to ask aloud the extent to which white supremacy has defined each of us. It is an essential, though as Hughes readily admits, controversial task. But one critical today in a rapidly changing America, an America clearly changing too fast for many, as we debate about who we are and what we will become."

—**Michael A. Anastasi,** vice president and editor, *The Tennessean*

"A fearless, well-researched, searing critique that shatters the underpinnings of white racial superiority in America and abroad."

—**Joseph Robinson Jr.,** president, Martin Luther King Leadership
   Development Institute

"*Myths America Lives By* is prophetic—not merely in the predictive sense, so evident in the first edition, but in the far more consequential sense of prophecy as calling us to repentance and to our better selves. This is a very fine book, offering both a searing critique and a summons to embrace our common humanity."

—**Randall Balmer,** author of *Redeemer: The Life of Jimmy Carter*

"This book is a critical examination of the ways in which we as Americans deceive ourselves regarding our history and our present. Hughes presents a compelling and convicting argument, demonstrating that recognizing and changing the myths that shape our shared lives is the only way for us to move forward. As this book details, the myth of white supremacy, and the accompanying sins of explicit, implicit, and systemic racism, has plagued our nation since its inception; it is time for us to construct a national identity that allows for full participation regardless of race, and deposes white supremacy from its position as an idol in our country."

—**Jim Wallis,** author of *America's Original Sin: Racism, White Privilege, and the Bridge to a New America* and editor-in-chief of *Sojourners* magazine

"The myth of white supremacy is the unrecognized enemy within. In *Myths America Lives By: White Supremacy and the Stories that Give Us Meaning*, Richard Hughes shows that the malignant notion that white people are superior to people of color is the grand myth that undergirds other myths we live by. In a smooth, clear narrative, Hughes moves through innumerable, precisely relevant, historical and religious sources. His argument, covering the sweep of U.S. history, is compelling and his conclusions disturbing."

—**Joel E. Anderson,** Chancellor-Emeritus and Scholar-in-Residence, Institute on
   Race and Ethnicity, University of Arkansas at Little Rock

"At the age of five, my clergy father took me to Little Rock, Arkansas to stand with nine black students as they tried to enter the doors of Central High School. I had no idea that I was witnessing history. All I remember is a moment when one of the students walked past me just as a white racist stepped forward to spit directly into her face. She did not blink in the face of this obscenity, but wiped her cheek and walked on. It would be many years before I fully understood the essential truth of this vitally important book—namely, that the myth of white supremacy is indeed the primal American myth, and that all our other myths are supported by it. We owe Richard Hughes a debt of gratitude for making it impossible to look away."

—**Rev. Dr. Robin Meyers,** author of *Spiritual Defiance: Building a Beloved Community of Resistance*

"In this era of Trump and ugly racist discourse it is easy for many responsible Americans to dismiss the rhetoric as foreign to their own values and integrity. In this magisterial expansion of his earlier path-breaking book *Myths Americans Live By*, Richard T. Hughes makes clear that such self-righteousness is a grave mistake. In beautifully-written, prophetic cadences Hughes calls on all of white America to examine themselves and see the painful truth that we are all infected with the highly contagious disease of white racism. Until this reality is faced squarely there can be no redemptive reconciliation. There is no other work that I am aware of that matches the wisdom of *Myths America Lives By: White Supremacy and the Stories that Give Us Meaning*."

—**Harry S. Stout,** Jonathan Edwards Professor of American Religious History, Yale University

"Hughes's thought-provoking *Myths America Lives By* is informed simultaneously by a personal and collective understanding of white supremacy that is essential to analyzing the interconnectivity of radicalization designed to permeate every aspect of life in the United States. In an era where increasingly lying is touted as a virtue, Myths challenges church, academy, and society to engage in a difficult but necessary dismantling of white supremacy as this country's national sin."

—**Angela Sims,** author of *Lynched: The Power of Memory in a Culture of Terror*

"In this major reworking of his valuable 2003 book, *Myths America Lives By*, Richard Hughes offers compelling evidence for the revelation (at least for most white Americans) that the pervasive but largely unacknowledged belief that white people are superior to black people stands at the heart of much of the dissonance and conflict in our national experience. In this time of heightened turmoil over race-related issues, the history and insight Hughes provides should enable faculty and students in American colleges and universities to see our country in a clearer light and to talk with each other with much greater understanding."

—**Joel Cunningham,** Vice-Chancellor Emeritus, Sewanee: The University of the South

"James Baldwin wrote in 1963 that 'everything white Americans think they believe must now be reexamined.' Perhaps it was the election of the appalling Donald Trump that has jarred an increasing number of thoughtful white American Christians to (re)examine the nature and depth of white American racism. Richard Hughes has done that reexamination humbly, and admirably, in this rewrite of his classic *Myths America Lives By*. He has now placed the myth of white supremacy at the center of his understanding of white American self-understanding, and has shown that white supremacism has inflected, and infected, all other American myths. He has done so, in large part, by listening very deeply to what black American leaders and writers have been saying all along. This book will cost Dr. Hughes many friends in white Christian America. It is a price worth paying. I strongly recommend this revised book. Every white Christian should read it."

—**David P. Gushee**, President, the American Academy of Religion

"Those who don't understand their history are destined to repeat it over and over again. If we want to break the cycle of American racism, we must confront our history and the myths that underlie it. Reading Richard Hughes's *The Myths America Lives By* is a good place to start. Well worth reading, and a useful primer for many college classrooms!"

—**Beverly Daniel Tatum**, author of *Why Are All the Black Kids Sitting Together in the Cafeteria? And Other Conversations about Race*

"Richard Hughes is a passionate truth teller. As an African American, I am grateful to him, a white person who is willing to present this clear analysis of the myth of white supremacy and all of its offsprings. This volume is a welcome resource to all who are laboring every day to forge the path to racial healing, justice, and reconciliation in America."

—**Catherine Meeks**, Executive Director, Absalom Jones Episcopal Center for Racial Healing

"In this enduring book, Richard Hughes breaks new ground and sharpens his efforts to make transparent the elusive freedom which has been rendered opaque by whiteness in the American imagination."

—**Raymond Carr**, assistant professor of theology and ethics, Pepperdine University

Myths America Lives By

Myths

America Lives By

SECOND EDITION

White Supremacy and the Stories that Give Us Meaning

RICHARD T. HUGHES

Foreword by **Robert N. Bellah**

New Foreword by **Molefi Kete Asante**

UNIVERSITY OF ILLINOIS PRESS
Urbana, Chicago, and Springfield

Library of Congress Cataloging-in-Publication Data

Names: Hughes, Richard T. (Richard Thomas), 1943–
    author. | Bellah, Robert N. (Robert Neelly), 1927–2013,
    writer of foreword. | Asante, Molefi Kete, 1942– ,
    writer of foreword.
Title: Myths America lives by: white supremacy and
    the stories that give us meaning / Richard T. Hughes;
    foreword by Robert N. Bellah; new foreword by Molefi
    Kete Asante.
Description: Second edition. | [Urbana, Illinois]:
    University of Illinois, [2018] | Includes bibliographical
    references and index.
Identifiers: LCCN 2018015287| ISBN 9780252042065
    (hardcover : alk. paper) | ISBN 9780252083754 (pbk. :
    alk. paper)
Subjects: LCSH: United States—History—Philosophy.
    | United States—Foreign relations—Philosophy.
    | United States—History—Religious aspects—
    Christianity. | National characteristics, American.
    | Nationalism—United States. | Myth—Political
    aspects—United States.
Classification: LCC E175.9 .H84 2018 | DDC 973—dc23
LC record available at https://lccn.loc.gov/2018015287

Ebook ISBN 978-0-252-05080-0

For Two of My Teachers

For Reverend Wayne Baxter
whose five little words,
"But I will help you,"
enlarged my world and
transformed my life.
(See "Conclusion")

And to honor the memory of
Professor James Noel (1948–2016)
whose twelve simple words,
"Professor, you left out the most
important of all the American myths,"
expanded my thinking, resulting in this
second edition of *Myths America Lives By.*

Most Americans are quick to condemn white supremacist organizations of every stripe. But few seem to discern the deeper problem we must address before we can rid ourselves of racism and racist behavior. That deeper problem is the topic of this book—the extent to which white supremacy has defined us all.

—Richard T. Hughes, September 2017

Contents

Foreword to the First Edition
by Robert N. Bellah   ix

Foreword to the Second Edition
by Molefi Kete Asante   xiii

Acknowledgments   xvii

1. The Great American Myths and a
   Different American Future   1

2. The Myth of the Chosen Nation:
   The Colonial Period   32

3. The Myth of Nature's Nation:
   The Revolutionary Period   60

4. The Myth of the Christian Nation:
   The Early National Period   82

5. The Myth of the Millennial Nation:
   The Early National Period   130

6. The Mythic Dimensions of American Capitalism:
   The Gilded Age   165

7. The Myth of the Innocent Nation:
   The Twentieth and Twenty-First Centuries   198

   Conclusion   239

   Index   243

Foreword to the First Edition

I have spent a good deal of my life thinking about the United States of America, its history, its role in the world, and above all its self-understanding in the light of religious belief. Since I have found it increasingly difficult to make sense of the changes that have occurred even in my own lifetime, I am happy to see that Richard Hughes is contributing so thoughtfully to a task that I have come to feel is almost beyond me. If we look at the history of our country in the last 250 years, we cannot but be truly amazed. In 1750 we were a set of thirteen small, sparsely settled, colonial dependencies at the fringe of what was fast becoming the greatest empire of the age. Our Declaration of Independence of 1776 was a presumptuous one in view of the enormous disparity in power between the American colonies and the home country. That we did indeed become independent in 1781 was due in no small part to the rivalry between Britain and the second-greatest colonial power of the day, France. We like to think that we gained our independence because of our own bravery alone, but it was an unlikely outcome had it not been for French assistance. Even after gaining our independence, we were a small country of no consequence in the larger world, and we very nearly lost our independence again during the War of 1812, the last time we suffered an attack on the continental United States before September 11, 2001.

During the nineteenth century, when we pushed our frontier across the continent and then, as a result of the Spanish-American War of 1898, gained a couple of overseas colonies (Puerto Rico and the Philippines), we still heeded the words of George Washington in his Farewell Address about avoiding "foreign entanglements." The Monroe doctrine, which attempted to declare the whole Western Hemisphere "off limits," so to speak, in the increasingly intense competition of the European powers for world empire, we saw as fending off foreign incursion more than creating an empire of our own. Though most Americans wanted to stay out of World War I, once we were drawn in we committed ourselves to it ferociously. But no sooner was it over than we withdrew once again into our cocoon. We even refused to join the League of Nations, the brainchild of our own President Woodrow Wilson, and isolationism was a powerful influence on American policy right up until Pearl Harbor.

Already by 1900 it had become evident that we were a world power, and our intervention in World War I was decisive. But for many Americans we were still that small agricultural nation of 1776, cut off, thank God, by two mighty oceans, from the corruption and fratricide of the Old World. World War II was in this regard a turning point. Although an undertone of isolationism exists in America even to the present day, from that time on most Americans knew we had to exercise leadership in the world, even if only for our own security. Soon after defeating world fascism, we took on the threat of world communism. The cold war for forty years brought us or our agents into every corner of the world outside the boundaries of the communist nations themselves. We called the noncommunist world the "free world," overlooking the dictatorial nature of many of the regimes we sponsored, and we saw ourselves as the leader of this free world, a far cry indeed from the role that Washington's Farewell Address had envisioned for us.

In 1989 the door on which we had been pushing for forty years suddenly and unexpectedly collapsed: There was no longer a communist world; the evil empire had vanished. It is true that there were a few remnant communist states around, but we could either quarantine them as in the case of North Korea and Cuba or befriend them as in the case of China and Vietnam. Things looked so rosy that some proclaimed "the end of history" and others resurrected the long-standing American hope that we could quietly withdraw from the world and tend to our own affairs. During the 1990s, the minuscule amount of foreign aid, 0.2 percent of GDP, the lowest among the rich nations, was cut in half to 0.1 percent of GDP. It might be amusing, if it were not so sad, that Americans when polled believed that we were spending 10 to 15 percent of our federal budget on foreign aid, and that we were doing too much.

It is not that the decade of the 1990s was entirely quiet. The Gulf War at the beginning of the decade (leading the first President Bush to declare a "new world order," much to the dismay of many Americans) and later in the decade several terrorist attacks on American facilities abroad, and even one at home—the 1993 bombing of the World Trade Center—reminded us that the world was still restless. But it was the terrifying attacks of September 11, 2001, that will probably prove to be another historical turning point, warning us unmistakably that we are part of the world and that we can ignore the rest of the world only at our gravest peril.

The question of what it means to be part of the world, however, remains unresolved. At the moment it is defined largely by the War on Terrorism and the exercise of American military power, explicitly or implicitly, everywhere in the world. But what other responsibilities do we have? Should we be concerned that the gap between the developed nations and the undeveloped nations grows greater every year, that half the world's population subsists on less than two dollars a day and one-sixth of the world's population (one billion people) subsists on less than one dollar a day? Should we be concerned with the fact that several so-called nations are at or near complete internal collapse? Our president has said that he doesn't believe in nation building, but can it be that there is no relation between collapsing nations and terrorism?

I have spoken so far as though our involvement with the world is primarily political and military, but that is far from the case. Economic globalization has been underway for a long time, but it has sped up enormously in recent decades and we are at the center of it. Our economy is the most dynamic in the world and the engine of world growth. Mirroring our economic influence is our cultural influence. American films, television, popular music, and the World Wide Web pervade the globe, and American English is the new international language. America is the center of a new kind of empire, but it is the only empire there is. Americans are, like it or not, citizens of that empire and responsible for the whole world.

Our reaction to September 11 suggests we are far from ready for that responsibility. After so devastating and brutal an attack, it is natural that we see ourselves as victims and respond with flag-waving patriotism, more concerned with homeland security than with global responsibility. Not since Pearl Harbor has America suffered such an attack, and not since the War of 1812, as I have said, have we suffered an attack on this continent. So it is natural now that we look within rather than contemplate the staggering job of leading the whole world.

It is precisely at this moment that Richard Hughes's book is so appropriate. In this hour of danger and anxiety he invites us indeed to look within, to examine the myths we have lived by, and to consider which of them we need to reaffirm and which to revise or even discard. But the inward gaze to which Hughes invites us is not merely so that we can better understand ourselves. It is also so that we can assess our cultural resources for taking on the role of world empire that has been thrust upon us. America's world power has no precedent; we could even say that everyone in the world today has two nationalities—the one they were born with and American. How are we going to cope with that?

Hughes has wisely argued that the myths that we have spun about ourselves, though containing much truth, can also be disabling unless critically reappropriated. John Winthrop saw us as a city on a hill, a light to the nations. We are, more than ever, a city on a hill. The eyes of all people are truly on us. But do we bring light or darkness, a blessing or a curse to the rest of the world? Hughes argues that all the myths he describes still have much to teach us, however critically we must now rethink them, except one: the myth of innocence. That we must discard. Neither our military nor our economic intervention in the rest of the world has been innocent. No empire with any duration has ever believed in its own innocence. Humility about who we are and what we can do is essential if we are to avoid the many disasters that await us.

Chosen it seems we are, if not by God then by geopolitics. But the historical example of that original Chosen People should warn us against turning our chosenness into triumphalism. Chosenness today is our burden, and we must think long and hard about how to bear it. I could make a similar case about the other myths that Hughes describes, but that is unnecessary, since the book itself is designed to do that.

I may add only one more comment. Hughes has included in his discussion of every American myth the perspective of African Americans, a perspective often sharply different from that of the majority population, a perspective of those who have many times taken the brunt of our history and seldom fully shared in its successes. I believe that in a moment when we are no longer just a nation, but in many respects the nation, those African American voices can be heard as speaking for the rest of the world, over which we exercise such power, but which often lacks even the simplest ingredients of our way of life.

Richard Hughes writes as a Christian and so do I. His book is a thoughtful contribution to a decision that all of us who are Christians must make: To what extent can we help America become a responsible empire and to what extent must we stand against empire altogether?

Robert N. Bellah

Foreword to the Second Edition

Our quest in this millennium is to come to terms with the nature of our heterogeneous postindustrial diversity. Richard Hughes has written a dynamic book that will reverberate for years to come because he has dared to put the red flag in front of the bull's eyes, and the sudden trauma of seeing the flag has shaken the foundations of our insidious comfort. As a nation, we are exposed and those who have held onto the myths that have sustained haughtiness are exposed the most, and those people who cannot shake the overarching Myth of White Supremacy are condemned to reap a whirlwind of historical distress, distortion, and social death.

The universe is said by scientists to be fourteen billion years old. The earth is computed to be four and a half billion years old. Sixty-five million years ago the last of the dinosaurs died after having lived on the earth for seventy-five million years. There were no humans of any variety on the earth when the dinosaurs ruled in the Jurassic Age.

Homo sapiens like us can be traced by DNA to a single mother in Africa. Physical differentiation based on separation of gene pools, climate, and random selection have, since 300,000 years ago when homo sapiens appeared, produced different phenotypes of homo sapiens. It is this fact, imbued with imagination, aggression, and the need to humiliate the enemy that has brought us to the brink of wanton murder of each other. Alas, Hughes has tried to demonstrate a more powerful path forward.

If a pantheon of brave white authors of this generation writing on race could ever be assembled, I believe that Richard Hughes would have to be in it. I know many others, some I still count as friends, but for the most part the majority of white authors are not simply victimized by the myth of white supremacy, they are sustainers of the myths wanting to believe that whites are superior to other people. When I read J. M. Blaut's *Eight Eurocentric Historians*, I understood how easy it was for white intellectuals to fall in line with the dominating myths as if they were natural. The historians identified by Blaut as sustainers of the European dominance idea were the ones that we had all been exposed to in our own college days.

All societies operate on the basis of myths. This is not original to the United States but what is new, innovative, and profoundly valuable is Richard Hughes's evaluation that many of the working myths of the United States are fully linked to the ideas of racism, patriarchy, and domination. Any action that is taken to lessen the effects of the most debilitating myths on the population must be seen in the light of a victory of an enlightened consciousness.

There is another level of mythic reality that haunts ideas of intercultural interaction and that is simply the fact that western notions grounded in Hughes's myths also are found in the popular memes constructed from ancient Greek myths. As a student of classical civilizations, I am aware of the importance of memes and myths that help us build linguistic, social, political, and ethical environments. In my opinion the Greek myths in the American society obliterate all other possibilities and reinforce the idea of European exclusivity in a multiethnic and multicultural world. In a quest for full communication, goodness, integrity, and intercultural education with respect for all people, I assert the value of understanding the place of memic and mythic realities in the creation of national and global communication equality. Hughes knows this and seeks to free the human spirit by opening us up to an awareness of aggressive myths that control much of what we think and do.

What I wish the readers of this provocative book would do as they read Hughes's beautifully written work is to examine how Greek memes are related to a transcultural reality. Do we have simply a monocultural response to our linguistic complexity and cultural diversity? It is not so much that we have to minimize the classical Greek heritage of the western world but we must consider the positive idea of a more robust American society where other memes are made possible. I am suggesting that it is necessary to be conscious of Zeus while simultaneously discovering the possibilities inherent in a more nuanced psychomythic linguistic reality.

Since humans construct linguistic and social environments with whatever baggage they bring or whatever they can find in the natural environment, we can reconstruct or add to such constructed environments. But first, we must understand the myths that we live by and the ways myths and memes have been used to build the current communication environment. City and street names, weekdays, planets, stars, and even corporations are characteristically central to the built linguistic environment. Thus, exposing the way Hughes's myths constrain us and the linguistic realities of Greek classics proscribe and prescribe our communication in fields such as medicine, sports, religion, and astronomy will reveal the intricate nature of our communication society.

The common nicknames for schools and hotels in the United States such as Athenas, Athenaeum, Athenians, Argonauts, Centaurs, Golden Griffins, Golden Rams, Griffins, Griffons, Phoenix, Tritans, Trojans, Spartans, and so forth are reflective of the built memic environment. Furthermore, words and terms that undergird the ethnocentric environment such as Achilles heel, Trojan horse, stentorian roar, Myrmidons, Troy, Scylla and Charybdis, and siren voices constitute a veritable canopy of symbols with no space for other cultural myths. One sees how this is augmented by ideas such as *a Cassandra* or *a Mentor* that are derived from the same rich western classical environment as other memes of culture. How to educate readers so that they are comfortable with other memes or myths from other cultures is the challenge of Richard Hughes's audience. What do we make of the space that is covered by names such as Atlas, Clotho, Cronos. Eros, Fortúna, Hypno, Chaos, Mars, Mercury, Narcissus, Calypso, Nymphs, Typhon, Vulcan, and Zephyr?

As a brief demonstration of how this works in society I draw the reader's attention to the common memes in our built linguistic environment. According to Plato, the name *Atlas* was also the name given to the first king of Atlantis, although this person is not identified as a son of Zeus but rather the son of Poseidon and the woman Cleito. Atlas was also a name given to the king of Mauretania.

So we also know that Clotho is one of the three fates. She spins and weaves while her sister Lachesis draws out and measures the thread and her sister Atropos cuts and designs the thread of life. Now we know something about the language where the words atropy and clothes are common.

One can take Cronos as another example. He was the leader and youngest of the first generation of Titans, the divine descendants of Uranus, the sky, and Gaia, the earth. He overthrew his father and ruled during the mythological Golden Age, until he was overthrown by his own son Zeus and imprisoned in Tartarus. Or consider the fact that Eros was the god of sexual desire and our society sails on the sea of this Greek primordial god, called the son of Aphrodite. In a modern sense, a Trojan is a condom and a computer virus but it is fully in the tradition of Greek mythology to speak of it as a trickster derived from the idea of the Trojan Horse. What I have just cited are the names by which we have come to understand our reality as presented in the West.

Our myths and memes, consequently, are at the fountain of our interaction. Fortunately or unfortunately, Fortūna, the Latin goddess with the Greek equivalent Tyche, was the goddess of fortune and the actual personification of luck. Richard Hughes has not chosen luck to support his thesis and analysis; but he has demonstrated for us the cornucopia of ideas that can be gained from a serious study of the overriding myths of a complex society rather than rolling the capricious Rota Fortúna and waiting to see where the ball lands.

Molefi Kete Asante
Philadelphia, November 18, 2017

Acknowledgments

In this book, I stand on the shoulders of scores of other scholars who have taught me much about the mythic history of the United States.

I stand indebted, first, to my major professor at the University of Iowa, James C. Spalding, who first taught me about William Tyndale's understanding of a national covenant and how that notion was subsequently mediated to an entire generation of Puritans, both in England and in America.

Two other scholars profoundly shaped the way I think about the United States. One was Sidney E. Mead, who taught me at the University of Iowa also and who mentored me through his published works and through extensive personal correspondence and conversation for three decades. The other scholar who helped shape the way I think about the United States is Robert N. Bellah, University of California, Berkeley, who taught me in 1975 in the summer seminar, "Civil Religion in America," sponsored by the National Endowment for the Humanities. Like Mead, Bellah has continued to teach me for all these years, mainly through his published works on American civic faith and the meaning of community in the United States. His book, *The Broken Covenant: American Civil Religion in Time of Trial*, helped me to conceive both the content and the structure of this text in both its first and second editions.

I also owe a special debt of gratitude to Professor Martin E. Marty, Fairfax M. Cone Distinguished Service Professor Emeritus of the History of Modern Christianity, University of Chicago, who, since the late 1980s, has taken a particular interest in my work and has offered me support, advice, and encouragement in countless ways. I never studied with Marty in a classroom setting, though I have been a student of his books and articles on American religious history for many years.

I also stand indebted to Professor Conrad Cherry, Distinguished Professor Emeritus in the Department of Religious Studies at Indiana University/Purdue University at Indianapolis, especially for his work on the mythic dimensions of the United States as reflected in his book, *God's New Israel: Religious Interpretations of American Destiny*.

I wish to thank Pepperdine University for two sabbaticals, one in the winter term of 1995 and the other in the fall term of 2001, both of which I devoted to this project.

I am especially grateful to A. J. Hughes for sharing important references, for offering helpful suggestions, and for preparing the manuscript of this text for submission to the publisher by merging the new content with the original.

A number of individuals, both scholars and lay people, read all or parts of the manuscript for the second edition of this text and offered valuable suggestions: Lee Camp, Raymond Carr, Jerry Collins, Perry Cotham, Joyce Davis, David Fleer, Richard Goode, Phyllis Hildreth, A. J. Hughes, Catherine Meeks, Sandra Parham, Ted Parks, Joseph Robinson, and Angela Sims.

Still and all, this book is mine and I must take final responsibility for its deficiencies.

As always, I wish to thank my wife, Jan, not only for her support for my work but also for the fact that she routinely interacts with me about ideas that matter and shares with me information that she knows will be helpful to my work. She has helped in these ways with reference to this book, just as she has with reference to everything I have sought to accomplish over the course of a long career and an even longer marriage. To her, I renew my ultimate devotion and offer my deepest thanks.

Myths America Lives By

CHAPTER ONE

The Great American Myths and a Different American Future

In her important book, *White Rage: The Unspoken Truth of Our Racial Divide*, Carol Anderson asks us to imagine what the United States might look like today if, instead of resisting racial equality and equal opportunity for people of color for so much of American history, the nation had actually worked to realize those ideals:

> Imagine if Reconstruction had actually honored the citizenship of four million freedpeople—provided the education, political autonomy, and economic wherewithal warranted by their and their ancestors' hundreds of years of free labor. . . . Imagine the educational prowess our population might now boast had *Brown [v. Board of Education]* actually been implemented. . . . Imagine if, instead of launching into spurious attacks about his citizenship and filling the blogosphere with racist simian depictions, the United States had been able to harness the awe-inspiring symbolism of our first black president.[1]

And while Anderson calls on Americans—both white and black—to "imagine" a better America, she also summons us to "choose a different future."

Anderson's call to "imagine" a better nation is clearly within our reach. But it may be far more difficult for Americans to "choose a different future," simply because "the future" that so many Americans have chosen for this nation since World War II is embedded in the Great American Myths which, all too often, we have hardened and absolutized into rigid orthodoxies from which we often permit little or no dissent.

The first edition of this book explored five of those myths:

- The Myth of the Chosen Nation—the notion that God Almighty chose the United States for a special mission in the world

- The Myth of Nature's Nation—the conviction that American ideals and institutions are rooted in the natural order, that is, in God's own intentions first revealed at the dawn of creation
- The Myth of the Millennial Nation—the notion that the United States, building on that natural order, will usher in a final golden age for all humankind
- The Myth of the Christian Nation—the claim that America is a Christian nation, consistently guided by Christian values
- And the Myth of the Innocent Nation—the conviction that, while other nations may have blood on their hands, the nobility of the American cause always redeems the nation and renders it innocent

Those myths typically function as a two-edged sword. On the one hand, our myths can remind us of our noblest ideals and can challenge us to realize the American promise. But an absolutized version of those myths seduces us into believing that we have, in fact, achieved those ideals and therefore have no need to "choose a different future."

As historian Eric Foner put it, "There is [in this country] a deeply ingrained notion of American exceptionalism. We are democratic. We believe in equality. We believe in opportunity. This is the land of all those things. So therefore, there is a tendency to forget about aspects of our history which don't fit that pattern." We forget about these things because they don't "fit the image that we want to have of the greatness of our own country."[2] And armed with an image of American greatness and nobility, the summons to "choose a different future" may strike many Americans as a rhetorical flourish at best and irrelevant at worse.

In addition to the five American myths I discussed in the first edition of this book, there is another myth—a myth that defines the nation in many ways and that makes it even more difficult for us to "choose a different future." To introduce that myth, I share the following story.

At the invitation of Professor Raymond Carr, one of my students when I taught at Pepperdine University, I participated in 2012 in a panel that reviewed James Cone's pathbreaking book, *The Cross and the Lynching Tree*, at the national meeting of the American Academy of Religion that convened that year in Chicago. As part of my presentation, I explored the five American myths discussed in the first edition of this book and explained how, from an early age, those myths had shaped not only my view of the American nation but also my understanding of black people and of race relations in the United States.

When I concluded my remarks and took my seat alongside the other panelists, the late James Noel, a professor of African American Christianity and

American religion at San Francisco Theological Seminary, leaned over and whispered, "Professor, you left out the most important of all the American myths."

"And what might that be?" I inquired.

"The Myth of White Supremacy," Noel replied.

My initial response to Noel's assertion underscores the subtle power of the Myth of White Supremacy, on the one hand, and why so many white Americans would likely reject Noel's claim out of hand, on the other. I had spent years thinking about the Great American Myths. I had taught classes and written books and articles on that subject. In the first edition of *Myths America Lives By*, I had done my best to assess the Great American Myths from the perspective of various blacks throughout the course of American history. And while I acknowledged the persistence of racism in American life, not once had I considered the notion of white supremacy as an idea that has been central to the American mythos. It simply never registered on my radar screen.

When Professor Noel told me that I had omitted the most important of all the American myths, therefore, my initial response was skepticism. I understood that there were avowed white supremacists, but I had always viewed them as standing on the margins of American life. To suggest that white supremacy was a defining American myth struck me as preposterous.

But as I reflected over many months on what Noel had said, and as I placed his assertion into the context of the Obama years, I began to see his point. I began to see that even whites like me—whites who strongly reject racist ideology—can escape the power of the white supremacist myth only with extraordinary effort, if at all. That is because assumptions of white supremacy are like the very air we breathe: they surround us, envelop us, and shape us, but do so in ways we seldom discern. Put another way, notions of white supremacy are so embedded into our common culture that most whites take them for granted, seldom reflecting on their pervasive presence or assessing them for what they are.

The fundamental argument of this book, therefore, is twofold—first, that the Myth of White Supremacy is the primal American myth that informs all the others and, second, that one of the chief functions of the other five myths is to protect and obscure the Myth of White Supremacy, to hide it from our awareness, and to assure us that we remain innocent after all.[3]

At this point, let me be clear. While I try in this book to state my case with clarity and conviction, I do not wish to suggest that those who disagree with me are racists. There is a vast difference between unconsciously appropriating the dominant myths of our culture, on the one hand, and consciously embracing racist attitudes, on the other. If I have one hope for this book, it is this—that it will encourage readers to examine their own hearts and minds in light of these cultural myths—including the Myth of White Supremacy—that to one degree or another have shaped us all.

Getting Our Bearings

David Billings's experience may differ in certain details from that of other whites, but his story can help us understand that when we speak in this book of white supremacy, we are not speaking of white nationalist groups that proclaim white supremacy from the rooftops. We are speaking, instead, of ourselves and of the common culture in which we live—a culture suffused with the assumption that, in most ways, whites are superior to blacks. Billings writes,

> As a white person, even in my youth, I was taught that everything of significance that had happened in the United States had been accomplished by white people. . . . I was brought up to think and see my white world as normal. Everybody else around me seemed to me to see the world in the same way. . . . My world-view, shaped by this internalized sense of racial superiority, meant that I saw history, morality, the will of God, and scientific truth as the special province of white people, usually white men. . . . More than [to] laws or customs, my very understanding of myself was bound to the idea of white supremacy.

Billings goes on to explain that in his world, "whites were not self-reflective about race."[4] But why should they have been? Some of them—perhaps many of them—had experienced hardship and persecution. But not a single negative dimension in their lives—neither poverty nor harassment nor brutal treatment nor lack of opportunity—was due to the color of their skin. To the contrary, the color of their skin insured that most of them would not face the same limitations that they, themselves, imposed on their African American neighbors. And if it did fall their lot to face such constrictions, it would not be for the same reasons. There was simply no incentive for them, therefore, to reflect on what it meant to be white or on the Myth of White Supremacy, which they simply took for granted. That is the meaning of white privilege at the most basic level.

Blacks, on the other hand, typically discerned that myth with keen insight. They have been forced to discern it, to reflect upon it, and to understand it, for that myth alone could provide to their minds the rationale for the realities of slavery, for Jim Crow segregation, for beatings and lynchings and castrations, and for denial of equal opportunity in a nation that claims that "all men are created equal."

White supremacy has worked powerfully not only on the bodies but also on the minds of blacks in the United States. A young woman—one of my students in recent years—told how a teacher once asked her a piercing question: "Why do you always draw white girls?" the teacher queried. Later that evening, my student recalled, "The image of my teacher kneeling down to ask the impossible question stomped through my mind and raged through my ears like a violent storm. The weight of the question bent me, splitting my mind and my heart."

And then she said this:

> When I was in high school, I would often do what many girls did. I would imagine myself years from now, getting ready for work early in the morning. The house was quiet, I would be tranquil but moving quickly to beat the traffic. I'd check the mirror in the foyer before leaving, straighten my perfectly pressed collar, twist the ring on my wedding finger so that the beautiful carved diamond would face the right way. I'd check my long and silky hair for any strands that had fallen out of the elaborate style I'd wrapped it in. I'd check my skin for imperfections.
>
> It was always the skin that grabbed me, that pulled me away. It was always then that I realized the beautiful, successful, loved woman in my dreams was white. I have never felt more gut wrenching shame than those times, when I was suddenly torn from my unreachable dream to face a reality that was impossible to ignore. I could not be white. I wasn't white. . . .
>
> It is harrowing to live with a stress you can never escape . . .—the fear that you will never be fully accepted.[5]

The experience of Malcolm X was like the experience of my student. When he was in the seventh grade in Lansing, Michigan, he recalled, "I didn't really have much feeling about being a Negro, because I was trying so hard, in every way I could, to be white."[6]

In point of fact, many American blacks, especially those born in the early-to-mid–twentieth century, internalized the judgment embodied in the demeaning phrase, "If you're white, you're right; if you're brown, stick around; if you're black, get back"—a phrase obviously rooted deeply in the Myth of White Supremacy.[7]

In her novel, *The Bluest Eye*, Toni Morrison tells the story of a young girl named Pecola to whom "it had occurred . . . some time ago that if her eyes . . . were different, that is to say, beautiful, she herself would be different. . . . Each night, without fail, she prayed for blue eyes. Fervently, for a year she had prayed. Although somewhat discouraged, she was not without hope. To have something as wonderful as that happen would take a long, long time."[8]

In one way or another, Pecola's experience reflected reality for millions of American blacks.

Twenty-three years after writing that novel, Morrison reflected on its meaning. "*The Bluest Eye*," she wrote, "was my effort to say something about . . . why she [Pecola] had not, or possibly ever would have, the experience of what she possessed and also why she prayed for so radical an alteration. Implicit in her desire was racial self-loathing. And twenty years later I was still wondering about how one learns that. Who told her? Who . . . had looked at her and found her so wanting, so small a weight on the beauty scale?"[9]

Self-loathing, indeed! James Baldwin (1924–1987) picked up on that same theme when he wrote to his nephew about Baldwin's father, his nephew's grandfather. "He had a terrible life," Baldwin asserted. "He was defeated long before he died because, at the bottom of his heart, he really believed what white people said about him."[10]

Catherine Meeks tells a similar story. Her illiterate father worked as a sharecropper and her family was poor. She often wondered why, as a young black woman, she "could not go to the front window at the Dairy Queen, try on the new dress that I wanted, or sit in the same waiting room with White people in our little rural Arkansas town."

But that was not the worst of it. When her brother Garland's appendix became infected, her father found someone to drive both of them to the nearest hospital in El Dorado, Arkansas. But because he was black, the hospital refused to treat Garland and instructed her father to drive him "to the 'charity' hospital" in Shreveport, some seventy miles away. "By the time my father could get someone to drive them there, Garland's appendix had become so infected that he was beyond saving. . . . He died soon after arriving [at the hospital]. He was twelve years old."

His role as a sharecropper rendered Meeks's father powerless economically, and his black skin rendered him powerless in a world defined by the Myth of White Supremacy. His inability to save his son only heightened those feelings, and all those realities, taken together, transformed him into an angry and bitter man.[11]

W. E. B. Du Bois (1868–1963) recalled that he first learned he was different when—as he put it—"the shadow swept over me," and he found himself "shut out from . . . [the world of whites] by a vast veil." He wondered, "Why did God make me an outcast and a stranger in mine own house?" That experience led him to speak of a "double-consciousness, this sense of always looking at one's self through the eyes of others, or measuring one's soul by the tape of a world that looks on in amused contempt and pity. . . . One ever feels his twoness,—an American, a Negro; two souls, two thoughts, two unreconciled strivings; two warring ideals in one dark body."[12]

These kinds of experiences, so common to blacks in the United States, help us understand why the black appraisal of the American nation is so different from that of most whites. The poet James M. Whitfield (1822–1871), born in New Hampshire to free parents, described black life in this country in the starkest of terms.

> America, it is to thee,
> Thou boasted land of liberty,—
> It is to thee that I raise my song,
> Thou land of blood, and crime, and wrong.
> It is to thee my native land,
> From which has issued many a band
> To tear the black man from his soil
> And force him here to delve and toil
> Chained on your blood-bemoistened sod,
> Cringing beneath a tyrant's rod.[13]

Sara G. Stanley (1837–1918) was born to a free and financially secure family in North Carolina. Nonetheless, she wrote in 1856 that the American ideal of liberty was, for her and her people, "a phantom, shadowy and indistinct—a disembodied form, impalpable to our sense of touch." She added, "In the broad area of this Republic, there is no spot, however small or isolated, where the colored man can exercise his God-given rights."[14]

Another free man, John Mercer Langston (1829–1897), wrote in 1845, "We have been in the habit of boasting of our Declaration of Independence, of our Federal Constitution, of the Ordinance of 1787, and various enactments in favor of popular Liberty, for so long, that we verily believe that we are a Free people." Yet, he concluded, the American people had been deceived. Because the spirit of slavery dominated the nation, there was no one—black or white—who enjoyed a "full share of Liberty."[15]

Charles Lenox Remond (1810–1873), an abolitionist from Massachusetts, proclaimed that "it does very well for nine-tenths of the people of the United States to speak of the awe and reverence they feel as they contemplate the Constitution, but there are those who look upon it with a very different feeling, for they are in a very different position. What is it to *them* that it talks about peace—tranquility—domestic enjoyments—civil rights?"[16]

William Wells Brown (1814–1884) was born in slavery in Kentucky but escaped at age 20 and fled to Boston where he became an abolitionist. To an audience in Great Britain in 1849, Brown affirmed,

Wherever the Constitution proclaims a bit of soil to belong to the United States, there it dooms me to be a slave the moment I set my foot upon it, and all the 20,000 or 30,000 of my brethren who have made their escape from the Southern States, and taken refuge in Canada or the Northern States, are in the same condition. . . . I cannot look at the Constitution or laws of America as a protection to me; in fact, I have no Constitution, and no country. I cannot, like the eloquent gentleman who last addressed you say—"I am bound to stand up in favor of America." I would to God that I could; but how can I? America has disenfranchised me, driven me off, and declared that I am not a citizen, and never shall be, upon the soil of the United States. Can I, then, gentlemen, stand up for such a country as that?[17]

This was the same William Wells Brown who reported his punishment for having run away from his master when he served as an enslaved person in Missouri: "I was tied up in the smokehouse, and was very severely whipped. After the major had flogged me to his satisfaction, he sent out his son Robert, a young man eighteen or twenty years of age, to see that I was well smoked. He made a fire of tobacco stems, which soon set me to coughing and sneezing. . . . After giving me what they conceived to be a decent smoking, I was untied and again set to work.[18]

The great abolitionist Frederick Douglass concurred with Brown's assessment of the United States when he said in 1847 that "I have no love for America, as such; I have no patriotism; I have no country." And if we were to ask Douglass why he felt as he did, he would tell us what he said then: "I am not thought of, spoken of, except as a piece of property belonging to some *Christian* slaveholder, and all the religious and political institutions of this country, alike pronounce me a slave and a chattel. Now, in such a country as this, I cannot have patriotism."[19]

Surely the American people in the twenty-first century can hear these nineteenth-century African American prophets and not be threatened. We can hear them with relative equanimity because today we know the words they spoke were true.

Yet most white Americans of earlier times could no more hear these voices of protest than white Americans in the twentieth century were able to hear comparable voices of protest in their own time and place. Many, for example, labeled Malcolm X a radical and then refused to take him seriously when he proclaimed in 1964:

I'm not a Democrat, I'm not a Republican, and I don't even consider myself an American. . . . No, I'm not an American. I'm one of the 22 million black people who are the victims of Americanism. One of the 22 million black people who are the victims of democracy, nothing but disguised hypocrisy. So, I'm not standing here speaking to you as an American, or a patriot, or a flag-saluter, or a flag-waver—no, not I. I'm speaking as a victim of this American system. And I see America through the eyes of the victim. I don't see any American dream; I see an American nightmare.[20]

Only seven years before Malcolm spoke these words, Richard Wright (1908–1960) affirmed that the meaning of black life in America was deeply and profoundly bound up with "race hate, rejection, ignorance, segregation, discrimination, slavery, murder, fiery crosses, and fear."[21] Many whites might read these words and imagine that Wright was exaggerating, that things have never been all that bad because, after all, this is America.

Molefi Kete Asante described African Americans as "the people of the Wilderness" which, he wrote, "is a metaphor for the feeling of economic, social, political, and professional abandonment that is often found in the inner cities, but can be found anywhere and everywhere bigotry creates the death of hope. . . . Some of us," he continued, "live in the deep inner recesses of the Wilderness from which it is almost impossible to escape. Others of us are on the shallow fringes . . . but know that at any moment we could slip back into the depths."[22]

What all these voices have sought to convey is that blacks and whites experience America in radically different ways, chiefly because the Myth of White Supremacy defines life for blacks in terms that whites can barely grasp.

To put all this a slightly different way—some years ago I saw the film, *The Help*, at a theater in a white suburb of Harrisburg, Pennsylvania. All the patrons were white, and when the film concluded, they broke into spontaneous applause, presumably cheering the "victory" that, by the end of the film, "the help" had scored over their white employers.

I shared this experience a few days later with a black friend, Wayne Baxter, the man to whom—along with Professor James Noel—I have dedicated this book. Baxter told me that he had seen the film as well, but in a theater filled almost entirely with blacks. And then he said this: "When the film was over, nobody clapped. Nobody clapped because the film portrayed the reality of their lives, the lives to which they would return when they left the theater."

What should we make of these two different perspectives—one black and one white—on the very same film? What should we make of the radically different perspectives—one black and one white—on the same American nation? What should we make of the fact that most blacks perceive the Myth of White Supremacy with startling clarity and view it as pervasive in American life, while most white Americans imagine that white supremacy is confined to the radical fringes of American culture?

That is the question that drives this book, and in the context of that question, I share the following story. A dear friend whose work—and whose intellect, character, and personhood—I hold in the highest esteem, upon reading an early draft of this book, wrote, "I fear that you may . . . undercut yourself by reaching too much [and] depicting this myth [of white supremacy] as the root problematic myth. . . . It seems somewhat arbitrary to me to give . . . white supremacy a sort of logical priority among the myths." Arguing, in effect, that I lack sufficient evidence to make such a bold assertion, he suggested that I eliminate the contention that white supremacy is the primal myth and argue instead that it merely overlaps and connects with the other American myths.

When I asked several black scholars to assess my friend's critique, they responded viscerally. They argued with passion that James Noel was right—that the Myth of White Supremacy *is the primal myth* in American life and history, and that to tell this story in any other way would be to speak untruth. Indeed, the evidence for the primacy of the Myth of White Supremacy is all around us if we are attentive. We find that evidence in the testimony of black Americans—a testimony that has been consistent from slave days until now.

So we return to the question that stands at the heart of this book: What should we make of two different perspectives—one black and one white—on the very same film? What should we make of the radically different perspectives—one black and one white—on the same American nation? And what should we make of the two different perspectives—one black and one white—on how I should treat the Myth of White Supremacy in this text?

The answer to these questions begins to emerge when we consider the meaning of "myth." The English word *myth* derives from the Greek word *mythos*, which literally means "story." Contrary to colloquial usage, a myth is not a story that is patently untrue. Rather, a myth is a story that, whether true or false, helps us discern the meaning and purpose of our lives and, for that reason, speaks truth to those who embrace it.

John H. Westerhoff III helps us understand this issue at greater depth when he recalls Peter Shaffer's play *Equus*, in which a psychiatrist tells his patient, "We need a story to see in the dark." Reflecting on that pregnant line, Westerhoff comments, "We all need such a story. Stories are the means by which we see reality. Without a story it would appear as if we lived in an unreal world. Without a story we cannot live. Without a story we cannot have community. . . . Without a story life makes no sense. The story that is foundational to our life provides us with the basis for our perceptions and for our faith. . . . Stories are the imaginative way of ordering our experience."[23]

Our national myths, then, are the stories shared in common by the American people—or at least by the majority of the American people—stories that convey, reinforce, and help us affirm commonly shared convictions regarding the purposes and meaning of the nation.

White supremacy, however, is not a story shared in common by *all* Americans but a story on which the American people are deeply divided. Most blacks understand the primacy of the Myth of White Supremacy because they have suffered its bitter fruit and know no other way to explain that experience. Whites, on the other hand, typically embrace this myth but, for the most part, do so unconsciously. Nothing in their experience has forced them to recognize this myth, much less to regard it as America's primal narrative.

Hubert Locke, an African American who served for many years as dean of the Evans School of Public Policy at the University of Washington, helps put the radical difference between black and white perceptions of white supremacy in perspective. "The core of the problem in America," he writes, "is the fact that black and white Americans live not in one nation, let alone 'under God,' but on two different planets. This is the only metaphor that accurately depicts the gulf that lies between the lives and experiences of black Americans and their white counterparts."[24]

The question we now must ask is this: How did the Myth of White Supremacy achieve such dominance in the United States? In his award-winning book, *Stamped from the Beginning: The Definitive History of Racist Ideas in America*, Ibram X. Kendi explains that the Myth of White Supremacy has been evolving for roughly 600 years and, for all that time, has served a single purpose—to justify and legitimate the enslavement, brutalization, oppression, torture, and marginalization of African men, women, and children.

In 1453, Gomes Eanes de Zurara of Portugal published the first book-length defense of the African slave trade.[25] From that small beginning, Europeans began to develop the racist stories that gave them meaning—stories that transformed vice into virtue, that recast criminal behavior as Christian charity, and that soothed the "Christian" conscience of western Europe.

And the stories kept coming. They came from explorers like Captain John Smith, literary elites like William Shakespeare, Christian thinkers like the New England Puritan divine Cotton Mather, scientific luminaries like Robert Boyle, and nation builders like Thomas Jefferson. They flourished during the sixteenth-century Reformation, the seventeenth-century religious wars, and the eighteenth-century Enlightenment, and they flourished on both sides of the Atlantic.

The stories ranged from tales of inherent black depravity to claims of black stupidity to affirmations that blacks had more in common with apes than with human beings. These stories rested on other equally malicious narratives—that black skin signaled a curse from God, or that black skin would return to its white and normal hues if exposed to colder climes. Each story reinforced the dominant themes—that blacks were fundamentally aberrant and whites were superior to blacks in every conceivable way.

Each new turn of history's massive wheel cemented those stories ever more firmly into the hearts and minds of whites in Europe and America alike. The layers upon layers of racialized history, stacked upon each other for some 600 years, amplified those stories and turned them into myths— the stories white people lived by, the stories that gave them meaning. And after influential white thinkers from both Europe and America reinforced, repeated, amplified, honed, and fine-tuned those stories for all those years, it would be a miracle had the doctrine of white supremacy not emerged as the dominant, defining, and primal myth in the American nation.[26]

Because African Americans discern the Myth of White Supremacy so clearly—and because they discern that myth in ways that most whites do not—I seek in this book to pay close attention to African American voices—to their analyses, their perceptions, and to their understandings of the racial divide in the United States.

But there is another reason why I want to listen carefully to the voices of black Americans on this matter—and why their voices play a significant role in this book. As a Christian, I understand that the one I seek to follow has asked us to see the world through the eyes of people who suffer oppression at the hands of the world's elites. Oppressed people will tell us the truth, I believe, in ways that the world's elites, the wealthy, and the power brokers typically will not. The elites will not because they have too much to lose. But oppressed people have nothing to lose and that is why we need to hear them clearly.

Obviously, not all African Americans see the world alike and there is no such thing as "*the* African American perspective" just as there is no such thing as "*the* white perspective." The debate between W. E. B. Du Bois and Booker T. Washington over the role of blacks in American life, briefly chronicled in chapter 6, symbolizes those differences. Still, the black voices cited in this book offer important perspectives on the black experience in American life.

While I could have turned to hundreds, even thousands, of black voices who have spoken of the pervasive nature of the Myth of White Supremacy in American life, I have lifted up in this text a sample of blacks who speak of this myth—and of how it informs the other American myths—with particular force and clarity. Accordingly, in the pages that follow, the reader will hear the voices of Michelle Alexander, Muhammad Ali, Carol Anderson, William Anderson, Molefi Kete Asante, James Baldwin, Wayne Baxter, Cornell Belcher, Rich Benjamin, Charles Blow, Senator Cory Booker, D. P. Brown,

William Wells Brown, Eldridge Cleaver, Ta-Nehisi Coates, James Cone, Anna J. Cooper, Angela Davis, Kelly Brown Douglas, Frederick Douglass, W. E. B. Du Bois, Michael Eric Dyson, Thomas Fortune, Sam Fulwood, Fred Gray, Forrest E. Harris Sr., Langston Hughes, Ibram X. Kendi, Coretta Scott King, Martin Luther King Jr., John Mercer Langston, Hubert G. Locke, Catherine Meeks, Anne Moody, Toni Morrison, James Noel, Nell Irvin Painter, Lucy Parsons, Yolanda Pierce, Charles Lenox Remond, Sara G. Stanley, Maria W. Stewart, B. T. Tanner, David Walker, Lesley Walker, Booker T. Washington, Ida B. Wells, Cornel West, James M. Whitfield, Albery A. Whitman, Gayraud Wilmore, Jeremiah Wright, Richard Wright, and Malcolm X.

Racial Attitudes in High Places

To help us grasp just how pervasive the Myth of White Supremacy has been in American life, it will be useful to recall the racial attitudes of several people who led the nation at various points in American history, even people widely credited with promoting racial equality in the United States.

Many of the Founders, including Thomas Jefferson and George Washington, owned slaves, and Jefferson—the man who penned the Declaration's immortal words, "We hold these truths to be self-evident, that all men are created equal"—also believed that blacks were "inferior to . . . whites in the endowments both of body and mind."[27] It is no wonder, then, that the United States government employed enslaved people as a significant part of the work force that built the White House and the United States Capital during the 1790s.

In 1857, Chief Justice Roger B. Taney wrote the "Opinion of the [United States Supreme] Court" regarding the Dred Scott decision. Taney read his own pro-slavery bias into the "Opinion of the Court" and, in many respects, misrepresented the American Founders. Still, "a long history of social and political practice, North and South, was on his side," as historian Matthew Frye Jacobson has noted,[28] and the "Opinion" Taney wrote helped shore up the Myth of White Supremacy in American life and culture for decades to come:

> It is difficult at this day to realize the state of public opinion in relation to that unfortunate race, which prevailed in the civilized and enlightened portions of the world at the time of the Declaration of Independence, and when the Constitution of the United States was framed and adopted. . . . They had for more than a century before been regarded as beings of an inferior order, and altogether unfit to associate with the white race, either in social or political relations; and so far inferior, that they had no rights which the white man was bound to respect. . . . This opinion was at that time fixed and universal in the civilized portion of the

white race. It was regarded as an axiom in morals as well as in politics, which no one thought of disputing, or supposed to be open to dispute.[29]

Only months after the Supreme Court handed down its Dred Scott decision, Abraham Lincoln, in a speech at Springfield, Illinois, called that decision "erroneous" and "based on assumed historical facts which were not really true." One of the assertions Lincoln thought untrue was Taney's contention regarding "the state of public opinion" with regard to blacks at the time of the founding:

> The Chief Justice does not directly assert, but plainly assumes, as a fact, that the public estimate of the black man is more favorable now than it was in the days of the Revolution. This assumption is a mistake. . . . As a whole, in this country, the change between then and now is decidedly the other way; and their ultimate destiny [the destiny of blacks] has never appeared so hopeless as in the last three or four years.[30]

Lincoln himself, however, contributed to that hopelessness when, in the following year in his debate with Stephen A. Douglas, he affirmed,

> I am not, nor ever have been, in favor of bringing about in any way the social and political equality of the white and black races; that I am not, nor ever have been, in favor of making voters or jurors of negroes, nor of qualifying them to hold office, nor to intermarry with white people; . . . There is a physical difference between the white and black races which I believe will forever forbid the two races living together on terms of social and political equality. And inasmuch as they cannot so live, while they do remain together there must be the position of superior and inferior, and I as much as any other man am in favor of having the superior position assigned to the white race.[31]

Following Lincoln's assassination in 1865, his vice president and the man who succeeded him as president—Andrew Johnson—wrote to Missouri Governor Thomas C. Fletcher that "this is a country for white men, and by God, as long as I am President, it shall be a government for white men."[32]

Some forty years later, while still the president of Princeton University and before his election as president of the United States, Woodrow Wilson repeated in his five-volume *History of the American People* the long-standing myth of the happy slave. In the midst of the Civil War, he wrote, "Great gangs of cheery negroes worked in the fields. . . . No distemper touched them; no breath of violence or revolt stirred them. There was, it seemed, no wrong they fretted under or wished to see righted. The smiling fields not yet trodden by the feet of armies still produced their golden harvests of grain under the hands of the willing slaves."

He spoke, too, of "the plain and wholesome simplicity of the planters' lives."[33] But the blacks who became officeholders during Reconstruction (1865–1877) were, Wilson affirmed, "men who could not so much as write their names and who knew none of the uses of authority except its insolence."[34]

Even though he was deeply critical of the terror the Ku Klux Klan wielded in the South following the war,[35] he seemed to excuse the activity of Klansmen in the organization's earliest years as mere pranks. He spoke of the "comrades" who "rode abroad at night when the moon was up: a white mask, a tall cardboard hat, the figures of man and horse sheeted like a ghost." He told how those night rides "threw the negroes into a very ecstasy of panic to see these sheeted 'Ku Klux' move near them in the shrouded night," and how "their comic fear stimulated the lads who excited it to many an extravagant prank."[36]

Once in the White House, Wilson resegregated the federal civil service that had been integrated for years following Reconstruction and held in the White House a private screening of the film, "Birth of a Nation," a film that praised the rise of the Klan as symbolic of the white South's resurgence after Reconstruction.[37]

These brief vignettes may help us grasp the role white supremacy has played, from time to time, even at the highest levels of government in the United States.

Digging Deeper

To press our inquiry even further, consider these three episodes—one from the nineteenth century, one from the twentieth century, and one from the twenty-first century. They are connected to one another by a single assumption—the notion that whites are superior to blacks and should therefore control the American nation.

In the *nineteenth century*, the Emancipation Proclamation brought euphoria to blacks all over the South. They would be free at last! But violent white resistance to black freedom exploded, prompting the federal government to launch an era of Reconstruction that sought to protect blacks with at least a measure of equal opportunity.

But Reconstruction only intensified the determination of southern whites to keep the formerly enslaved people "in their place" which, for many whites, meant utter subservience and abject poverty. Once Reconstruction ended in 1877, the white South passed a series of Black Codes that sought to re-enslave African Americans—to make them "slaves in everything but name," as W. E. B. Du Bois put it.[38] The codes forced blacks to sign labor contracts, binding them to long hours with little or no pay. The contracts functioned as proof of employment, and any black caught without that proof was typically arrested for vagrancy and auctioned to the highest bidder. Any form of protest, defiance, or even a plea for higher wages or better working conditions could trigger ruthless whippings. And as Carol Anderson explains, these codes "were not the work of extreme secessionists . . . [but were crafted by] some of the South's most respected judges, attorneys, and planters."[39]

In the *early twentieth century*, thousands of African American citizens of the United States fled the Deep South—the scene of countless beatings, lynchings, castrations, immolations, and other forms of harassment, intimidation, and murder—and took refuge in Greenwood, Oklahoma, a suburb of Tulsa, where they believed they would be safe. There they built what came to be known as Black Wall Street—the most affluent all-black community in America at the time with hundreds of successful businesses including restaurants, grocery stores, movie theaters, libraries, law offices, a hospital, a bank, schools, and a post office, along with their churches.

Then, on the night of June 1, 1921, a mob of whites firebombed this community from the ground and the air. As Linda Christensen tells the story,

> During the night and day of the riot, deputized whites killed more than 300 African Americans. They looted and burned to the ground 40 square blocks of 1,265 African American homes, including hospitals, schools, and churches, and destroyed 150 businesses. White deputies and members of the National Guard arrested and detained 6,000 black Tulsans who were released only upon being vouched for by a white employer or other white citizen. Nine thousand African Americans were left homeless and lived in tents well into the winter of 1921.[40]

The sun rose the next morning to reveal the corpses of murdered blacks and the smoldering ruins of a once-prosperous community destroyed by fire.[41]

In the *early twenty-first century*—on January 20, 2009—Barack Hussein Obama became the first black president of the United States. Ninety-five percent of African Americans had voted for him and when his victory was apparent, they were euphoric. But virtually no one was prepared for what would follow.

On January 16, 2009, commentator Rush Limbaugh set the stage for the next eight years when he told his radio audience, "I hope he fails."[42] Limbaugh placed that statement in the context of his opposition to what he regarded as Obama's liberal policies, but the other inescapable context was this singular fact—that the man Limbaugh hoped would fail was the first black president of the United States.

Only four days later, on January 20, 2009—the day the new president was inaugurated—leading Republicans in the House and the Senate vowed to obstruct every proposal and initiative that Obama might propose, regardless of merit. They made this pledge even though the nation faced at that time what came to be known as the Great Recession—the most severe economic downturn since the Great Depression of the 1930s[43] which, by any measure, called for collaboration, not obstruction.

At the grassroots level, opposition to Obama was vile and potentially deadly. Routinely portrayed as "other," as somehow different from mainstream America, as foreign-born, as a Muslim, and as a man who hated his country, Obama suffered during his first year in office a 400 percent increase in death threats when compared with threats against the life of his predecessor, George W. Bush.[44] At a Wall Street event in February 2015, former New York mayor Rudy Giuliani summed up the attitudes toward Obama embraced by many whites: "I do not believe, and I know this is a horrible thing to say, but I do not believe that the president loves America. He doesn't love you. And he doesn't love me. He wasn't brought up the way you were brought up and I was brought up through love of this country."[45]

Then, in 2016, the American people, by virtue of the Electoral College,[46] elected to the presidency a man who had built his political career on the utterly false and disproven claim that the nation's first black president had been born in Kenya and therefore occupied the White House illegally.

What we witness in all these episodes is a common pattern in American life. Indeed, Carol Anderson argues that every time blacks have made notable gains, white America has undermined those gains and forced blacks to take one step backward for every two steps forward.

As she wrote in a *Washington Post* editorial,

> White rage recurs in American history. It exploded after the Civil War, erupted again to undermine the Supreme Court's *Brown v. Board of Education* decision and took on its latest incarnation with Barack Obama's ascent to the White House. For every action of African American advancement, there's a reaction, a backlash.[47]

The "trigger," she argues, is always "black advancement. It is not the mere presence of black people that is the problem; rather, it is blackness with ambition, with drive, with purpose, with aspirations, and with demands for full and equal citizenship."

The heart of the problem, she continues, is not the Klan. It's "the courts, the legislatures, and a range of government bureaucracies."[48] Indeed, "White rage doesn't have to wear sheets, burn crosses, or take to the streets. Working the halls of power, it can achieve its ends far more effectively, far more destructively."[49]

Her summary of the white response to the landmark Supreme Court decision in *Brown v. Board of Education*, striking down segregation in America's public schools, offers a case in point:

> The truth is that when the *Brown v. Board of Education* came down in 1954 and black children finally had a chance at a decent education, white authorities didn't see children striving for quality schools and an opportunity to fully contribute to society; they saw only a threat and acted accordingly, shutting down schools, diverting public money into private coffers, leaving millions of citizens in educational rot, willing even to undermine national security in the midst of a major crisis—all to ensure that blacks did not advance.[50]

Anderson does not argue—and I do not wish to argue—that life for African American citizens of this country has not improved since the 1950s, for certainly it has. But that improvement should not obscure the legitimacy of her thesis—that vast inequalities still remain, that systemic racism is far from eradicated, that prejudice against blacks still runs deep in American life, and that whites in this country have resisted, and often successfully resisted, every major gain that blacks have made over the course of American history. As Molefi Kete Asante observed in 2009, "While there has been change, the fundamental white supremacist position of society has never been relinquished."[51] And Forrest E. Harris Sr., president of Nashville's American Baptist College—an institution that produced scores of student leaders for the Civil Rights Movement—affirmed in 2017 that "the systematic history of white supremacy remains the nation's chief moral problem at a deeper level than ever before."[52]

How White Supremacy Informs and Shapes the Great American Myths

For virtually all Americans, the nation draws its primary meaning from the American Creed—the affirmation in the Declaration of Independence of what that document calls the "self-evident" truths that "all men are created equal, that they are endowed by their Creator with certain unalienable rights, that among these are Life, Liberty, and the pursuit of Happiness." The American Creed is also a myth since it, too, tells a story that lends purpose and meaning to the nation—the story of a God, best discerned through the light of nature, who created all men equal and bestowed upon them those "unalienable rights."

But beyond the American Creed, the nation also draws meaning from what I call in this book "the Great American Myths"—the myths that affirm the United States as a chosen nation, as nature's nation, as the millennial nation, as a Christian nation, and as an innocent nation.

The nation works well when most Americans believe that the American Creed and the Great American Myths work in harmony, reinforcing and supporting each other. But when large numbers of Americans believe that the myths are skewed in favor of one segment of the population against another, or when they believe that the myths stand at odds with the American Creed and undermine its promise, precisely at that point, the meaning of the nation is compromised at best and undermined at worst.

And that is precisely what happens when the Myth of White Supremacy stands at the heart of the nation's self-understanding. Those who discern the role white supremacy plays in shaping the contours of the Great American Myths understand how those myths can rob the American Creed of its meaning, power, and promise.

And *discernment* is key. As mentioned earlier, the Myth of White Supremacy is like the air we breathe, surrounding us, enveloping us, and shaping us, but in ways we seldom discern. The same is true for the other American myths. In this country, they, too, are like the air we breathe. No one sits us down and teaches us these myths. Rather, they belong to the ethos of our culture and most of us accept them reflexively with no critical reflection on their meaning or function at all. And that is what makes those myths so potentially dangerous. If critically examined and nuanced, they have the potential for good. But when accepted uncritically, as they so often are, they have potential for great harm.

Because most white Americans embrace these myths uncritically, most also fail to discern the extent to which white supremacy defines and shapes the myths that, in turn, define and shape the nation. For that reason, it will be useful in this introductory chapter to briefly explore some of the ways in which white supremacy defines and undergirds each of the Great American Myths.

While we will look at each of the myths individually, it must be said from the outset that the Great American Myths are interconnected and interdependent, forming a complex web of meaning. One can hardly speak, for example, of the Myth of the Chosen Nation without also speaking of the Myth of the Christian Nation since chosenness assumes a Judeo-Christian God who did the choosing. Likewise, one can hardly speak of the Myth of the Chosen Nation without also speaking of the Myth of Nature's Nation, since America believes itself chosen precisely because it claims to conform itself to the natural order of things.

Or again, the Myth of the Innocent Nation depends on perceptions of national righteousness which find their deepest roots in the nation's supposed Christian identity, on the one hand, and its conformity to the natural order of things, on the other.

With that complex web of interconnectedness in mind, we must now look briefly at each of the Great American Myths and the relation they sustain to the Myth of White Supremacy.

The Chosen Nation

The extent to which white supremacy defined the Myth of the Chosen Nation from an early date, for example, is easy enough to demonstrate. The America chosen by God to illumine the world with the great truths of democracy and self-government was from the beginning a white America that excluded people of color. Abraham Lincoln may well have spoken truth when he argued that, over the long term, "the Declaration contemplated the progressive improvement in the condition of all men everywhere." But for the short term, Stephen A. Douglas had it right, at least if we judge by the words and actions of the Founders. "No man," Douglas claimed, "can vindicate the character, motives and conduct of the signers of the Declaration of Independence except upon the hypothesis that they referred to the white race alone, and not to the African, when they declared all men to have been created equal."[53]

How could blacks believe that God chose the United States to illumine the world with the truths of democracy and self-government when they were locked out of the very democracy with which the nation hoped to illumine the rest of the world? When, for example, they were denied the vote until the Fifteenth Amendment was ratified in 1870? Or when, following ratification of the Fifteenth Amendment, state and local governments routinely defied the Fifteenth Amendment through literacy tests and the poll tax, measures not struck down until the Voting Rights Act of 1965? Or when many states still practice voter suppression through voter identification requirements, the gerrymandering of Congressional districts, and reducing the hours when voting places are open?

The only way white America could justify the claim that God had chosen a nation built on racial discrimination to enlighten the rest of the world was to build into its identity as a chosen nation the assumption that whites are, in fact, superior to blacks in every conceivable way and that God had therefore chosen the whites, not the blacks, for this special mission in the world.

In the final analysis, the Myth of the Chosen Nation was built on two components—religion (the Judeo-Christian heritage) and blood (Anglo-Saxon blood). While this book will focus on the religious underpinnings of the Myth of the Chosen Nation, Kelly Brown Douglas has shown that the Myth of the Chosen Nation was built squarely on racial claims that centered on the alleged purity and morality of the Anglo-Saxon people. As Douglas writes, "the stewards of the Anglo-Saxon myth were compelled to realize that the Anglo-Saxon capacity for morality and free institutions was not an accident. It was an innate capacity. It was in the blood. Morality and freedom flowed through Anglo-Saxon veins."[54]

Nature's Nation

The Myth of White Supremacy likewise undergirded the notion that the United States was nature's nation—a nation whose ideals and institutions are rooted in God's own intentions, revealed at the dawn of creation. Thomas Jefferson succinctly stated the Myth of Nature's Nation in the Declaration of Independence when he wrote that "Life, Liberty, and the pursuit of Happiness" were "self-evident" truths, grounded in "Nature and Nature's God" and therefore embedded in the natural order of things.

But Jefferson himself predicated the Myth of Nature's Nation squarely on the Myth of White Supremacy when he wrote in his *Notes on the State of Virginia* "that the blacks, whether originally a distinct race, or made distinct by time and circumstances, are inferior to the whites in the endowments both of body and mind." Like the promise of "Life, Liberty, and the pursuit of Happiness," Jefferson regarded the inferiority of black people as a self-evident truth, also grounded in nature. "It is not their condition, then, but nature, which has produced the distinction," he wrote.[55]

Blacks have always understood the extent to which the notion of white supremacy has distorted the Myth of Nature's Nation. Michael Eric Dyson, Georgetown University professor and well known media commentator, for example, has argued that "the real unifying force in our national cultural and political life, beyond skirmishes over ideology, is white identity masked as universal, neutral and, therefore, quintessentially American."[56] Dyson therefore placed the Myth of White Supremacy squarely into the myth that the United States, historically dominated by whites, is rooted in the natural order of things, in the way things are meant to be.

Now we can grasp what James Cone meant when he recalled his childhood and adolescent years in Bearden, Arkansas. "The white folks of Bearden did not think of themselves as being cruel or unjust to black people," Cone wrote. Instead, "they regarded the social and political arrangements that they maintained as an expression of *the natural orders of creation* [italics mine]."[57]

Now we can grasp why so many Americans sought to portray President Barack Obama as other, as foreign, as alien, as Muslim, and as one who hated his own country. Obama simply did not fit the natural norm of white supremacy—long an unspoken qualification for a president of the United States.

A Christian Nation

Because the Christian faith, by definition, transcends color, ethnicities, and national boundaries, and because—at the very same time—the United States had built its identity, wealth, and power on racial subjugation, the only way America could embrace the Myth of the Christian Nation was to whiten it as well, doing unspeakable violence to the cardinal precepts of the Christian religion. And the only way the nation could protect itself from the implications of this devastating contradiction was to embrace—however subtly and however unconsciously—the notion of white supremacy as somehow compatible with the Christian religion.

No one discerned this trick the nation had played on itself more insightfully than Frederick Douglass, once enslaved but who, during the days of American slavery, became one of the most powerful voices for abolitionism. "Between the Christianity of this land, and the Christianity of Christ," Douglass wrote,

> I recognize the widest possible difference—so wide, that to receive the one as good, pure, and holy, is of necessity to reject the other as bad, corrupt, and wicked. . . . I love the pure, peaceable, and impartial Christianity of Christ: I therefore hate the corrupt, slaveholding, women-whipping, cradle-plundering, partial and hypocritical Christianity of this land. Indeed, I can see no reason, but the most deceitful one, for calling the religion of this land Christianity.[58]

A Millennial Nation

The Myth of the Millennial Nation argued that, through the power of its example—through the power of freedom and democracy in action—the United States would inspire men and women around the globe to throw off the yoke of tyranny until the entire world would enter a golden age—a millennium—of freedom and self-government. But since slavery and, later, Jim Crow segregation told the world, in effect, that America lied when it presented itself as a nation defined by freedom and democracy, the nation had no choice but to whiten its millennial vision, leaving blacks out of the equation altogether. The only way the nation could cope with such a radical contraction that stood at the heart of its own self-image was to embrace—however subtly and however unconsciously—the notion of white supremacy as a defining component of the Myth of the Millennial Nation.

An Innocent Nation

It must now be obvious why the Myth of White Supremacy stands at the heart of the Myth of American Innocence. The very idea of innocence stands at odds with the practice of racial discrimination. The only way, therefore, to claim innocence and practice racial discrimination at one and the same time is to argue—or failing the will to make the argument, to believe implicitly and without conscious reflection—that white people are by nature superior to blacks. In this way, the Myth of American Innocence rests squarely on the presupposition of the Myth of White Supremacy.

How, Then, Might We Respond?

Many white Americans would like to believe that their nation is sufficiently virtuous that God Almighty would choose the United States to inspire and uplift the rest of the world.

They would like to believe that the bedrock principles on which this nation is built are rooted in "Nature and Nature's God," as the Declaration put it, that our core national values simply reflect the natural order of things, an order that God from the beginning built into the structure of the universe.

They would like to believe that, because our values reflect that natural order, we will progressively enlighten the world with the principles of freedom and democratic self government until the whole world is free.

And even though this nation is religiously pluralistic, they would like to believe that this nation is in sync with the noblest principles of the Christian religion—the religion that has shaped this nation in countless ways since 1776.

The problem is that the Myth of White Supremacy, so deeply woven into the warp and woof of the fabric of the nation, stands as a rebuttal to each of these myths, allowing us to discern—if we have eyes to see—that the Myth of American Innocence, while telling a story that gives us meaning, is also a myth in the popular sense of the term—a falsehood.

The question that cries out for an answer, then, is this: How might the nation respond to such deep contradictions in our national sense of meaning? Three possible responses present themselves as alternatives.

The Cynical Response

Cynicism—the belief that the nation is hopelessly mired in these contradictions and that the Great American Myths are therefore meaningless—is the first possible response.

To understand this response more fully, we might ask, "What would happen to the United States if we entered a period when no one could agree on the meaning of America, when a large number of Americans were cynical about the American Creed, and when—in short—the spiritual glue that had bound the nation together in previous years had broken apart, crumbled, and collapsed?"

In *The Broken Covenant*, Robert N. Bellah (1927–2013) argued that America has experienced three such periods. The time of the founding was one of those periods, since it was by no means clear that the American people could actualize the American Creed.

Before and during the Civil War, many Americans asked the obvious question, "How can we claim a commitment to the proposition that 'all men are created equal' when millions of Americans are kept in bondage simply because of the color of their skin?" One of the leading abolitionists of that time, William Lloyd Garrison, called the Constitution "a pact with the devil" that ought to be abolished, since the Founders had failed to outlaw slavery when they had the opportunity to do so. Garrison's opinion on the meaning and purpose of America typified the feelings of many abolitionists of that period.

Then, during the 1960s, many Americans raised similar concerns. "How can we take seriously the nation's commitment to the American Creed," they asked, "since for a hundred years after the Civil War, white Americans still treat black Americans as second-class citizens with no significant rights whatsoever? And how can we take seriously the nation's commitment to the American Creed in the face of America's military venture in Vietnam?" Many believed that venture to be an unjust war, fought mainly to protect American investments abroad.

Bellah described these three periods as times "of testing so severe that not only the form but even the existence of our nation has been called in question."[59] Bellah, of course, was right, for if Americans fought over the fundamental meaning of the nation—a meaning that had ceased to be clear— then it is obvious that the glue that held the nation together was rapidly deteriorating, and America stood in peril of disintegration.

The problem sometimes ran even deeper than this, for some Americans, both during the 1860s and the 1960s, essentially stripped the nation of any meaningful myths at all. The myths, they said, were nothing but lies, meant only to deceive the public and maintain the power and privileges of an established class. If Westerhoff was right when he claimed "Without a story we cannot live" and "Without a story life makes no sense," then it is obvious that those who stripped the nation of its myths also stripped the nation of its capacity to survive.

Here we find the enduring problem that the fundamentalists of the left, who can find no good in America whatsoever, have posed. If Americans in significant numbers finally conclude that the American story is both false and bankrupt, precisely at that point the nation is in danger of disintegration.

The Absolutist Response

The absolutist response essentially argues that the nation has fully realized the meaning of its myths and stands in no need of improvement. This response has emerged at a variety of critical periods in American history. For example, some responded to the tumult of the 1960s with uncritical affirmations of the nation's righteousness and offered this pointed advice to the nation's dissidents: "America: love it or leave it." A similar dynamic emerged in the aftermath of the September 11, 2001, terrorist attacks on the Pentagon and the World Trade Center. Few at that time wished to hear what was wrong with America, and few could bear to engage in national self-examination.

Thus, for example, the American Council of Trustees and Alumni, founded by Lynne Cheney and committed, in part, to the "free exchange of ideas on campus," nonetheless issued a report that roundly condemned university professors who called for a more thoughtful approach to that crisis than dividing the world neatly between the forces of good and the forces of evil.[60] Some of the comments the report found unacceptable were these:

[We should] build bridges and relationships, not simply bombs and walls.
—speaker at Harvard Law School

[O]ur security can only come by using our national wealth, not for guns, planes, and bombs, but for the health and welfare of our people, and for people suffering in other countries.
—professor emeritus, Boston University

If we perpetuate a cycle of hate and revenge, this conflict will escalate into a war that our great-grandchildren will be fighting.
—professor of anthropology, Brown University

[W]e need to hear more than one perspective on how we can make the world a safer place. We need to understand the reasons behind the terrifying hatred directed against the United States and find ways to act that will not foment more hatred for generations to come.
—professor emerita of women's studies, University of Chicago

The absolutist response also ignores or willfully dismisses as false the pervasive reality of white supremacy. The irony of that response is the fact that, while it seeks to affirm the American Creed, it simultaneously undermines one of the most precious of all American rights—the right to dissent.

The Future-Oriented Response

There is one more possible response to the question, "How might the nation respond to the fact that the Myth of White Supremacy so completely contradicts and undermines the promise of both the American Creed and the Great American Myths?"

To abandon the myths as the cynics do is to abandon the nation as well. And to absolutize the myths as many conservatives do is to restrict dissent, shackle the Bill of Rights, undermine the American Creed, and warp the very meaning of the American nation.

A far more constructive approach calls for a twofold response. First, through a process of careful discernment, attention to American history, and serious introspection, Americans must come to terms with their Myth of White Supremacy. And through that process, they must reject it, once and for all.

At the very same time, Americans must find in their Great American Myths a redemptive potential and ask how they might realize the potential of those myths in a responsible way.

In his 1895 book, *Why Is the Negro Lynched?*, the great abolitionist Frederick Douglass asked how the nation could solve its racial dilemma. While the particular circumstances in 1895 differ from those the nation confronts in the twenty-first century, the principles that guided his answer still ring true today. "How can this problem be solved?" Douglass asked and answered:

> I will tell you how it cannot be solved. It cannot be solved by keeping the Negro poor, degraded, ignorant and half-starved. . . . It cannot be solved by keeping back the wages of the labourer by fraud. . . . It cannot be done by ballot-box stuffing, by falsifying election returns, or by confusing the Negro voter by cunning devices. It cannot be done by repealing all federal laws enacted to secure honest elections.

How, then, could it be done?

> Let the white people of the North and South conquer their prejudices. Let the Northern press and pulpit proclaim the gospel of truth and justice against the war now being made upon the Negro. Let the American people cultivate kindness and humanity. . . . Let them give up the idea that they can be free while making the Negro a slave. Let them give up the idea that to degrade the coloured

man is to elevate the white man. . . . In the language of ex-Senator [John James] Ingalls: "Let the nation try justice and the problem will be solved."[61]

Douglass, in effect, charged the American people with living out the meaning of the American Creed. And based on the spirit of these admonitions, he also charged them, in effect, with living out the richest possible meaning of the Great American Myths.

To argue, for example, that God—or at least some power beyond themselves—chose the American nation for a special mission in the world may be a useful idea if the American people can imagine that God chose this nation in the same way that God chose every other nation—not for power or dominance or might, but for healing and reconciliation and to promote the common good among all people, both within and outside of America's borders.

To argue that the bedrock principles held by this nation conform to the natural order of things may be a useful theme if Americans can discern in the natural order what their Pledge of Allegiance asserts—that this is "one nation, under God, with liberty and justice for all."

And the claim that the United States is a Christian nation can be useful as well if this admittedly pluralistic nation were to embody not only the basic principles of the Christian faith but the basic principles of all the world's great religions—compassion for the oppressed, welcome for strangers, and justice for the poor.

If the United States were to embrace those ideals in those ways, then perhaps the Myth of the Millennial Nation—the claim that the American nation will in some way help promote those same ideals throughout the world—might make some sense.

In the meantime, Reinhold Niebuhr reminded us years ago that nations, like all other human institutions, typically seek to preserve their wealth and power and share that power and resources with others only under duress.[62] That observation should chasten whatever expectations we may have regarding the virtue of the American nation and remind us that of all the American myths, the myth of innocence is certainly false.

At the same time, four of the Great American Myths, like the American Creed to which they point, can surely drive our aspirations, for without those aspirations, the historic meaning of the American experiment has no sustainable future.

Notes

1. Carol Anderson, *White Rage: The Unspoken Truth of Our Racial Divide* (New York: Bloomsbury, 2016), 163–164.

2. Eric Foner, CNN, December 28, 2016, https://www.youtube.com/watch?v=ovRKKeUDafs, accessed December 29, 2016.

3. The argument of this book is similar, though hardly identical, to that of Joe Feagin who posits a "white racial frame," which he defines as "a perspectival frame" embedded both in our individual minds and our "collective memories and histories" that "helps people make sense out of everyday situations." This "perspectival frame," he argues, dates to the seventeenth century; extends "across white divisions of class, gender, and age"; and "has provided the vantage point from which white Americans have constantly viewed North American society." Indeed, Feagin argues that "for most whites . . ., the white racial frame is more than just one significant frame among many; it is one that has routinely defined a way of being, a broad perspective on life, and one that provides the language and interpretations that help structure, normalize, and make sense out of society." Joe R. Feagin, *The White Racial Frame: Centuries of Racial Framing and Counter-Framing* (second edition, New York: Routledge, 2013), 3, 10–11.

4. David Billings, *Deep Denial: The Persistence of White Supremacy in United States History and Life* (Roselle, N.J.: Crandall, Dostie and Douglass Books, Inc., 2016), 13–14.

5. Lesley Walker, "Words," essay in "Learning to Tell Our Stories," an honors first-year seminar at Lipscomb University, fall, 2016.

6. Malcolm X as told to Alex Haley, *Autobiography of Malcolm X* (New York: Grove Press, 1964), 31.

7. Telephone conversation with Joseph Robinson, executive director of the Martin Luther King Jr. Leadership Development Institute, Harrisburg, Pennsylvania, September 5, 2017.

8. Toni Morrison, *The Bluest Eye* (New York: Plume, 1994; first published 1970), 46.

9. Ibid., 209–210.

10. James Baldwin, *The Fire Next Time*, in Toni Morrison, ed., *James Baldwin: Collected Essays* (New York: Library Classics of the United States, 1998), 291.

11. Catherine Meeks, "Why Is This Black Woman Still Talking about Race?" in Catherine Meeks, ed., *Living into God's Dream: Dismantling Racism in America* (New York: Morehouse Publishing, 2016), 35–36.

12. W. E. B. Du Bois, *The Souls of Black Folk*, in *Three Negro Classics* (New York: Avon Books, 1965), 214–215.

13. Quoted in Richard Wright, *White Man, Listen! Lectures in Europe, 1950–1956* (1957: reprinted, New York: HarperPerennial, 1995), 82.

14. Sara G. Stanley, "What to the Toiling Millions There, Is This Boasted Liberty?" (1856), in *Lift Every Voice: African American Oratory, 1787–1900*, ed. Philip S. Foner and Robert James Branham (Tuscaloosa: University of Alabama Press, 1998), 286.

15. John Mercer Langston, "There Is No Full Enjoyment of Freedom for Anyone in This Country" (1845), in Foner and Branham, *Lift Every Voice*, 274–275.

16. Charles Lenox Remond, "For the Dissolution of the Union" (1844), in Foner and Branham, *Lift Every Voice*, 206.

17. William Wells Brown, "I Have No Constitution and No Country" (1849), in Foner and Branham, *Lift Every Voice*, 215–216.

18. William Wells Brown, *Narrative of William W. Brown, a Fugitive Slave* (1847), in *African American Voices: The Life Cycle of Slavery*, ed. Steven Mintz (St. James, N.Y.: Brandywine Press, 1999), 136.

19. Frederick Douglass, "Speech on American Anti-Slavery Society" (1847), in Foner and Branham, *Lift Every Voice*, 248.

20. Malcolm X, "The Ballot or the Bullet" (1964), in *Malcolm X Speaks*, ed. George Breitman (New York: Grove Weidenfeld, 1965). For an extended commentary on this statement from Malcolm X, see James H. Cone, *Martin and Malcolm and America: A Dream or a Nightmare* (Maryknoll, N.Y.: Orbis Books, 1991).

21. Wright, *White Man, Listen!* 83, 79.

22. Molefi Kete Asante, *Erasing Racism: The Survival of the American Nation* (second edition, New York: Prometheus Books, 2009), 117, 130.

23. John H. Westerhoff III, *A Pilgrim People: Learning through the Church Year* (Minneapolis: Seabury Press, 1984), 3–4.

24. Hubert G. Locke, *Searching for God in Godforsaken Times and Places: Reflections on the Holocaust, Racism, and Death* (Grand Rapids: Eerdmans, 2003), 47.

25. Gomes Eanes de Zurara, *The Chronicle of the Discovery and Conquest of Guinea, 1453,* cited in Ibram X. Kendi, *Stamped from the Beginning: The Definitive History of Racist Ideas in America* (New York: Nation Books, 2016), 22–23.

26. Kendi, *Stamped from the Beginning*, Kendi's book won the 2016 National Book Award for nonfiction. In tracing "the history of racist ideas in America," he invariably chronicles in great detail the growth and development of the Myth of White Supremacy. Every page contributes to our understanding of that process.

27. Thomas Jefferson, *Notes on the State of Virginia* (Philadelphia: Prichard and Hall, 1788), 138–143.

28. Matthew Frye Jacobson, *Whiteness of a Different Color: European Immigrants and the Alchemy of Race* (Cambridge: Harvard University Press, 1998), 30.

29. Chief Justice Roger B. Taney, "Opinion of the Court" in *Dred Scott v. Sandford*, 1857, http://www.let.rug.nl/usa/documents/1826–1850/dred-scott-case/chief-justice-taney.php, accessed January 30, 2017.

30. Abraham Lincoln, "Speech on the Dred Scott Decision," Springfield Illinois, June 26, 1857, http://teachingamericanhistory.org/library/document/speech-on-the-dred-scott-decision/, accessed September 1, 2017.

31. Abraham Lincoln, "Fourth Debate with Stephen A. Douglas," Charleston, Illinois, September 18, 1858, https://www.nps.gov/liho/learn/historyculture/debate4.htm, accessed August 9, 2017.

32. Reported in the *Cincinnati Enquirer* and cited in Hans Louis Trefousse, *Andrew Johnson* (New York: W. W. Norton and Company, 1997), 236.

33. Woodrow Wilson, *A History of the American People*, vol. 4: *Critical Changes and Civil War* (New York: Harper and Brothers, 1902), 250–251, 270.

34. Ibid., vol. 5: *Reunion and Nationalization* (New York: Harper and Brothers, 1902), 49.

35. Ibid., 62–64.

36. Ibid., 59–60.

37. William Keylor, "The Long-Forgotten Racial Attitudes and Policies of Woodrow Wilson," *Professor Voices: Commentary, Insight, & Analysis*, Boston University, March 4, 2013, http://www.bu.edu/professorvoices/2013/03/04/the-long-forgotten-racial-attitudes-and-policies-of-woodrow-wilson/, accessed August 13, 2017.

38. W. E. B. Du Bois, *Black Reconstruction in America: 1865–1880*, introduction by David Levering Lewis (New York: Touchstone, 1995), 167.

39. Anderson, *White Rage*, 19–20.

40. Linda Christensen, "Burning Tulsa: The Legacy of Black Dispossession," *Teaching a People's History: Zinn Education Project*, May 28, 2013, https://zinnedproject.org/2013/05/burning-tulsa-the-legacy-of-black-dispossession/, accessed July 16, 2017.

41. "What Happened to Black Wall Street on June 1, 1921?" *San Francisco BayView: National Black Newspaper*, http://sfbayview.com/2011/02/what-happened-to-black-wall-street-on-june-1-1921/, accessed January 14, 2017.

42. "Limbaugh: I Hope He Fails," rushlimbaugh.com, https://www.rushlimbaugh.com/daily/2009/01/16/limbaugh_i_hope_obama_fails/, accessed January 15, 2017.

43. Azmat Khan, "The Republicans' Plan for the New President," *Frontline*, January 15, 2013, http://www.pbs.org/wgbh/frontline/article/the-republicans-plan-for-the-new-president/, accessed January 15, 2017. On the GOP's avowed resistance to Obama, see Michael Grunwald, *The New New Deal: The Hidden Story of Change in the Obama Era* (New York: Simon and Schuster, 2013).

44. Anderson, *White Rage*, 156.

45. John Perr, "The Othering of the President," *Daily Kos*, February 22, 2015, http://www.dailykos.com/story/2015/02/22/1365647/-The-othering-of-the-president, accessed January 15, 2017.

46. While Donald Trump won the Electoral College, Hillary Clinton, the Democratic nominee, won the popular vote by 2.9 million votes.

47. Anderson, "Ferguson Isn't about Black Rage against Cops. It's White Rage against Progress," *Washington Post*, August 29, 2014, https://www.washingtonpost.com/opinions/ferguson-wasnt-black-rage-against-copsit-was-white-rage-against-progress/2014/08/29/3055e3f4–2d75–11e4-bb9b-997ae96fad33_story.html?utm_term=.4d1a9a3e8550, accessed September 10, 2014.

48. Anderson, *White Rage*, 3.

49. Ibid., 3.

50. Ibid., 5.

51. Asante, *Erasing Racism*, 123.

52. Forrest E. Harris Sr., "The Future That Threatens Us and the Future That Calls Us to Change—Both are Here," in "The President's Blog," http://www.abcnash.edu/about/presidents-blog, accessed September 24, 2017. The leaders of the Freedom

Movement who were also students at American Baptist College included, for example, Julius Scruggs, Bernard Lafayette, Jim Bevels, William Barbee, and John Lewis.

53. Abraham Lincoln, and Lincoln quoting Douglas, "Speech on the Dred Scott Decision," Springfield, Illinois, June 26, 1857, http://teachingamericanhistory.org/library/document/speech-on-the-dred-scott-decision/, accessed September 1, 2017.

54. Kelly Brown Douglas, *Stand Your Ground: Black Bodies and the Justice of God* (Maryknoll: Orbis Books, 2015), 21. Anyone who doubts the veracity of this argument should read Brown's immensely compelling and informative book that connects the ancient myth of Anglo-Saxon exceptionalism, rooted in Tacitus's *Germania*, published in 98 C.E., to the murder of Tryvon Martin on February 26, 2012

55. Thomas Jefferson, *Notes on the State of Virginia*, ed. William Peden (Chapel Hill: University of North Carolina Press, 1955), 138–143.

56. Michael Eric Dyson, "What Donald Trump Doesn't Know about Black People," *The New York Times*, December 17, 2016, http://nyti.ms/2hTedjR, accessed December 17, 2016.

57. James Cone, *My Soul Looks Back* (New York: Orbis, 1985), 18.

58. Frederick Douglass, *Narrative of the Life of Frederick Douglass, an American Slave, Written by Himself* (1845; New York: Signet Books, 1968), 120.

59. Robert N. Bellah, *The Broken Covenant: American Civil Religion in Time of Trial* (New York: Seabury, 1975), 1.

60. "Defending Civilization: How Our Universities Are Failing America and What Can Be Done about It," a project of the Defense of Civilization Fund (Washington, D.C.: American Council of Trustees and Alumni, 2002), 1. The quotation is from the mission statement at the council's Web site, http://www.goacta.org/missionframeset.html; accessed January 23, 2003.

61. Frederick Douglass, *Why Is the Negro Lynched?* (1895; repr. London: Forgotten Books, 2012), 34–35.

62. Reinhold Niebuhr, *Moral Man and Immoral Society: A Study in Ethics and Politics* (New York: Charles Scribner's Sons, 1932).

CHAPTER TWO

The Myth of the Chosen Nation
The Colonial Period

Among the most powerful and persistent of all the myths that Americans invoke about themselves is the myth that America is a chosen nation, the idea that lies at the heart of American exceptionalism. What seems lost today are the profoundly religious origins of this vision. It is one thing to claim that America is exceptional in its own eyes. It is something else to claim that America is exceptional because God chose America and its people for a special mission in the world.

The Myth of the Chosen Nation has its oldest and deepest roots in the Hebrew Bible where the book of Deuteronomy reports that God spoke to the Jews as follows:

> The Lord your God has chosen you out of all the peoples on the face of the earth to be his people, his treasured possession. The Lord did not set his affection on you and choose you because you were more numerous than other peoples, for you were the fewest of all peoples. But it was because the Lord loved you and kept the oath he swore to your forefathers that he brought you out with a mighty hand and redeemed you from the land of slavery, from the power of Pharaoh king of Egypt. (Deut. 7:6–8, NIV)

In time, the American people would appropriate this myth for themselves and the land in which they lived. How that happened—and how that theme is deeply rooted in the notion of white supremacy—are the subjects of this chapter.

The English Reformation

In order to understand how the Myth of the Chosen Nation migrated from ancient Israel to the United States, it is important to turn the clock back some five hundred years to England during the early sixteenth century. There, a man named William Tyndale popularized the notion that England stood in a covenant relationship with God. If England obeyed God's commands, it would be blessed. If not, it would be cursed. Implied in this notion of a national covenant was the assumption that England, like Israel of old, had been chosen by God for a special mission in the world.

Henry VIII

Our story begins with Henry VIII, King of England from 1509 to 1547. Dismayed because his queen, Catherine of Aragon, had not given birth to a male heir to the English throne, and enamored of another woman, Anne Boleyn, Henry asked the pope for a divorce. When the pope refused, Henry, in effect, fired the pope, proclaimed himself head of the church in England, and demanded that his archbishop of Canterbury, Thomas Cranmer, ratify the divorce. In taking these actions, Henry not only divorced his wife. He also divorced England from the Roman Catholic Church. In its place, he created the Church of England, often known as the Anglican Church and, in America, as the Episcopal Church.

All this took place in 1534, seventeen years after Martin Luther had drafted the Ninety-five Theses and launched the Protestant Reformation. By breaking with the Roman Catholic Church, Henry opened the door for reformation in England, but Henry had little interest in real reform. He was interested mainly in divorcing Catherine and marrying Anne Boleyn, and if the only way to achieve those objectives was to break with the pope, then so be it. Though Henry had broken with the pope, he was devoutly Catholic in almost every other way and strenuously resisted the Protestant movement. The Church of England in its earliest years, therefore, resembled the Catholic Church, but without the pope.

If there was to be serious reform, therefore, it had to begin in other quarters, far from the courts of the King. As early as 1519, visions of reform stirred in the minds of several Cambridge University scholars who met regularly in a local pub, the White Horse Tavern, to drink beer and discuss the ideas of Martin Luther.[1] For several years, William Tyndale played a prominent role in that group and rapidly developed a deep admiration for Luther and his teachings. He also determined to translate the New Testament into English so that his own people could read it firsthand. When he approached the Bishop of London for permission to undertake this project, the bishop rejected his proposal out of hand. Tyndale therefore left England for Germany, where he took up residence in Wittenberg in 1524. There he learned from Luther himself and worked on his English translation of the New Testament.

That translation appeared in print in 1526. Tyndale wrote an assortment of prefaces and prologues that he included with that text, explaining to the reader how the New Testament should best be understood. Because Tyndale was so devoted to Luther's theology, these prefaces clearly identified the Lutheran notion of "justification by grace through faith" as the central, overarching theme of the New Testament. Since Henry VIII so strongly resisted all things Protestant, that particular Bible never enjoyed much circulation in England.

In 1530 Tyndale published the Pentateuch (five books of Moses) as a pocket book. In translating the book of Deuteronomy, Tyndale was especially struck with the theme of covenant. There, he found the story of a God who had made a covenant, or an agreement, with his chosen people. Essentially, that covenant embodied God's promise to bless his people if they remained faithful to him but to curse them if they disobeyed him and followed other gods. This was not for Tyndale just one more biblical saga. Rather, it was the very essence of the biblical saga and a story terrifying in its implications. The twenty-eighth chapter of Deuteronomy, especially, struck fear into Tyndale's heart. That chapter tells, first, of the blessings that would come upon Israel if the Israelites obeyed all of God's commands. Tyndale translated that material in the following way: "Blessed shalt thou be in the town and blessed in the fields, blessed shall be the fruit of thy body, the fruit of thy ground and the fruit of thy cattle, the fruit of thine oxen, and thy flocks of sheep, blessed shall thine almery be and thy store. Blessed shalt thou be, both when thou goest out, and blessed when thou comest in." On the other hand, that chapter also tells (verses 22–29) that God would send the most devastating curses upon Israel if it violated its covenant with God:

> And the Lord shall smite thee with swelling, with fevers, heat, burning, weathering, with smiting and blasting. And they shall follow thee, until thou perish. . . .
> And the Lord shall plague thee before thine enemies. Thou shalt come out one way against them, and flee seven ways before them, and shalt be scattered among all the kingdoms of the earth. And thy carcase shall be meat unto all manner fowls of the air and unto the beasts of the earth. . . .
> And the Lord shall smite thee with the botches of Egypt and the emerods, scall and manginess, that thou shalt not be healed thereof. And the Lord shall smite thee with madness, blindness and dazing of the heart. And thou shalt grope at noonday as the blind gropeth in darkness, and shalt not come to the right way.[2]

Upon reading these words, Tyndale exclaimed, "A christian man's heart might well bleed for sorrow at the reading of it, for fear of the wrath that is like to come upon us according unto all the curses which thou there readest. For according unto these curses hath God dealt with all nations, after they were fallen into the abominations of blindness."[3]

In 1534 Tyndale issued a second edition of the New Testament. Because the Old Testament notion of national covenant had now shaped his thinking so profoundly, Tyndale substantially rewrote for his 1534 New Testament the prologues and prefaces he had composed for the 1526 edition. While still maintaining a strong belief in justification by grace through faith, Tyndale now argued that the central theme of scripture is the covenant God has made with his people. When Tyndale's Bible came from the press, Henry was preoccupied with Catherine, Anne, and the pope. As a result, it did not face the restrictions the 1526 edition had encountered. It therefore achieved a significant circulation among literate English people.

It is difficult to overestimate the importance of that 1534 New Testament, for it helped define and popularize in England the concept of the national covenant. Tyndale did not restrict the covenant to ancient Israel but envisioned the possibility that God had extended His covenant to England as well. "The general covenant wherein all other are comprehended and included is this," he wrote. "If we meek ourselves to God, to keep all his laws, after the example of Christ: then God hath bound himself unto us to keep and make good all the mercies promised in Christ, throughout all the scripture."[4]

He made this point especially clear in his preface to the book of Jonah, published separately probably in 1531. He argued there that in years past, God had sent prophets to England, but England had refused to repent. "Gildas preached repentance unto the old Britains that inhabited England," Tyndale wrote. "[T]hey repented not, and therefore God sent in their enemies upon them . . . and destroyed them. . . . Wicliffe preached repentance unto our fathers not long since: they repented not for their hearts were indurate." Then Tyndale made the crucial point: "And now Christ to preach repentance, is risen yet once again out of his sepulcher in which the pope had buried him and kept him down with his pillars and poleaxes and all disguisings of hypocrisy. . . . And as I doubt not of the examples that are past, so am I sure that great wrath will follow, except repentance turn it back again, and cease it."[5]

Tyndale never claimed that England was God's chosen people, but the theme of the national covenant implied as much. After all, God had struck a covenant with ancient Israel precisely because he had chosen Israel from all the nations of the earth. Tyndale's vision of covenant, therefore, was the soil in which the notion of chosenness would slowly germinate until, finally, it would spring full-blown in the United States.

One can hardly overestimate the importance of the various biblical materials that Tyndale translated and made available to his compatriots. Never having seen or read the Bible in their own language, an entire generation of English people eagerly devoured both his translations and his commentaries. And through his prologues and prefaces, Tyndale became a preacher to the nation. By the time Henry VIII died and Edward VI took the throne (1547), the notion that England was in some sense a chosen people, standing in covenant relation with God, had become a working assumption for many English people.

Edward and "Bloody" Mary

Edward VI (1547–1553) was only nine years old when he became king of England, a fact that allowed the king's Privy Council extraordinary powers. Because some on the Council favored the Protestant cause, the king and his Council suppressed Catholicism and implemented Protestant reforms with astonishing rapidity. Quick to compare their nation with ancient Israel, many in England saw in Edward a reflection of Josiah, the eight-year-old king of Israel who reestablished the laws of God and, on the basis of those laws, initiated far-reaching reforms (2 Kings, chapters 22 and 23). Clearly, the Myth of the Chosen People was working its way into the English imagination.

Still, Edward VI was not altogether certain what it might mean for England to keep covenant with God. He therefore instructed Thomas Cranmer, his archbishop of Canterbury, to consult Heinrich Bullinger, the successor to Ulrich Zwingli, the great Protestant reformer in Zurich, Switzerland. In effect, Bullinger replied, "You must restore the primitive church." Others sustained that advice. Martin Bucer, a leading Christian humanist and Reformed theologian from Strasbourg, for example, wrote a treatise, *De Regno Christi* ("The Kingdom of Christ"), which he dedicated to King Edward. There, Bucer argued that by emulating the ancient Christian faith, England could become the kingdom of Christ.

Many during Edward's reign linked Tyndale's covenant theology to the Reformed emphasis on primitive Christianity. England could keep the covenant, they argued, but only if England abolished human traditions in religion and restored the ancient Christian faith. In this way, Reformed Protestantism first began to shape British religious thought.

When Edward died in 1553, Mary Tudor (1553–1558), daughter of Henry VIII and Catherine of Aragon, became queen. Deeply resentful of both her father and the Protestant faith, Mary determined to turn England back to the Church of Rome. She thought she could achieve that objective through the sheer force of persecution. She therefore executed hundreds of Protestants, earning for herself the sobriquet "Bloody Mary."

Many Protestants, fearing for their lives, fled England, hoping to live in peace abroad as long as Mary was on the throne. These Marian Exiles, numbering some 800 in all, took up residence in several cities on the continent, among them Strasbourg, Basel, Frankfurt, and Geneva. While abroad, they pondered Tyndale's claim that God would curse England if the nation wandered from his will. Since they could regard the deaths of so many godly Protestants only as a curse, the pressing question emerged, "What did we do, or fail to do, that we should deserve such devastation from the hand of God?"

The answer seemed clear. They had not restored the ancient Christian faith as Bullinger and others had advised. Instead, they had settled for mere reform. Many exiles therefore determined that when Mary died, they would return to England and devote themselves to a thoroughgoing restoration of the ancient Christian faith. Only by taking such a course might England be saved from divine wrath to come.

This was a radical goal, for those who took this position hoped to replace the Anglican establishment with a church that conformed at every significant point to an ancient model revealed, they thought, in the biblical text. When one realizes that the Anglican Church was now the legally established church in England and that it functioned as a civic faith for the English people, one then sees what a radical—and risky—objective these visionaries undertook.

The radicals who took this position were England's earliest Puritans. Prior to the exile, there had been no Puritans in England at all. There had been Catholics on the one hand and Protestants on the other, and Protestants had been uniformly Anglican. Now, however, there emerged from the very bosom of the Anglican establishment a Puritan party that would rival the Church of England for religious control of the realm. While some of these Puritans would eventually break from the Church of England, others—still wearing the label "Anglican"—sought to subvert that church from within.

There are two other aspects of Puritanism that deserve mention here. First, Puritans always defined themselves over against Roman Catholic tradition, and they quarreled with the Church of England mainly because it retained so many Catholic practices. To the Puritans, Catholics had defiled and corrupted the ancient church. They viewed the pope as antichrist and Catholic clerics as vermin from the bottomless pit. To restore the ancient faith therefore meant to abandon every vestige of Catholic practice and to return to biblical norms that predated the rise of the papacy.

Elizabeth I, James I, and Charles I

Mary died in 1558 and Elizabeth I, the daughter of Henry VIII and Anne Boleyn succeeded her. Elizabeth would rule over England for forty-five years—from 1558 to 1603. How ironic it was that Henry divorced Catherine because she had given birth to no male heirs to the British throne and then married Anne who bore Elizabeth, destined to rule for almost half a century as one of the greatest monarchs in British history.

Upon Elizabeth's accession to the throne, the Puritans returned home and launched what amounted to a virtual revolution. It was not a revolution with guns, but one of words and propaganda, fought on three separate fronts. First, they secured for themselves strategic teaching positions in the English universities, especially Cambridge, where they could shape the thinking of the next generation of clerics. Second, they sought appointments to some of England's most influential pulpits, where they could shape the thinking of the general population. And third, they wrote. They wrote books, pamphlets, and broadsides. Propaganda poured from their pens as they sought to explain why England must abolish a church built on tradition and restore a church built on God's word.

The Puritans did not at that time separate from the Church of England. Instead, they worked inside the established order, seeking to bring change from within. So while their hopes and objectives made them Puritans, their actual membership made them Anglicans.

Elizabeth, then, inherited a volatile situation. She had Puritans on her left and Catholics on her right, both agitating for special privilege. Elizabeth, however, resolutely cast her lot with the Anglican establishment, what historians call the via media or middle way. From time to time, she made minor concessions to the Puritans designed to pacify them. But for the most part, she ignored their demands and thwarted their agenda.

By the 1580s and 1590s, long before Elizabeth's reign was complete, the Puritans found themselves thoroughly discouraged. Some began to argue that they had pursued the wrong strategy from the beginning. It would never work, they said, to seek reform from *within* the Church of England. Instead, they must *separate* from the Church of England and establish a true church, one that conformed to the word of God at every point. The Puritans who took this position soon became known as the Separatists.

The Separatists' decision was momentous, for they thereby abandoned all hope of controlling the national church and purging that church of Catholic tradition. In the meantime, however, many other Puritans continued their efforts to transform the Anglican establishment from within.

After a long and fruitful reign, Elizabeth died in 1603, and James I succeeded her until 1625. Since 1567, James had ruled Scotland as James VI. There he developed an intense dislike of all things Puritan, having known all too well the Scottish version of the Puritan party. He therefore determined, as he once put it, to "harry them out of the land." James harassed the Puritans and made their lives extraordinarily difficult. He blocked publication of their books. He deprived Puritan ministers of their livings. He even encouraged Anglican clerics to burn two "heretics" at the stake. It is little wonder that a colony of Puritans left England for Leyden in the Netherlands in 1608 and then settled Plymouth Colony, Massachusetts, in 1620. This was the earliest Puritan settlement in America.

James I died in 1625, and his son, Charles I, assumed the throne. Charles ruled until 1649. From the beginning, Charles made himself enormously unpopular with the Puritans. In the first place, Charles adopted an openly pro-Catholic, anti-Puritan policy. He married a Catholic princess, Henrietta Maria, and built for her a Catholic chapel in the heart of London. From the Puritan perspective, such actions by the king could only bring upon England the wrath of God. In addition, Charles appointed as his archbishop of Canterbury a man resolutely opposed to the Puritan movement, William Laud. And if his father, James, had harassed the Puritans, Charles persecuted them, sometimes viciously. It is easy to see, therefore, why another wave of Puritans fled England in 1630 to establish a second settlement in America: the Massachusetts Bay Colony.

Finally, the Puritans who settled New England—both Plymouth in 1620 and Massachusetts Bay Colony in 1630—were neither Presbyterians nor Separatists. Instead, they were Congregationalists, that is, members of the Church of England who sought to reform that church according to a congregational model of church polity.

The Covenant People in America

Americans have shrouded in myth the reasons for the Puritan migration to the New World. Every school child learns that the Puritans settled America for the sake of freedom. To a degree, that is true. The freedom the Puritans envisioned, however, was a far cry from the freedom Americans prize today. The Puritans sought freedom for themselves but for no one else.

To acknowledge that Puritans came to the New World in order to secure freedom for themselves still misses the principal motivation for their migration. Puritans never sought freedom for its own sake as Americans do today.

They rather sought freedom to place themselves under the absolute control of the law of God, revealed in scripture.

But why? Why was that concern so important, and why could they not pursue that objective in England? The answer to those questions points us once again to William Tyndale's covenant theology. As far as the Puritans could see, the English crown had little interest in keeping covenant with God. Since 1558, when Elizabeth took the throne, the Puritans had done everything in their power to bring England to repentance and to hold forth clearly the way of the ancient church. More than sixty years had elapsed since then, and little had changed. A host of events made this clear—the refusal of the crown to cooperate with the Puritan agenda, the repression of Puritan literature, the harassment of Puritan ministers, Charles's flirtations with the Catholic faith, and his marriage to a Catholic princess. All these things convinced them that God's wrath hung heavy over England's future.

The Puritans had one more card to play. They could flee into the American wilderness, erect there a church that conformed to biblical norms, and hold that example forth for the English to see and perhaps even to emulate. This would be a last-ditch attempt to rescue England from the wrath of God.

Within a very few years, however, New England Puritans generally despaired of any hope of meaningful change in Old England. A clear example of this sentiment appears in a sermon that Thomas Hooker, Founder of Connecticut, preached to friends and acquaintances gathered at the dock to bid him farewell as he departed England for the New World in 1633. Hooker claimed that God would soon turn his back on England, apparently to accompany the Puritans to a land where people took his law with greater seriousness. "God is going," he told his friends and well-wishers, "his glory is departing, England hath seen her best days, and now evil days are befalling us. God is packing up his gospel because nobody will buy his wares nor come to his price."[6]

Even in New England, Puritans built their experiment squarely on the concept of covenant. No one made this point more clearly than did John Winthrop, first governor of Massachusetts Bay Colony, who assembled the Puritans on the deck of the ship *Arbella* and preached them a sermon before they set foot on dry land. "Thus stands the cause between God and us," he told them. "We are entered into a Covenant with him for this work. . . . Now if the Lord shall please to hear us, and bring us in peace to the place we desire, then hath he ratified this Covenant and sealed our Commission."[7]

As Winthrop understood the notion of covenant, however, it had little to do with special privilege and everything to do with responsibilities for one another. In fact, he explained that *covenant* meant that "we must be knit together in this work as one man, we must entertain each other in brotherly affection, . . . we must delight in each other, make others' conditions our own, rejoice together, mourn together, labor and suffer together, always having before our eyes our Commission and Community in the work." If the Puritans would fulfill the covenant in these ways, he said, "We shall find that the God of Israel is among us."

The Chosen People in the Promised Land

In the colonies, however, the metaphor of the covenant pointed more and more to the notion of chosenness. After all, the Myth of the Chosen Nation had lingered in the shadows of covenantal thought ever since the days of Tyndale. Now, in the American colonies, it stepped forward into the full light of day.

There were several reasons for this. First, New England Puritans believed that other Protestants had accomplished mere reform, while they alone had successfully restored the ancient church. John Robinson, pastor of the Leyden pilgrims, affirmed, for example, that the Puritan way was "cast in the apostolical and primitive mould, and not one day nor hour younger, in the nature and form of it, than the first church of the New Testament." And John Cotton, a leading minister in the Massachusetts Bay Colony, smugly claimed that the New England churches were as close as could be to what "the Lord Jesus [would erect] were he here himself in person." Here we find a prime example of a concept I introduced in chapter 1—the notion of absolutizing a myth, that is, assuming that one has completely realized in one's own experience the meaning of a given myth and that no growth or improvement is needed. Little wonder that Cotton Mather, a third-generation Puritan minister, could proclaim to Old England, "Let us humbly speak it, it shall be profitable for you to consider the light which from the midst of this outer darkness is now to be darted over unto the other side of the Atlantic Ocean."[8]

Second, New England Puritans now found themselves isolated both geographically and spiritually. While initially hopeful that their holy experiment might prompt England to serious reform, that hope soon turned to despair. Separated from their homeland by perilous waters and thousands of miles, Puritans in New England grew increasingly certain that the English monarch and the majority of the English people would not support their cause. From the Puritan perspective, the English church remained entrenched in Catholic tradition and practice and refused to conform itself to the ancient Christian faith. New Englanders therefore found themselves isolated spiritually and felt they stood alone against the world. Because they stood alone in covenant with God, they found it easy to think of themselves as a chosen people.

Third, since the days of Tyndale, English Protestants had drawn a parallel between England and ancient Israel. Now, in their migration to New England, Puritans found that parallel even more compelling. Centuries ago, for example, God had led the Jews out of Egypt, through the Red Sea, and into the Promised Land. Now God led the Puritans out of England, across the Atlantic Ocean, and into another promised land. The Puritans made the most of this comparison. In the Puritan imagination, England became Egypt, the Atlantic Ocean became the Red Sea, the American wilderness became their own land of Canaan, and the Puritans themselves became the new Israel.

The "Chosen People," Native Americans, and African Americans

If one imagines one's tribe or clan or nation a chosen people, then it is also clear that others are not. The Puritans' view of themselves as a chosen people took on particular significance in this regard with respect to both Native Americans and enslaved people, transported against their will from the African continent. It simply never occurred to New England's Puritans to include anyone in the orbit of chosenness but themselves—white, English-speaking people from Great Britain—and that is why they took such pains to exclude all people of color within their borders.

If ancient Israel had encountered "heathen tribes" in the land of Canaan, the Puritans thought of native peoples in the same terms. William Bradford, the governor of Plymouth Colony, for example, described the land and its inhabitants like this: "What could they [Puritans] see [upon landing] but a hideous and desolate wilderness, full of wild beasts and wild men—and what multitudes there might be of them they knew not."

This description suggests that the Puritans attributed to the land and its native occupants two very different meanings. On the one hand, New England was a promised land, now to be inhabited by God's new Israel. At the same time, Puritans believed that Satan ruled the wilderness areas of the world and its inhabitants. Only when the gospel penetrated these regions would the tyranny of Satan recede. Puritans therefore believed that God had called them to dispel the influence of Satan in this new, promised land.

The well-known Puritan poet Michael Wigglesworth gave clear expression to this conviction in his verse of 1662, "God's Controversy with New England."

> Beyond the great Atlantick flood
> There is a region vast,

A country where no English foot
In former ages past:
A waste and howling wilderness,
Where none inhabited
But hellish fiends and brutish men
That devils worshiped.

This region was in darkness plac't
Far off from heavens light,
Amidst the shadows of grim death
And of eternal night.
For there the Sun of righteousness
Had never made to shine
The light of his sweet countenance,
And grace which is divine:

Until the time drew nigh wherein
The glorious Lord of hostes
Was pleasd to lead his armies forth
Into those forrein coastes.
At whose approach the darkness sad
Soon vanished away,
And all the shaddows of the night
Were turned to lightsome day.[9]

Even though Puritans viewed Native Americans as agents of Satan, they also believed that God could use Native Americans as agents of mercy and hospitality to his chosen people. Puritans, therefore, seldom viewed native hospitality as marks of their inherent goodness, but as evidence of the power of God in an otherwise depraved people. For these reasons, Puritans seldom took Native Americans very seriously. They sometimes spoke of the land that Native Americans had occupied for many generations as "vacant." John Cotton, for example, defended Puritan occupation of Native American lands in the following terms: "Where there is a vacant place, there is liberty for the son of Adam or Noah to come and inhabit, though they neither buy it, nor ask their leaves. . . . In a vacant soil, he that taketh possession of it, and bestoweth culture and husbandry upon it, his right it is. And the ground of this is from the Grand Charter given to Adam and his posterity in Paradise, Genesis 1:28. Multiply and replenish the earth, and subdue it."[10] The truth is, New England Puritans seldom had to buy native lands or wrest them from Native Americans by military might. Instead, smallpox epidemics so greatly reduced and subdued native populations that Puritans encountered little resistance to their settlements in the early years.

If New England's Puritans jealously guarded the notion of a chosen people as applicable to themselves alone, and if they took pains to exclude Native Americans from that orbit, they also took every conceivable step to prevent blacks from assimilating into their society and into their story.

In the first place, they assumed the facticity of the mythic "Curse of Ham," based on Genesis 9:20–27. That text tells how Ham, one of Noah's three sons, saw his father drunk and naked in his tent and told his two brothers. When Noah awoke, he said, "Cursed be Canaan; a slave of slaves shall he be to his brothers."

While this text never mentions either race or skin color, numerous readers over the course of many centuries have erroneously claimed that Ham was the father of African people and that Noah's curse therefore doomed Africans to perpetual servitude. Samuel Willard, minister of South Church Boston, appealed to that myth when he flatly affirmed that "all servitude began in the curse." Famed New England pastor Cotton Mather also appealed to that myth when he said of enslaved blacks in New England that "it is God who caused them to be servants."[11]

White supremacy and superiority were simply assumed in this interpretation, and the New England colonies sought to operationalize that difference in status in a variety of ways, including statutes that barred black and white intermarriage. Thus, a 1705 Massachusetts law entitled, "An Act for the Better Preventing of a Spurious and Mixed Issue," stipulated that "none of her Majesty's English or Scottish subjects, nor of any other Christian nation, within this province, shall contract matrimony with any negro or mulatto; nor shall any person, duly authorized to solemnize marriage, presume to join any such in marriage, on pain of forfeiting the sum of fifty pounds."

In time, other colonies took similar steps. A 1717 Maryland law therefore decreed that "any white man or white woman who shall intermarry . . . with any negro or mulatto, such white man or white woman shall become servants during the term of seven years, and shall be disposed of . . . as the justices of the county court, where such marriage so happens, shall think fit."[12]

Throughout the colonies, whites viewed both Native Americans and African Americans as fundamentally inferior beings, completely unfit for either citizenship or inclusion in the orbit of chosenness, which whites had appropriated to themselves.

The Legacy of the Myth of the Chosen Nation

The notion that God had chosen the people of New England for a special mission in the world intensified over the years and eventually became central to the white American imagination. This happened for one fundamental reason: the Puritans told a focused, compelling, and convincing story that no other immigrant group could match. Nevertheless, it was a story with which many immigrant groups could identify. In numerous books, treatises, and sermons, the Puritans told how God had led them from oppression into a promised land. Immigrants from all over Europe—and from other parts of the world as well—found this story immensely compelling and adopted it as if it were their very own. In this way, the Myth of the Chosen Nation became a permanent part of the white American consciousness.

Obviously, African Americans did not come to these shores as immigrants but as people forcibly enslaved. They therefore devised an entirely different chosen-people myth, a myth that rejected the standard narrative that whites loved to rehearse. Later in this chapter, we will explore the alternative "chosenness" myth that blacks claimed as their own.

The Creation of the "White People" Myth

In the meantime, it is crucial to grasp the fact that what I have called the "white American consciousness" had nothing to do with color. Instead, it had everything to do with politics and privilege.

It only takes a moment's thought to realize that no one is truly "white." People we often think of as "white" actually range in skin tone from light to dark. Likewise, people we often think of as "black" range in skin tone from light to dark as well. What, then, could the terms, "white" and "black," possibly mean when applied to human beings?

The answer to that question begins to emerge when we consider the point made by Nell Irvin Painter: "Today . . . biologists and geneticists . . . no longer believe in the physical existence of races—though they recognize the continuing power of racism (the belief that races exist, and that some are better than others."[13]

The notion that race and color signify real biological differences has been a powerful myth in the western world and one with a long and complex history, which Painter traces in detail in her book, *The History of White People*. Rather than corresponding to anything biological, these notions are essentially political, intended to signify who was superior and who was inferior on a sliding scale of human value. While the imperial nations of Europe vied with each other for colonial dominance in Africa and Asia, they all agreed on one theme that linked them together—"the presumed racial superiority of the colonizing white nations and the racial inferiority of the colonized darker nations," as David Billings put it.[14]

That pattern persisted in North America where Puritans and other British settlers drew a line—first, between themselves and the darker-skinned Native Americans and, later, between themselves and the darker-skinned Africans. And the color line they drew was intended to function as a barrier that would separate the privileged from those denied privilege.

American blacks have always understood that "there is no such thing as white people," that "whiteness is made up, and that white history disguised as American history is a fantasy, as much a fantasy as white superiority and white purity," as Michael Eric Dyson put it.[15]

And since there is no such thing as "white people," Ta-Nehisi Coates wrote perceptively of "people who have been brought up hopelessly, tragically, deceitfully, to believe that they are white." Believing that they are white, Coates observed, not only reinforces their sense of privilege—it also reinforces their "power of domination and exclusion," which "is central to the belief in being white, and without it, 'white people' would cease to exist for want of reasons."

Coates's point explains why some southern whites, believing that a rigidly held color line would protect their power and privilege, devised what is known as "the one-drop rule"—that one drop of African blood makes one black—a rule that segregated white from black "even if it meant," as Coates observed, "that their own blue-eyed sons would live under the lash."[16]

While originating in European colonialism, the color line that divided "white" from "black" became much more difficult to draw with any semblance of accuracy when some 28 million people, including Slovaks, Russians, Poles, and others from southern and eastern Europe immigrated to the United States from the 1880s to the 1920s. With skin tones often darker than most from northern Europe, their presence in the United States significantly blurred the color line that earlier immigrants from northern and western Europe had sought to draw with such precision.

Religion emerged as a factor as well. Were Russian Jews, for example, "white"? What about Orthodox Christians from Greece, or Roman Catholics from Italy? Would they be regarded as "white" or as "ethnics"? A similar question emerged with reference to Asian and Hispanic immigrants. To draw a line between "white" and Asian, on the one hand, or between "white" and Hispanics, on the other, proved to be a fruitful way to deny immigrants access to the privileges that "white" people typically enjoyed. But when immigrant peoples were grafted onto the tree called "white," as many were, power and privilege followed.[17]

It is no wonder, then, that many of those immigrants sought to identify with the myth of America as a chosen nation. To claim that story was a way to claim for themselves the myth of "whiteness" and all the privileges pertaining thereunto. One example will suffice. Many white Protestants in the United States resisted Jewish immigration, especially from eastern Europe, in the mid–nineteenth century. But Rabbi Isaac Mayer Wise nonetheless immigrated to America from Bohemia in 1846. Here he became the paramount spokesperson for Reform Judaism, a form of Judaism that sought to adapt the Jewish heritage to modern culture. Ironically, this Jewish leader—this nineteenth-century representative of the Chosen People of the biblical text—could speak of the wars that whites waged against the Native American population as "the wars of 'the Israelites against the Philistines,' of 'God's chosen people against the Indian Gentiles.'" Further, Wise argued that "George Washington and his heroic compatriots were the chosen instruments in the hands of Providence, to turn the wheel of events in favor of liberty forever."[18] In this speech, Wise articulated the myth that he, like millions of immigrants to these shores, ultimately learned from the Puritans of New England. And by claiming that myth, he claimed for himself and the Jewish community for which he spoke the power and privilege that typically belonged to "white" America.

The Myth of the Chosen People in the Revolutionary Period

Since the Puritans told their story so often and so well, one should not be surprised to find the Myth of the Chosen Nation central even to the thinking of the American Founders. In fact, when Congress appointed a committee of Franklin, Jefferson, and Adams to design a seal for the United States, Franklin suggested a seal that would portray "Moses lifting his hand and the Red Sea dividing, with Pharaoh in his chariot being overwhelmed by the waters, and with a motto in great popular favor at the time, 'Rebellion to tyrants is obedience to god.'" No less concerned than Franklin to link the United States to the image of ancient Israel, Jefferson suggested "a representation of the children of Israel in the wilderness, led by a cloud by day and a pillar of fire by night."[19]

Images of the children of Israel and of America as a chosen people likewise informed the rhetoric of the Revolution. In a sermon with the significant title "God Arising and Pleading His People's Cause," for example, Abraham Keteltas, a preacher in Newburyport, Massachusetts, told his congregation in 1777, "Our cause is not only righteous but, most important, it is God's own cause. It is the grand cause of the whole human race. . . . If the principles [adopted] . . . by the American colonies . . . were universally adopted and practiced upon by mankind, they would turn a vale of tears into a paradise of God." Keteltas had by no means finished with that rhetorical flourish.

He went on. The cause of the American Revolution, he proclaimed, "is the cause of truth against error and falsehood, the cause of righteousness against iniquity, the cause . . . of benevolence against barbarity, of virtue against vice. . . . In short, it is the cause of heaven against hell. . . . It is the cause for which heroes have fought, patriots bled, prophets, apostles, martyrs, confessors, and righteous men have died. Nay, it is a cause for which the Son of God came down from his celestial throne and expired on a cross."[20]

Keteltas was not unique in his presentation of these themes. Nicholas Street, for example, preached a sermon in East Haven, Connecticut, in 1777, in which he claimed that God had sent the Revolutionary War to scourge the colonies for their sins. He entitled that sermon, appropriately enough, "The American States Acting Over the Part of the Children of Israel in the Wilderness and Thereby Impeding Their Entrance into Canaan's Rest."

Then, in 1796, twenty years after the Revolution, another patriot named John Cushing spoke at a Fourth of July celebration at Ashburnham, Massachusetts. He told the crowd that in all of history, "God dealt with no people as with Israel. But in the history of the United States, particularly New England, there is as great similarity perhaps in the conduct of Providence to that of the Israelites as is to be found in the history of any people."[21] And Jefferson, in his second inaugural address, once again appealed to the image of ancient Israel as an appropriate model for the United States. "I shall need," he proclaimed, "the favor of that Being in whose hands we are, who led our fathers, as Israel of old, from their native land and planted them in a country flowing with all the necessaries and comforts of life."[22]

What must now be noted is that the Founders and virtually all whites during the Founding period viewed white Americans as the ones whom God had chosen and took great pains to keep blacks out of that equation. Thomas Jefferson, for example, hoped that blacks would "be removed" out of this country, "beyond the reach of mixture" so "the blood of his master" would not be stained. Indeed, he wrote that "amalgamation with the other color produces a degradation to which no lover of his country, no lover of excellence in the human character can innocently consent."[23]

Further, Article 1, Section 9, of the Constitution allowed each state to import enslaved people until 1808, and Article 4, Section 2, affirmed that any "Person held to Service or Labour in one State," having escaped to another state, must be "delivered up on Claim of the Party to whom such Service or Labour may be due." Likewise, the Naturalization Act of 1790 limited the right of American citizenship "to aliens being free white persons."[24] As David Billings notes, "The 1790 racial exclusionary act would be the primary reason the US would become an overwhelmingly white majority nation."[25]

In May 1792, Congress passed the First and Second Militia Acts, the second of which stipulated that "every free able-bodied white male citizen" be enrolled in the militia, thereby rejecting blacks from the defense of the nation.[26] In that very same year, Congress authorized construction of the White House, using the labor of enslaved blacks. As Randall Robinson writes, "To erect the building that would house the art that symbolized American democracy, the United States government sent out a request for one hundred slaves. . . . In exchange for the slaves' labor the government agreed to pay their owners five dollars per month per slave."[27]

It seems obvious that while many whites viewed their nation as chosen by God, as a new Israel chosen for a special mission in the world, they viewed blacks as inferior beings, barred from participation in the privileges of the chosen nation, but chosen instead for subjugation and bondage.

There is a sense in which the bondage to which many whites believed God had consigned black people became a self-fulfilling prophecy: bondage begat ever more restrictive bondage, oppression begat ever more brutal repression, and slavery rendered blacks less than human in the eyes of many whites. As Winthrop Jordan noted,

> The enormous toll of Negro life must have caused many white men to withdraw in silent horror, to refuse to admit identity with a people they were methodically slaughtering year after year. . . . To the horrified witness of a scene of torture, the victim becomes a "poor devil," a "mangled creature." He is no longer a man. He can no longer be human because to credit him with one's own human attributes would be too horrible.[28]

The Myth of the Chosen People after the Revolution

Intellectuals and literary elites, no less than politicians, have resorted to the myth of the Chosen People to describe the United States. Herman Melville in his novel *White Jacket* (1850) depicted Americans as "the peculiar, chosen people—the Israel of our time; we bear the ark of the liberties of the world. . . . God has predestinated, mankind expects, great things from our race. . . . Long enough have we been skeptics with regard to ourselves, and doubted whether, indeed, the political Messiah had come. But he has come in *us*, if we would but give utterance to his promptings."[29]

By the time Americans fought the Civil War, the Myth of the Chosen Nation continued to hold an extraordinary power over the American imagination—so powerful, in fact, that both northerners and southerners appealed to this motif to legitimate their cause. Numerous examples could be given, but two will suffice.

Henry Ward Beecher, son of the famed Lyman Beecher, brother of Harriet Beecher Stowe (author of *Uncle Tom's Cabin*), and one of America's most popular pulpit preachers in the mid–nineteenth century, has been described as "that magnificent weathervane of respectable opinion."[30] In a sermon preached at Plymouth Church of Brooklyn in 1861, he explicitly drew the comparison between the northern states and ancient Israel. He reflected on the fact that God had "brought the Egyptians behind the children of Israel" as Israel prepared to cross the Red Sea. Then he made his point. "And now our turn has come. Right before us lies the Red Sea of war. It is red indeed. There is blood in it. We have come to the very edge of it, and the Word of God to us to-day is, 'Speak unto this people that they go forward.'"[31]

Benjamin Palmer served as the first moderator of the General Assembly of the Presbyterian Church in the Confederate States of America. In a sermon he delivered in 1861, Palmer also appealed to the Myth of the Chosen Nation, in this case on behalf of the South: "Eleven tribes sought to go forth in peace from the house of political bondage: but the heart of our modern Pharaoh is hardened, that he will not let Israel go. In their distress, with the untried sea before and the chariots of Egypt behind, ten millions of people stretch forth their hands before Jehovah's throne, imploring him to 'stir up his strength before Ephraim and Benjamin and Manasseth, and come and save them.'"[32]

At the end of the nineteenth century, patriots in the Spanish-American War once again appealed to the Myth of the Chosen Nation to justify American intervention in Cuba and the Philippines. Senator Orville Platt of Connecticut, for example, expressed on the floor of the U.S. Senate his conviction that "the same force was behind our army at Santiago and our ships in Manila Bay that was behind the landing of the Pilgrims on Plymouth Rock," adding that "we have been chosen to carry on and to carry forward this great work of uplifting humanity on earth."

Among those who sought to justify American involvement in the Philippines, no one employed the Myth of the Chosen Nation with greater force—and no one linked it more explicitly to white supremacy—than Albert Beveridge, senator from Indiana from 1899 to 1911. According to Beveridge,

God has not been preparing the English-speaking and Teutonic peoples for a thousand years for nothing but vain and idle self-contemplation and self-admiration. No. He made us master organizers of the world to establish system where chaos reigned. He has given us the spirit of progress to overwhelm the forces of reaction throughout the earth. He has made us adept in government that we may administer government among savage and senile peoples. Were it not for such a force as this the world would relapse into barbarism and night. And of all our race He has marked the American people as His chosen nation to finally lead in the redemption of the world.[33]

In this passage, several things seem obvious. First, Beveridge defines America strictly in terms of "English-speaking and Teutonic peoples." This conception of America has no room for people of color. This point is fundamental to the thesis of this book, for in making the claim that "English-speaking and Teutonic peoples" were God's "chosen nation to finally lead in the redemption of the world," Beveridge implicitly defined people of color as "the other"—those people who were not chosen and who needed to be redeemed.

Second, in the rhetoric of Beveridge, the earlier definition of covenant that for so many years had accompanied the Myth of the Chosen Nation now disappeared. John Winthrop, for example, argued in the seventeenth century that "we are entered into a Covenant with him [God] for this work" and defined "this work" as love for the neighbor. By the late nineteenth century, Beveridge argued that America was God's "chosen nation to finally lead in the redemption of the world."

One finds here little if any sense of responsibility to the neighbor and certainly nothing comparable to Winthrop's assertion that "we must be knit together in this work as one man, we must entertain each other in brotherly affection, . . . we must delight in each other, make others' conditions our own, rejoice together, mourn together, labor and suffer together, always having before our eyes our Commission and Community in the work."

Instead, we find in Beveridge only the claim that the Teutonic peoples of America were the "master organizers of the world" who would "administer government among savage and senile peoples." Here one finds only an appeal to power, domination, and control. No wonder that H. Richard Niebuhr could write in 1937 that "the old idea of American Christians as a chosen people who had been called to a special task was turned into the notion of a chosen nation especially favored. . . . As the nineteenth century went on, the note of divine favoritism was increasingly sounded."[34] In this sense, the American people absolutized the Myth of the Chosen Nation. It is precisely that understanding of chosenness as divine favoritism that would continue to dominate the thinking of many Americans through the twentieth century and into the twenty-first.

African Americans and the Myth of the Chosen People

Because white Americans increasingly embraced the Myth of the Chosen Nation as a sign that the Almighty had favored them with power, dominion, and control, minority peoples often had to devise alternate but comparable myths in order to survive in a hostile and alien culture. The enslaved African

American population was a case in point, and their creation of alternate Chosen People myths provided a telling critique of the dominant white understandings.

Like the whites, enslaved blacks also identified with the saga of ancient Israel. If whites, however, imagined themselves a new Israel in a promised land, enslaved blacks identified with Israel in Egyptian bondage, longing for deliverance to the Promised Land. In this way, the white South became Egypt, the land of oppression, and the North became the Land of Canaan, flowing with milk and honey.

If whites celebrated John Winthrop and other Puritan leaders as "Moses" who had led them into the Promised Land, blacks eagerly looked for just such a Moses who would lead them out of the house of bondage. From time to time, such a "Moses" emerged. Nat Turner, Denmark Vesey, and a man known only as Gabriel announced themselves as messianic liberators who would overpower the white population and lead enslaved people to freedom. During the days of the Underground Railroad, "conductors" did just that, smuggling blacks out of the South to freedom in the northern states. One of the most famous of those conductors, Harriet Tubman, soon acquired the designation "Black Moses."

Sometimes blacks identified not just the South, but also the entire American nation as the "house of bondage," symbolized by Egypt or, alternatively, Babylon. For example, Maria W. Stewart, a pamphleteer and activist, suggested in an 1833 lecture at the African Masonic Hall in Boston that "America has become like the great city of Babylon, for she has boasted in her heart, 'I sit as a queen, and am no widow, and shall see no sorrow.'" By invoking the Babylon imagery, Stewart drew on Revelation 18–19, a biblical text that called down God's judgment on regimes that oppress the righteous and build their empires on the blood and toil of enslaved people. "She [America] is indeed a seller of slaves and the souls of men," Stewart continued. "She has made the Africans drunk with the wine of her fornication; she has put them completely beneath her feet, and she means to keep them there." God, Stewart claimed, would soon deliver the blacks from the house of bondage. "The oppression of injured Africa has come up before the Majesty of Heaven; and when our cries shall have reached the ears of the Most High, it will be a tremendous day for the people of this land; for strong is the arm of the Lord God Almighty."[35]

Often, enslaved blacks celebrated the theme of liberation from the house of bondage in their hymnody. To sing these songs was risky business, however, since white overseers often punished them severely if they spoke of escape. To fool the overseers, therefore, blacks routinely employed the metaphors of heaven and the afterlife when they spoke of liberation. They were interested in heaven, to be sure, but they also longed for freedom in this life. And so they sang songs like this one:

> I got shoes, you got shoes,
> All God's children got shoes.
> When I get to heaven, gonna put on my shoes,
> Gonna walk all over God's heaven.

Sometimes they described the Underground Railroad as a chariot and sang songs like these:

> Good news, chariot's comin',
> Good news, chariot's comin',
> Good news, chariot's comin',
> And it's coming for to carry me home.

Or again,

> Swing low, sweet chariot,
> Comin' for to carry me home,
> Swing low, sweet chariot,
> Comin' for to carry me home.
>
> If you get there before I do,
> Comin' for to carry me home.
> Tell all my friends I'm comin' too.
> Comin' for to carry me home.

By the late twentieth century, many African Americans still identified themselves as a chosen people bound for the Promised Land. On the evening before he was assassinated in 1968, Martin Luther King Jr., for example, identified himself with Moses and his black audience as a latter-day children of Israel. He told a crowd of striking sanitation workers and their supporters that "He's allowed me to go up to the mountain. And I've looked over. And I've seen the promised land. I may not get there with you. But I want you to know tonight, that we, as a people will get to the promised land."[36]

At the same time, some black Americans, at various times in American history, devised alternate chosen people myths in order to cope in the United States. For example, in order to counter the popular nineteenth-century notion that God through Noah had cursed the descendants of Ham with black skin and perpetual servitude, William Anderson published a book in 1857 that argued just the reverse. According to Anderson, the first people on earth were black, and whiteness, not blackness, was the fruit of God's curse. He ignored the story of the curse of Ham and focused instead on 2 Kings 5:27 where the prophet Elisha cursed his servant, Geházi, for both greed and lying. White skin first appeared, Anderson claimed, when—as the text records—Geházi "went out from [Elisha's] presence a leper, as white as snow." That account proved to Anderson that whiteness was a "disease."[37]

Another alternate myth is "Yacub's History," a narrative from the Nation of Islam, otherwise known as the Black Muslim tradition, founded in Detroit in 1930. Thousands of Americans learned of "Yacub's History" through Alex Haley's *Autobiography of Malcolm X*, the riveting biography of the most visible national leader of the Nation of Islam for roughly ten years before his assassination in 1965.[38]

According to this narrative, the first human beings on earth were black. Then, some 6,600 years ago, an angry and bitter scientist named Mr. Yacub decided to seek revenge on his peers. He therefore created through selective breeding and genetic manipulation "a devil race—a bleached-out, white race of people." The people that resulted from this effort were "pale-skinned, cold-blue-eyed devils—savages, nude and shameless; hairy, like animals, they walked on all fours and they lived in trees." The devil race wreaked so much havoc that blacks finally rounded them up, marched them to Europe, and placed them in caves. Once they left the caves, they grew strong, ruled the earth, and exploited other peoples around the world.[39]

The meaning of this myth is clear. Blacks are good and, since they came from the hand of God, they were the world's first human beings. Whites, on the other hand, are evil, and since they came from the hand of a mad scientist, they constitute an aberration on the natural order of things.

If one imagines that this story is nothing more than a fanciful tale, one should hear Malcolm explain its significance to the black community, especially to black prisoners:

> Among all Negroes, the black convict is the most perfectly preconditioned to hear the words, "the white man is the devil."
>
> You tell that to any Negro. Except for those relatively few "integration"-mad so-called "intellectuals," and those black men who are otherwise fat, happy, and deaf, dumb, and blinded, with their crumbs from the white man's rich table, you have struck a nerve center in the American black man. He may take a day to react, a month, a year; he may never respond, openly; but of one thing you can be sure—when he thinks about his own life, he is going to see where, to him, personally, the white man sure has acted like a devil. . . .
>
> You let this caged-up black man start thinking, the same way I did when I first heard Elijah Muhammed's teachings: let him start thinking how, with better breaks when he was young and ambitious he might have been a lawyer, a doctor, a scientist, anything. You let this caged-up black man start realizing,

as I did, how from the first landing of the first slave ship, the millions of black men in America have been like sheep in a den of wolves. That's why black prisoners become Muslims so fast when Elijah Muhammed's teachings filter into their cages by way of other Muslim convicts. "The white man is the devil" is a perfect echo of that black convict's lifelong experience.[40]

James Baldwin corroborated Malcolm's assessment: "One did not need to prove to a Harlem audience that all white men were devils. They were merely glad to have, at last, divine corroboration of their experience, to hear—and it was a tremendous thing to hear—that they had been lied to for all these years and generations, and that their captivity was ending, for God was black."[41]

Whether they embraced alternate myths or not, virtually all blacks categorically rejected the myth that, of all the nations and peoples of earth, God chose white America as a special agent to bring freedom and democracy to the world. Richard Wright offers a case in point. Correctly discerning the connections between the Myth of the Chosen Nation and the kind of Christianity whites had practiced for centuries, Wright asked in 1957, "How do I feel about the white man's vaunted claim . . . that he has been called by his God to rule the world and to have all overriding considerations over the rest of mankind, that is, colored men?" He answered,

I was born a black Protestant in the most racist of all the American states: Mississippi. I lived my childhood under a racial code, brutal and bloody, that white men proclaimed was ordained of God, said was made mandatory by the nature of their religion. Naturally, I rejected that religion and would reject any religion which prescribes for me an inferior position in life.[42]

In 2015, Ta-Nehisi Coates, whose people for generations had been locked out of the myth of American chosenness, explained to his young son why he could never embrace that myth or even the alternate myth that enslaved people embraced in their hymns and spirituals. "Here is what I would like for you to know," Coates wrote to his son:

In America it is traditional to destroy the black body—*it is heritage*. Enslavement was not merely the antiseptic borrowing of labor—it is not so easy to get a human being to commit their body against its own elemental interest. And so enslavement must be casual wrath and random manglings, the gashing of heads and brains blown out over the river as the body seeks to escape. It must be rape so regular as to be industrial. There is no uplifting way to say this. I have no praise anthems, nor old Negro spirituals. . . .

There is no them without you, and without the right to break you they must necessarily fall from the mountain, lose their divinity, and tumble out of the [American] Dream. And then they would have to determine how to build their suburbs on something other than human bones, how to angle their jails toward something other than a human stockyard, how to erect a democracy independent of cannibalism. But because they believe themselves to be white, they would rather countenance a man choked to death on film under their laws. And they would rather subscribe to the myth of Trayvon Martin, slight teenager, hands full of candy and soft drinks, transforming into a murderous juggernaut.[43]

Conclusions

It is clear that the Myth of the Chosen Nation has been a powerful theme in American life. It is also clear that this myth can serve good and constructive purposes when yoked to the notion of covenant, for "covenant" implies responsibilities to other human beings. In the United States, however, the Myth of White Supremacy has done far more than the notion of "covenant" to shape and define the Myth of the Chosen Nation.

Further, it is possible to take seriously the notion of covenant in the context of one's immediate peers and fail to extend that covenant understanding to a larger circle of humanity. In this case, the myth of the Chosen Nation can justify oppression of those outside the bounds of the covenant, as surely as if there were no conception of covenant at all. In spite of John Winthrop's words to the Massachusetts Puritans who settled Bay Colony—"we must delight in each other, make others' conditions our own, rejoice together, mourn together, labor and suffer together"—the Puritans who heard that speech understood that the notion of covenant encompassed them and them alone. Accordingly, they excluded from the outset both Native Americans and enslaved Africans from their covenant and their notion of themselves as the chosen people. In this way, the Myth of the Chosen Nation became an absolutized badge of privilege and power, justifying oppression and exploitation of those not included in the circle of the chosen.

Many white Americans over the years have failed to see the liabilities inherent in the Chosen Nation mythology—that cut loose from the chastening effects of covenant duties, this myth can cripple the American Creed and its promise that *all human beings* "are created equal, that they are endowed by their Creator with certain unalienable rights, that among these are Life, Liberty, and the pursuit of Happiness." Still, the notion that God chose America for power and privilege has seemed to many Americans altogether obvious and beyond dispute. How and why that myth could appear virtually self-evident to so many Americans for so many years are questions we will seek to answer in the following chapter.

Notes

1. For a discussion of these men and their contributions, see William A. Clebsch, *England's Earliest Protestants, 1520–1535* (New Haven: Yale University Press, 1964), esp. 42 and 139.

2. William Tyndale, trans., *Tyndale's Old Testament* (New Haven: Yale University Press, 1992), 292–293.

3. William Tyndale, "A Prologue into the Fifth Book of Moses Called Deuteronomy," in Tyndale, *Tyndale's Old Testament*, 256.

4. William Tyndale, "W. T. unto the Reader," in Tyndale, *Tyndale's New Testament*, ed. David Daniell (New Haven: Yale University Press, 1989), 4.

5. William Tyndale, "The Prologue to the Prophet Jonas," in Tyndale, *Tyndale's Old Testament*, 634–635. On Tyndale and his translations, see James C. Spalding, "Restitution as a Normative Factor for Puritan Dissent," *Journal of the American Academy of Religion* 44 (March 1976): 47–63.

6. Thomas Hooker, "The Danger of Desertion, a Farewell Sermon Preached Immediately before His Departure [1633] Out of Old England," in Winthrop Hudson, ed., *Nationalism and Religion in America* (New York: Harper and Row, 1970; orig. pub. London, 1641), 25.

7. John Winthrop, "A Modell of Christian Charity," in Conrad Cherry, ed., *God's New Israel: Religious Interpretations of American Destiny* (revised and updated edition, Chapel Hill: University of North Carolina Press, 1998), 40.

8. Robert Ashton, ed., *The Works of John Robinson, Pastor of the Pilgrim Fathers* (Boston: Jonathon Cape, 1851), 2:43; Cotton Mather, *Magnalia Christi Americana; or, The Ecclesiastical History of New England* (London, 1702), 1:26–27.

9. Michael Wigglesworth, "God's Controversy with New England," in Cherry, ed., *God's New Israel*, 42–43.

10. John Cotton, "God's Promise to His Plantations" (1630), *Old South Leaflets*, No. 53 (Boston, 1896), 6, cited in Charles M. Segal and David C. Stineback, *Puritans, Indians, & Manifest Destiny* (New York: G. P. Putnam's Sons, 1977), 31–32.

11. Samuel Willard, "Sermon CLXXIX [24 August 1703]," in *A Compleat Body of Divinity in Two Hundred and Fifty Expository Lectures on the Assembly's Shorter Catechism* (Boston: B. Green and S. Kneeland, 1726), 613; and Cotton Mather, *The Negro Christianized: An Essay to Excite and Assist That Good Work, the Instruction of Negro-Servants in Christianity* (Boston: B. Green, 1706), 32.

12. Cited in Chief Justice Roger B. Taney, "Opinion of the Court," in *Dred Scott v. Sandford*, 1857, http://www.let.rug.nl/usa/documents/1826–1850/dred-scott-case /chief-justice-taney.php, accessed January 30, 2017.

13. Nell Irvin Painter, *The History of White People* (New York: W. W. Norton and Company, 2010), xii.

14. David Billings, *Deep Denial: The Persistence of White Supremacy in United States History and Life* (Roselle, N.J.: Crandall, Dostie and Douglass Books, Inc., 2016), 49–50.

15. Michael Eric Dyson, *Tears We Cannot Stop: A Sermon to White America* (New York: St. Martin's Press, 2017), 44–45.

16. Ta-Nehisi Coates, *Between the World and Me* (New York: Spiegel and Grau, 2015), 6 and 42.

17. On the process of grafting darker-skinned Europeans into the category of "whiteness," see Matthew Frye Jacobson, *Whiteness of a Different Color: European Immigrants and the Alchemy of Race* (Cambridge: Harvard University Press, 1998).

18. Isaac Mayer Wise, "Our Country's Place in History," in Cherry, ed., *God's New Israel*, 230.

19. Irving L. Thompson, "Great Seal of the United States," *Encyclopedia Americana*, XIII (1967), 362.

20. Abraham Keteltas, "God Arising and Pleading His People's Cause," in Hudson, ed., *Nationalism and Religion in America*, 49 and 52.

21. John Cushing, "A Discourse Delivered at Ashburnham, July 4, 1796, in Hudson, ed., *Nationalism and Religion in America*, 18.

22. Thomas Jefferson, Second Inaugural Address in A. E. Bergh, ed., *The Writings of Thomas Jefferson*, X (Washington, D.C.: The Thomas Jefferson Memorial Association, 1907), 217.

23. Thomas Jefferson, *Notes on the State of Virginia*, 1783, ed. William Peden (Chapel Hill: University of North Carolina Press, 1955), 143; and Jefferson to Edward Coles, Monticello, August 25, 1814, cited in Winthrop D. Jordan, *White over Black: American Attitudes toward the Negro, 1550–1812* (Chapel Hill: University of North Carolina Press, 1968), 547, n. 5. These statements are especially striking in light of the fact that, several years after expressing those opinions, Jefferson apparently fathered several children by an enslaved woman, Sally Hemings. While the Jefferson-Hemings liaison is open to dispute, most historians agree that Jefferson fathered Hemings's children.

24. "An act to establish an uniform Rule of Naturalization," March 26, 1790, http://www.mountvernon.org/education/primary-sources-2/article/naturalization-acts-of-1790-and-1795/, accessed August 7, 2017.

25. Billings, *Deep Denial*, 29–30.

26. Constitution Society, http://www.constitution.org/mil/mil_act_1792.htm, accessed April 15, 2017.

27. Randall Robinson, *The Debt: What America Owes to Blacks* (New York: Penguin Putnam Inc., 2000), 3.

28. Jordan, *White over Black*, 233.

29. Herman Melville, *White Jacket, or the World in a Man-of-War*, 1850 (Boston: St. Botolph Society, 1892), 144.

30. Sidney E. Mead, *The Lively Experiment: The Shaping of Christianity in America* (New York: Harper and Row, 1963), 143.

31. Henry Ward Beecher, "The Battle Set in Array," in Cherry, *God's New Israel*, 171–172.

32. Benjamin Palmer, "National Responsibility Before God," in Cherry, *God's New Israel*, 184. For Palmer's use of the Israel motif, see Richard T. Hughes, "A Civic The-

ology for the South: the Case of Benjamin M. Palmer," in Hughes and C. Leonard Allen, *Illusions of Innocence: Protestant Primitivism in America, 1639–1875* (Chicago: University of Chicago Press, 1988), 194–195.

33. *Congressional Record*, XXXIII (Washington, D.C.: Government Printing Office, 1900), 711.

34. H. Richard Niebuhr, *The Kingdom of God in America*, 1937 (New York: Harper and Row, 1959), 179.

35. Maria W. Stewart, "An Address Delivered at the African Mason Hall, Boston, February 27, 1833," in "Productions," a pamphlet published in 1835, in Richard Newman, Patrick Rael, and Phillip Lapsansky, eds., *Pamphlets of Protest: An Anthology of Early African American Protest Literature, 1790–1860* (New York: Routledge, 2001), 127.

36. Martin Luther King Jr., "I See the Promised Land," April 3, 1968, in James Melvin Washington, ed., *A Testament of Hope: The Essential Writings and Speeches of Martin Luther King, Jr.* (San Francisco: HarperSanFrancisco, 1986), 286.

37. William Anderson, *Narrative of William J. Anderson . . . Containing Scriptural Views of the Origin of the Black and of the White Man*, 1857, cited in Emerson B. Powery and Rodney S. Sadler Jr., *The Genesis of Liberation: Biblical Interpretation in the Antebellum Narratives of the Enslaved* (Louisville: Westminster John Knox Press, 2016), 102–106.

38. The definitive biography of Malcolm X is Manning Marable, *Malcolm X: A Life of Reinvention* (New York: Penguin Books, 2011).

39. Malcolm X as told to Alex Haley, *The Autobiography of Malcolm X* (New York: Ballantine Books, 1964), 164–167.

40. Haley, *Autobiography of Malcolm X*, 164–67.

41. James Baldwin, "The Fire Next Time," in Toni Morrison, ed., *Baldwin: Collected Essays* (New York: Library Classics of the United States, 1998), 315.

42. Richard Wright, *White Man, Listen! Lectures in Europe, 1950–1956* (New York: HarperPerennial, 1957), 54–55.

43. Coates, *Between the World and Me*, 103–105.

CHAPTER THREE

The Myth of Nature's Nation
The Revolutionary Period

Studying the myths that have shaped the American people quickly leads one to realize that from one important perspective, at least, the revolutionary and early national periods (between 1776 and 1825) stand at the center of American self-understanding, for several reasons. First, the myths that emerged in those years seemed so self-evident, especially to Americans of European descent, that it was difficult to contest them at all. The American experiment simply reflected the way things were meant to be.

Second, the myths that emerged in this period had about them a certain timeless quality. Americans in the revolutionary and early national periods rooted their identity in a golden age of the past and a golden age yet to come. They stood, as it were, with one foot in the dawn of time and the other in the world's evening shadows. Defined by the beginning of the world, they would define its end, ushering in a final golden age of peace, justice, and democratic self-government. Like a bridge that spanned a mighty river, they spanned in their imaginations the particularities of time and place that had molded all cultures and civilizations except their own. They therefore thought themselves untouched in significant ways by the power of human history.

At one level, of course, everyone knew that Europe, especially Britain and France, had profoundly shaped the political structures of the United States. At another level, however, many believed that the American Founders simply exploited a design they found in nature itself, a design as old as creation, rooted in the mind of God.

Because these myths were so thoroughly ahistorical and seemed so completely self-evident, they had the capacity to absorb and reshape other American myths that were more obviously rooted in a particular past. The Myth of the Chosen Nation, for example, had its roots in the particularities of Israel's past and the English Protestant experience. In the context of the early national period, however, chosenness became a self-evident truth that helped to undergird the doctrine of manifest destiny. Or again, by the late nineteenth century, the doctrine of free enterprise capitalism emerged not as one economic system among others, but as a fundamentally natural system, rooted in the way things were meant to be. For all these reasons, myths born of the revolutionary and early national periods have defined American culture in far-reaching ways and, by any measure, stand at the center of American life.

What were these myths? There were two. One emerged especially in the revolutionary period. The other emerged especially in the early years of the nineteenth century. One looked to the beginning of time. The other looked to its end. I will explore the first of these myths in this chapter and the other in chapter 5.

Nature's Nation

We shall call the myth that emerged in the revolutionary period the Myth of Nature's Nation.[1] It had its deepest roots in the European Enlightenment, especially in Britain. The early seventeenth century provides the backdrop for understanding this development.

Enlightenment Backgrounds to the Myth of Nature's Nation

If the sixteenth century had been a period of religious reformation, the seventeenth century was a period marked by religious warfare. Before the Reformation, religious wars were virtually unthinkable, since one monolithic faith—the Roman Catholic Church—dominated western Europe. This dominance dated from the fourth century when, in 313 CE, the emperor Constantine's Edict of Milan legalized Christianity and when, in 380 CE, the emperor Theodosius made the Christian faith the official religion of the Roman Empire. For the next 1,100 years and more, therefore, the monolithic power of a single religious faith virtually guaranteed that if war marred the face of western Europe, it would not be rooted in differences between Christians.

Then, in the sixteenth century, Christianity in western Europe fragmented into competing faiths. Two embryonic Christian movements—Lutheran and Reformed—soon rivaled the Catholic Church for dominance in Western Europe. This situation was complicated by the fact that most Europeans—with the notable exception of the Anabaptists—still believed that a single state church was crucial to the welfare of the social and political order. The question quickly arose, therefore, of which church would serve as the legally established religion of a given state.

By the early seventeenth century, Europeans sought to resolve this question on the field of battle. The first religious war erupted in France in the late sixteenth century and pitted Catholics against Calvinists. Then, from 1618 to 1648, the Thirty Years' War virtually devastated the entire European Continent as Catholics and Protestants vied for power and control. In England, the Puritan Revolution erupted in 1640 and raged for the rest of the decade. This seventeenth-century background is crucial to understanding the Enlightenment of the eighteenth century.

In 1624 an Englishman named Edward Lord Herbert of Cherbury sought to find a way to resolve the religious crisis in Europe apart from bloodshed. In his book, *De Veritate*, he argued that the Bible stood at the heart of the problem. Before the sixteenth century, he observed, there had been only one version of the Bible, the Latin Vulgate, for which the church provided the single, official interpretation. With one version of the Bible and a single, unified interpretation, there was no theological basis for schism or for war.

Then, in the course of the Reformation, Herbert explained, religious leaders like Martin Luther and William Tyndale translated the Bible into the languages of the people. With that development, the Bible became an open book, subject to a variety of interpretations. The diverse interpretations legitimated the religious schisms that ultimately led to war. Under these circumstances, Herbert warned, religious warfare was inescapable.

Yet, Herbert noted, God had authored two books, not just one. If the first book was complex, the second was simple. If the first was susceptible to a variety of interpretations, the second was crystal clear to everyone who read it. In fact, the truths taught by this second book were self-evident. If the first book was the Bible, the second was the world of nature.

Herbert believed that nature taught the fundamental truths that stood at the heart of all religious faiths. Nature taught, for example, that God exists. Who could possibly observe the finely tuned symmetry of the natural world and conclude there was no God? Or again, nature taught the existence of a moral order that defined right and wrong. No one needed to read the Bible or any other religious text to learn that he or she should lead a virtuous life, or to discover that he or she should not kill or steal or abuse another human being, Herbert argued. One needed only to heed the laws God had written on the human heart. Nature also taught, Herbert believed, that human beings should repent of wrongdoings and that God would reward the righteous and punish the wicked after death.

Then Herbert asked what to him was the pivotal question: Who could possibly quarrel with these propositions? Would Catholics disagree with these truths? Would Protestants? The answer obviously was "no," since these themes, Herbert thought, stood at the center of all religious faiths. Further, in Herbert's view, these notions were self-evident to the rational mind. Herbert therefore suggested that Christians of all persuasions place the book of nature at center stage and relegate the Bible to the wings. In this way, Christians could rob religious warfare of its theological basis and help put an end to the wars of religion.

Herbert's objectives were fundamentally pragmatic and not theological at all. Herbert's question was simply this: "How can we put an end to the killing?" His answer was to reduce religion to a set of self-evident essentials upon which all reasonable human beings could agree. By arguing for a religion grounded in nature and knowable through the powers of reason, Herbert helped give birth both to the English Enlightenment and to English Deism.

These two phenomena—the Enlightenment and Deism—were related but were not the same. The term *Enlightenment* refers to a broad philosophical outlook that especially valued the powers of human reason and flourished in the eighteenth century. It manifested itself in many parts of Europe and even in the American colonies. In the context of the Enlightenment worldview, natural science as we know it today took root and flowered.

On the other hand, the term *Deism* refers to a particular religious perspective that reflected the Enlightenment worldview. Deism focused exclusively on the deity, that is, on God. In Herbert's zeal to seek religious truth in nature alone, for example, he scuttled all those doctrines that could be known only from the biblical text. In Deism, therefore, theologies about Jesus Christ as the Son of God went out the window. So did any teachings about the Holy Spirit. All that was left was God—a God who could be known through human reason, attentive to the natural order. This was the meaning of Deism.

In America, Deism institutionalized itself in the Unitarian Church. The word *Unitarian* says it all, for Unitarians affirmed the unity of God and rejected the trinitarian notion of God the Father, God the Son, and God the Holy Spirit. Put another way, they focused their faith on God alone.

When Herbert's *De Veritate* appeared in 1624, few in England took it seriously. After all, while the continent was embroiled in the Thirty Years' War, England was still at peace and would remain so for another sixteen years. Few in England, therefore, saw the urgency of the issues Herbert raised.

By the 1640s, however, when the streets of London ran red with the blood of young soldiers, giving their lives for religious zealotry, Herbert's arguments suddenly made a great deal of sense. Others now took up Herbert's banner and argued that authentic Christianity had little to do with the mysteries found in scripture but everything to do with the simple, rational, self-evident truths taught in nature.

John Toland, for example, wrote an influential book in 1696 that he called *Christianity Not Mysterious*. He argued that authentic Christianity could be discerned in nature by the rational mind. He therefore rejected any so-called religious truths that originate in revelation, outside the sphere of human reason.

The English Deistic tradition reached its pinnacle in a work by Mathew Tindal, published in 1730: *Christianity as Old as the Creation; or, the Gospel a Republication of the Religion of Nature*. If the gospel was a republication of nature's truths, Tindal asked, why bother with the gospel at all? Why not focus instead on God's second book, the book of nature?

The Religious Views of America's Founders

At this point, one might ask, how is any of this pertinent to the American myths that emerged in the founding years of the United States? The relevance becomes apparent when one takes note of the fact that the United States, born as it was in 1776, is a child of the eighteenth-century Enlightenment. Even more to the point, most of the American Founders embraced some form of Deism.

To suggest that most of the American Founders embraced some form of Deism is not to suggest that they did not *think of themselves* as Christians, for most certainly they did. Jefferson, in fact, argued that his own Deist sentiments represented the heart of Jesus's teachings and the purest form of Christianity. In addition, Michael Novak has demonstrated how the biblical tradition informed in significant ways the political ideas of the Founders.[2] Still, it is difficult to describe all the Founders as "orthodox Christians" when many rejected classic Christian doctrines like the divinity of Jesus.

Thomas Jefferson is a notable case in point. Though technically not a Founder, Jefferson was part of the founding generation, was the principal author of the Declaration of Independence, and was held in the highest esteem by his peers. His religious views, therefore, are worth noting.

One finds Jefferson's religious perspectives mainly in his private correspondence. In a letter to Benjamin Waterhouse, dated June 26, 1822, for example, Jefferson wrote,

The doctrines of Jesus are simple, and tend all to the happiness of man.

1. That there is one only God, and he all perfect.
2. That there is a future state of rewards and punishments.

3. That to love God with all thy heart and thy neighbor as thyself is the sum of religion. . . .

But compare with these the demoralizing dogmas of Calvin.

1. That there are three Gods.
2. That good works, or the love of our neighbor, are nothing.
3. That faith is everything, and the more incomprehensible the proposition, the more merit in its faith.
4. That reason in religion is of unlawful use.
5. That God, from the beginning, elected certain individuals to be saved, and certain others to be damned; and that no crimes of the former can damn them; no virtues of the latter save.[3]

In a letter to Jared Sparks, dated November 4, 1820, Jefferson described the teachings of traditional Christian orthodoxy as "metaphysical insanities . . ., mere relapses into polytheism, differing from paganism only by being more unintelligible." On the other hand, he argued in that same letter that "the religion of Jesus is founded in the unity of God. . . . Thinking men of all nations rallied readily to the doctrine of one only God, and embraced it with the pure morals which Jesus inculcated."[4] Put another way, Jefferson believed that Jesus taught religious truths that harmonized beautifully with the truths proclaimed by God's second book, the book of nature.

On the other hand, Jefferson claimed, Christian orthodoxy emerged centuries after Jesus when Christian leaders embellished his simple teachings for the sake of profit and power. Accordingly, Jefferson wrote to Mrs. Harrison Smith on August 6, 1816, "There would never have been an infidel, if there had never been a priest. The artificial structures they have built on the purest of all moral systems, for the purpose of deriving from it pence and power, revolts those who think for themselves."[5]

Unmistakably, one finds in Jefferson the perspectives of a classic Deist.

Because he believed so strongly in the moral teachings of Jesus, Jefferson in 1803 extracted from the New Testament those teachings of Jesus that he thought reflected the essence of Christian faith. This book has been called "The Jefferson Bible."

As a Deist, Jefferson strongly advocated religious toleration. In a letter to Miles King, dated September 26, 1814, he wrote:

I must ever believe that religion substantially good which produces an honest life, and we have been authorized by one whom you and I equally respect, to judge of the tree by its fruit. Our particular principles of religion are a subject of accountability to our God alone. I inquire after no man's, and trouble none with mine. . . . Nay, we have heard it said that there is not a Quaker, or a Baptist, or a Presbyterian or an Episcopalian, a Catholic or a Protestant in heaven; that on entering that gate, we leave those badges behind, and find ourselves united in those principles only in which God has united us all.[6]

One finds in Benjamin Franklin very similar perspectives. A single passage will suffice. To Ezra Stiles, the president of Yale University, Franklin wrote, "Here is my creed. I believe in one God, Creator of the Universe. That He governs it by His providence. That He ought to be worshipped. That the most acceptable service we render Him is doing good to His other children. That the soul of man is immortal, and will be treated with justice in another life respecting its conduct in this. These I take to be the principal principles of sound religion." Here, Franklin claimed for himself the central themes of classic Deism. But he went on:

> As to Jesus of Nazareth . . . I think the system of morals and his religion, as he left them to us, the best the world ever saw or is likely to see; but I apprehend it has received various corrupt changes, and I have, with most of the present dissenters in England, some doubts as to his divinity; though it is a question I do not dogmatize upon, having never studied it, and think it needless to busy myself with it now, when I expect soon an opportunity of knowing the truth with less trouble. I see no harm, however, in its being believed, if that belief has the good consequence, as probably it has, of making his doctrines more respected and better observed; especially as I do not perceive that the Supreme [Being] takes it amiss, by distinguishing the unbelievers in His government of the world with any peculiar marks of His displeasure.[7]

What difference did it make that those in the founding generation embraced Deism to the extent that they did? The answer to that question lies in the potential that religion held for the new nation. On the one hand, religion was a potential asset. As Franklin noted in the passage just cited, religious beliefs helped to sustain moral behavior, and that could only be good for the state.

Religion also presented serious liabilities, since so many competing Christian traditions existed in the colonies on the eve of the Revolution. Puritans, Presbyterians, Baptists, Quakers, Anglicans, Catholics, Lutherans, Methodists, Dutch Reformed people, and more—all these traditions, imported from Europe, had taken root in the American colonies. This diversity stood in marked contrast to the religious situation in Europe where, typically, for one state only one established church existed.

In addition, many of the churches in the colonies had held legally established status back in Europe, or at least had sought that status for themselves. This was true of Catholics, Anglicans, Puritans, Lutherans, and various churches descended from the Reformed tradition. Now, with the birth of the new nation, each of these churches nurtured the hope that it might become the established church of the United States. Precisely those kinds of ambitions and hopes had fueled the wars of religion back in Europe in the seventeenth century. It was hardly inconceivable that religious wars, or at least serious religious conflicts, might erupt in the new nation. But what could anyone do to prevent them?

The Founders had several options. Obviously, they could have made one church the legally established church of the United States. That course of action, however, would have undermined their vision of what America should become—a land where its citizens were free to believe what they chose to believe. On the other hand, they could have provided for complete freedom of religion. That provision, however, would have opened the door once again to the potential for religious conflict. Then what could be done?

Here, the Deism that characterized the founding generation served the nation remarkably well. Like Herbert of Cherbury, the Founders asked the pragmatic question, "How can we prevent religious conflict, even religious bloodshed?" To answer that question, they turned directly to their Deist faith and, like Herbert, sought to reduce religion to a set of self-evident essentials upon which all reasonable people could agree.

Nowhere was this strategy more apparent than in Thomas Jefferson's Declaration of Independence. In fact, in that document Jefferson borrowed a page from Herbert of Cherbury and other Deistic thinkers and grounded America's religious faith squarely in a Deistic perspective. For example, he clearly affirmed in that document the existence of God. "All Men," he wrote, "*are created* equal [and] . . . are endowed by their *Creator*" [italics mine] with certain rights. He even identified this God as "Nature's God," that is, the God all human beings can know through nature.

Second, Jefferson affirmed the existence of a self-evident moral order. "We hold these Truths to be self-evident," he wrote, "that all Men are created equal, that they are endowed by their Creator with certain unalienable Rights, that among these are Life, Liberty, and the Pursuit of Happiness." In this context, he grounded the right of the colonies to break their political bonds with Britain as a right to which they were entitled by "the Laws of Nature and of Nature's God."

What Jefferson did not say is as important as what he said. He said nothing in the Declaration about Jesus, or the Trinity, or the church, or the Virgin Mary, or Moses, or Buddha, or Mohammed. He did not appeal to the New Testament, the Hebrew Bible, the Koran, or to any other body of sacred scripture. Instead, he rooted the American Revolution in the existence of a

God, apparent to all human beings in nature, and in a moral order that he proclaimed as self-evident.

While the American Creed, therefore, is grounded in certain ways in biblical metaphysics, as Michael Novak has pointed out, it has little to do with historic Christian orthodoxy. This point is worth noting in light of the frequently heard claim that America is a Christian nation. The truth is, the American Creed is rooted squarely in a Deistic worldview that was common to the eighteenth century.

By appealing to this perspective, Jefferson sought to place on the nation's center stage a minimal religious vision that virtually all Americans in his day could affirm. At the same time, he sought to banish to the wings of the national stage those religious themes that were important to certain denominations or faiths but not to the American people at large. In this way, he believed, Americans could embrace a religious faith that could unite them, not divide them.

How successful was this strategy? Immensely so. From Jefferson's day to this, many Americans have commonly claimed that it makes very little difference what particular religious faith one embraces, just so long as one believes in God and lives a good moral life. These are the values of eighteenth-century Deism, made incarnate in the Declaration of Independence.

If anything, therefore, the Declaration made Deism America's national faith. In part, this was Jefferson's intent. This should not be surprising in light of Jefferson's prediction, confided to James Smith in a letter dated December 8, 1822, "I confidently expect that the present generation will see Unitarianism become the general religion of the United States."[8] Jefferson could make that prediction only because Unitarianism was the institutional embodiment of the Deist faith, a religion broad enough, he thought, to embrace all Americans willing to take "Nature and Nature's God" as the standard for their lives. And he imagined that all reasonable Americans would embrace just that option.

In 1791 the Bill of Rights, the first ten amendments to the Constitution of the United States, became effective. First among those amendments was Article I, which contained this affirmation: "Congress shall make no law respecting an establishment of religion, or prohibiting the free exercise thereof."

While Article I of the Bill of Rights did not ground its provisions in an explicitly Deistic frame of reference as had the Declaration, it did put legal teeth into one of the Declaration's main concerns. It disallowed any possibility that the federal government could ever make one single faith the established religion of the nation. Further, it applied to the realm of religion one of the truths that the Declaration had proclaimed as "self-evident"—the right to liberty. In other words, it denied to the federal government the right to "prohibit the free exercise" of religion on the part of any citizen. Finally, if the Declaration had *implicitly* pushed denominational religion to the wings of the national stage, the First Amendment to the Constitution made that point explicit: as far as the government was concerned, religion was simply off limits.

The First Amendment thereby provided the classic American doctrine of separation of church and state. It is a gross mistake nonetheless to imagine that separation of church and state also meant the separation of religion from culture. To make that mistake is to ignore the power both of the American Creed and of the various American myths. It is to ignore as well the many ways in which religious assumptions, often unspoken, have shaped the common life of the United States.

If one sought to illustrate the role religion has played in American culture, one could find no better example than the case of the First Amendment itself. It may appear ironic that the secularizing provisions of the First Amendment grew from deep religious convictions, but that is nonetheless the case.

First, James Madison, author of the Bill of Rights, clearly embraced the sentiments of Deism. In 1785, Madison wrote his famous "Memorial and Remonstrance," protesting a proposal that Virginia assess upon all citizens a tax that would support the Christian religion. In that document we can clearly discern Madison's religious commitments that would later undergird the First Amendment. Madison started with the assumption that "before any man can be considered as a member of Civil Society, he must be considered as a subject of the Governor of the Universe." He therefore argued that freedom of religion "is in its nature an unalienable right. It is unalienable," he said, because "it is the duty of every man to render to the Creator such homage, and such only, as he believes to be acceptable to him." This, Madison believed, was one of those truths taught by "Nature and Nature's God."[9]

Partly on that ground, Madison rejected the Virginia proposal that government has the right to raise a religious tax. On that same ground, he argued in the First Amendment that "Congress shall make no law respecting an establishment of religion, or prohibiting the free exercise thereof."

There is another sense in which the secularizing provisions of the First Amendment grew from deep religious convictions. For example, in colonies with established churches, Baptists and Methodists suffered severe disabilities because they refused to support the legally established faith. Because they sought religious freedom for themselves, dissenters like Baptists and Methodists made common cause with Deists in their effort to abolish religious establishments wherever they were found. It is doubtful, in fact, that people like Jefferson and Madison could have won religious freedom to the extent that they did without the support of those dissenting Christians.

Once religious freedom became a reality, however, many of those same dissenting Christians grew fearful that a nation without explicitly Christian supports might lack the moral character necessary to survive. They therefore snuggled up to those Christians of established churches who had treated them so badly for so long. Together, those two groups now launched an attack on the Deist perspective in which religious freedom was grounded. I will explore that development more fully in the following chapter.[10]

Elaborating the Myth of Nature's Nation

Because the American Founders grounded the American experiment in their vision of "Nature and Nature's God," it was easy to imagine that the United States simply reflected the way God himself intended things to be from the beginning of the world. In other words, the American system was not spun out of someone's imagination or contrived by human wit. Instead, it was based on a natural order, built into the world by God Himself.

Jefferson said as much when he spoke of "self-evident truths." John Adams concurred when he affirmed that "the United States of America have exhibited, perhaps, the first example of governments erected on the simple principles of nature." The fullest expression of this conviction came from Jefferson's friend and confidant, Thomas Paine, who announced that "the case and circumstance of America present themselves as in the beginning of the world." Indeed, Paine wrote, "We are brought at once to the point of seeing government begin, as if we had lived in the beginning of time. The real volume, not of history, but of facts, is directly before us, unmutilated by contrivance, or the errors of tradition."[11] Here one finds the Myth of Nature's Nation full blown.

At its core, this myth encouraged Americans to ignore the power of history and tradition as forces that shaped the nation. Paine's words epitomize this perspective: when we live in the United States, it is "as if we had lived in the beginning of time." Here was a nation untouched by the hand of human tradition, a nation that had escaped the molding power of history and culture, a nation that had sprung, as it were, directly from the hand of God. At the most fundamental level, therefore, American identity derived not from British history and culture, not even from ancient Greece and Rome, but from nature, formed directly by the Creator.

If one would like a graphic example of how this myth has found expression in American popular culture, a film that appeared in the late 1980s, *Rocky IV*, is particularly instructive. In this film, Rocky, an American boxer, goes to the Soviet Union to fight the Russian giant, Drago. A marvelous sequence depicts the two fighters training for the bout. Rocky trains in the Siberian wilderness. He lifts logs, drags heavy boulders, and runs on mountaintops. Clearly he is the natural man. On the other hand, Drago trains in a high-tech gym, full of the latest scientifically produced equipment. If Rocky is natural, Drago is contrived, a creature of human design and ingenuity.

Finally, the fight begins before a huge crowd of Muscovites. The fight is hardly underway before Drago begins to pummel Rocky unmercifully. It appears as though Rocky has more than met his match and will surely fall before the great Russian giant. But then, suddenly, Rocky gets a second wind. Boom! Boom! He lands a right, then a left, then another right. Drago stumbles, and finally falls. Suddenly, we see an American flag unfurl and we hear a chant go up from this crowd of Russian spectators: "Rocky! Rocky! Rocky!" It is clear what has happened. The Russians have witnessed the irresistible power of the American, the Natural Man.

Precisely because the Myth of Nature's Nation downplayed the power of history and tradition, it found a ready and receptive audience among many American Christians. The Reformed tradition, as I have noted, revered the founding period of the Christian faith. While Reformed Christians did appeal to Calvin and other leaders in the sixteenth-century Reformation, those leaders carried weight only to the extent that they pointed beyond themselves to Scripture and the first Christian age. Significantly, Christians from the Reformed tradition enjoyed extraordinary strength in the early national period throughout the United States. Puritans in New England, Presbyterians and Dutch Reformed Christians in the Middle Colonies, and Baptists in the South were all bona fide representatives of the Reformed tradition.

In addition, a variety of new Christian movements emerged in the United States in the early national period, and almost all of them claimed to have restored the ancient Christian faith in all its purity. Quite apart from the Enlightenment, therefore, fascination with pure beginnings abounded among American Christians in the early nineteenth century. These Christians shared with Deists a bias that favored the authority of the founding age, however that age might be defined. No wonder that the Myth of "Nature's Nation" captured the American imagination in the early nineteenth century.

Critiquing the Myth of Nature's Nation

In so many ways the Myth of Nature's Nation failed to deliver on its promise of liberty and justice for all. The reason for this failure is easy enough to grasp: Those who embraced this myth all too often found in nature their own cultural traditions and then defended those traditions as fundamentally natural.

A Philosophical Critique

Carl Becker made this point many years ago when he wrote that "in the eighteenth-century climate of opinion, whatever question you seek to answer, nature is the test, the standard: the ideas, the customs, the institutions of men, if ever they are to attain perfection, must obviously be in accord with those laws which 'nature reveals at all times, to all men.'" Becker went on to note that the problem lay in the fact that those Enlightenment philosophers who embraced nature as the standard for civilization "do not know that the 'man in general' they are looking for is just their own image, that the principles they are bound to find are the very ones they start out with. That is the trick they play on the dead."[12]

Examples of Becker's point abound. Becker himself offers one striking example when he notes that the natural-rights philosophy "had been, and could again be . . . effectively used as a justification of revolutionary movements." But revolution was precisely what nineteenth-century Americans did not want. They had fought one revolution and that was enough. Now their greatest concern was "to preserve the independence they had won, the institutions they had established, the 'more perfect Union' they had created."[13]

Of course, the political and cultural traditions they had created were deeply rooted in a white, male, European, and Protestant frame of reference. Regardless, those who embraced these traditions and institutions now defended them in the language of natural rights and ideals. In this way, they absolutized their very particular cultural traditions and then heralded those traditions as both natural and universal, and therefore as the standard for all human beings in all places in all times. Not only did they absolutize their cultural traditions; they absolutized the myth as well. The Myth of Nature's Nation at its best affirms that *all men* are created equal. In its absolutized form—the form that prevailed for many years following the nation's founding—this myth confined the "inalienable rights" that belonged to "all men" to all white men who owned property, even as it suggested that certain civilizations are grounded in the laws of nature, while others are simply contrived.

One finds another poignant example of Becker's point in the stance of Indiana senator Albert Beveridge. Eager to legitimate America's colonizing ventures at the end of the nineteenth century, Beveridge grounded those ventures in the self-evident laws of nature. In this vein, he spoke in glowing terms of "this self-evident and contemporaneous truth: *Every progressive nation of Europe to-day is seeking lands to colonize and governments to administer. . . .* France declined only when she abandoned that natural law of national power and progress." Accordingly, he spoke of "that universal law of civilization which requires of every people who have reached our high estate to become colonizers of new lands."[14]

The Myth of Nature's Nation has always held enormous implications for racial stratification in the United States, encouraging whites to claim that white supremacy was normal and in keeping with the way things were meant to be. Frederick Buechner, for example, recalls that in 1946 his time in the Army was almost finished and the discharge ceremony was about to begin. The group about to be discharged had lined up alphabetically when, suddenly, the officer in charge called Buechner aside, pointed out that the man at the front of the line was black, and asked Buechner to please line up in front of him. Buechner did as he was told, "accustomed as we all of us were in those days to accepting such things as simply the way the world worked."

Many years later, Buechner acknowledged the cruel irony implicit in his action. "Even if I had considered . . . [protesting]," he wrote, "I doubt I would have protested for fear that it might somehow endanger my own getting out of the Army then and there. So I went and stood where I had been told and within moments stepped out of the chapel as free a man as it is possible to be in a country where not everybody is free."[15]

It must be clear by now why and how the Myth of Nature's Nation was a two-edged sword, cutting in two very different directions. On the one hand, it promised "life, liberty, and the pursuit of happiness" as "unalienable rights" for "all men" and grounded those rights squarely in "Nature and Nature's God." On the other hand, it defined nature in Eurocentric terms that especially served the interests of a white male population descended from European stock.

An African American Critique

Thomas Jefferson held racial perspectives in line with most whites during the founding years and no one understood this point better than David Walker, born in Wilmington, North Carolina, in 1785. Walker's father was enslaved, but since his mother was free, he also was free in the eyes of the law. Nonetheless, Walker fled the slaveholding South and took up residence in Boston where, in 1827, he opened a store selling old clothes. In 1829 he published the first thoroughgoing critique of slavery written by a black man. He called his book *Walker's Appeal . . . to The Coloured Citizens of the World*.

Walker's book is notable for many reasons, but especially because he opposed Thomas Jefferson head-on and thereby exposed the ambiguities in the Myth of Nature's Nation. He pointed his readers, on the one hand, to the Declaration of Independence that declared that all men were created equal.

Then he quoted extensively from another document, *Notes on the State of Virginia*, where Jefferson argued that blacks were *by nature* inferior to whites.

Jefferson resolutely opposed the institution of slavery, which, in his judgment, degraded both enslaved blacks as well as their masters. He therefore claimed there was no more urgent business than the eradication of this barbaric practice. Despite his opposition to slavery, he compromised his conviction for a variety of reasons and consented to the extension of slavery into the territories of the United States. Finally, he died with scores of enslaved people working his property at Monticello. Paradoxically, he was never able to free himself of the institution he so much despised.[16]

Though he hoped for the abolition of slavery in his lifetime, he thought very poorly of those human beings who had been enslaved. In his *Notes on the State of Virginia*, he explored the supposed makeup of African Americans in considerable detail, speaking first of their physical characteristics:

> Are not the fine mixtures of red and white, the expressions of every passion by greater or less suffusions of colour in the one, preferable to that eternal monotony, which reigns in the countenances, that immoveable veil of black which covers all the emotions of the other race? Add to these, flowing hair, a more elegant symmetry of form, their own judgment in favour of the whites, declared by their preference of them, as uniformly as is the preference of the Oran-ootan for the black women over those of his own species. The circumstance of superior beauty, is thought worthy attention in the propagation of our horses, dogs, and other domestic animals; why not in that of man?

When Jefferson turned to the emotional makeup of blacks, he said this:

> A black, after hard labour through the day, will be induced by the slightest amusements to sit up till midnight, or later, though knowing he must be out with the first dawn of the morning. . . . They are more ardent after their female [than whites]: but love seems with them to be more an eager desire, than a tender delicate mixture of sentiment and sensation. Their griefs are transient. Those numberless afflictions, which render it doubtful whether heaven has given life to us in mercy or in wrath, are less felt, and sooner forgotten with them. In general, their existence appears to participate more of sensation than of reflection.

Regarding the mental characteristics of blacks, Jefferson wrote, "Comparing them by their faculties of memory, reason, and imagination, it appears to me, that in memory they are equal to the whites; in reason much inferior, as I think one could scarcely be found capable of tracing and comprehending the investigations of Euclid; and that in imagination they are dull, tasteless, and anomalous." He concluded by advancing the theory that blacks are fundamentally inferior to whites, and that the differences between the two races are rooted *in nature*. "I advance it therefore as a suspicion only," he wrote, "that the blacks, whether originally a distinct race, or made distinct by time and circumstances, are inferior to the whites in the endowments both of body and mind." Further, "it is not their condition, then, but nature, which has produced the distinction."[17]

Benjamin Franklin concurred and registered his opinion that "almost every Slave . . . [was] by Nature a Thief." That consideration, along with others, led him to conclude that the United States should be populated chiefly by "White People."[18]

Whether David Walker was familiar with Franklin's assertions we do not know, but he had read Jefferson, and recognizing Jefferson's standing among American whites, he understood the importance of his words. Jefferson's efforts to root the inferiority of blacks *in nature*, Walker wrote, "has in truth injured us more, and has been as great a barrier to our emancipation as any thing that has ever been advanced against us." Indeed, Walker surmised that Jefferson's remarks had "sunk deep into the hearts of millions of the whites, and never will be removed this side of eternity."[19]

Walker, of course, was right. A generation later, Frederick Douglass, a man formerly enslaved but later turned abolitionist leader, would complain,

> The chief and recognized builders of the Republic, almost without exception, openly condemned . . . the system of Slavery as a great moral and political evil, alien to the laws of nature. But how different from this is the sentiment of the present, among our public men! What was regarded as a curse at the beginning, is now cherished as a blessing. . . . Those who denounced the accursed thing at the beginning, were deemed wise, humane and patriotic. Those who denounce it now, are called disorganizers, enemies of the Union, "freedom-shriekers," "negro-worshippers," infidels and traitors. The contrast is striking and instructive.[20]

In David Walker's judgment, therefore, "unless we try to refute Mr. Jefferson's arguments respecting us, we will only establish them."[21]

Throughout his book, he sought to do precisely that. To Jefferson's reference to "oran-ootans," Walker responded, "Have they [the whites] not, after having reduced us to the deplorable condition of slaves under their feet, held us up as descending originally from the tribes of *Monkeys* or *Orang-Outangs*? O! my God! I appeal to every man of feeling—is not this insupportable? Is it not heaping the most gross insult upon our miseries, because they have got us under their feet and we cannot help ourselves?"[22] When Walker read Jefferson's affirmation that blacks were inferior to whites, both in mind and body, he was amazed that Jefferson would "speak so of a set of men in chains. I do not know what to compare it to," he wrote, "unless, like putting one wild deer in an iron cage, where it will be secured, and hold another by the side of the same, then let it go, and expect the one in the cage to run as fast as the one at liberty."[23]

It was difficult to argue against sheer prejudice. The best Walker could do, therefore, was to affirm his own humanity, and that of other enslaved people: "Are we MEN!!—I ask you, O my brethren! are we MEN? Did our Creator make us to be slaves to dust and ashes like ourselves? Are they not dying worms as well as we? Have they not to make their appearance before the tribunal of Heaven, to answer for the deeds done in the body, as well as we?"[24]

The proof of who was inferior and who was not, Walker suggested, was to be found in moral behavior, and on that score, he claimed that whites had failed miserably. Whether in Greece, Rome, Gaul, Spain, or Britain, he argued, "the whites have always been an unjust, jealous, unmerciful, avaricious and blood-thirsty set of beings, always seeking after power and authority." In a line that anticipated the twentieth-century Black Muslim affirmation that "the white man is the devil," Walker affirmed that, for the most part, whites have acted "more like devils than accountable men." In terms of moral behavior, Walker wondered "whether they are *as good by nature* as we are or not. Their actions . . . have been the reverse."[25]

Walker turned Jefferson's arguments upside down. The fact that whites found it necessary to keep blacks in chains was the strongest possible argument for the full humanity of African American people:

> Man, in all ages and all nations of the earth, is the same. Man is a peculiar creature—he is the image of his God, though he may be subjected to the most wretched condition upon earth, yet the spirit and feeling which constitute the creature, man, can never be entirely erased from his breast, because God who made him after his own image, planted it in his heart; he cannot get rid of it. The whites knowing this, they do not know what to do; they know that they have done us much injury, they are afraid that we, being men, and not brutes, will retaliate, and woe will be to them.[26]

With an ironic twist on the theme of Nature's Nation, Walker claimed that whites had made themselves the "natural enemies" of blacks through the "outrages" they had committed "upon human nature."[27] Finally, Walker raised before his readers the Declaration of Independence itself:

> See your Declaration Americans!!! Do you understand your own language? Hear your language, proclaimed to the world, July 4th, 1776—"We hold these truths

to be self evident—that *ALL* men are created EQUAL!! *that they are endowed by their creator with certain unalienable rights; that among these are life, liberty, and the pursuit of happiness!!"* Compare your own language above, extracted from your Declaration of Independence, with your cruelties and murders inflicted by your cruel and unmerciful fathers on ourselves on our fathers and on us, men who have never given your fathers or you the least provocation!!![28]

Walker's words of protest, as powerful as they were, still fell on deaf ears. According to the sketch of his life that accompanies Walker's *Appeal*, "This little book produced more commotion among slave-holders than any volume of its size that was ever issued from an American press. They saw that it was a bold attack upon their idolatry, and that too by a black man who once lived among them." Little wonder, then, that "a company of Georgia men . . . bound themselves by an oath, that they would eat as little as possible until they had killed the youthful author." Walker died in 1830 at the age of 34, apparently a victim of murder.[29]

When Walker unmasked the Myth of Nature's Nation, he stood shoulder to shoulder with millions of American blacks, both then and now, who have discerned the hypocrisy of that narrative.

The father of black liberation theology, James Cone, for example, recalled that in his home town of Bearden, Arkansas, the ruling whites "regarded the social and political arrangements that they maintained as an expression of the natural orders of creation."[30] Richard Wright recalled how white people, in his experience, firmly believed "that the past domination of Europe over . . . [Asia and Africa] was natural and justified by the racial structure of life and history itself."[31] Toni Morrison turned the myth of white America as nature's nation upside down when, in her novel *Song of Solomon*, two blacks discuss the barbarity of white behavior directed against blacks. When Milkman tells Guitar that "people who lynch and slice off people's balls—they're crazy, Guitar, crazy," Guitar responds,

> That's like saying they were drunk, Or constipated. Why isn't cutting a man's eyes out, cutting his nuts off, the kind of thing you never get too drunk or ignorant to do? Too crazy to do? Too constipated to do? And more to the point, how come Negroes, the craziest, most ignorant people in America, don't get that crazy and that ignorant? No, White people are unnatural. As a race they are unnatural. And it takes a strong effort of the will to overcome an unnatural enemy.[32]

Ta-Nehisi Coates, in particular, showed how the Myth of Nature's Nation, when applied to race, obscures the evil of racism and renders it innocent. Coates affirmed that

Americans believe in the reality of "race" as a defined, indubitable feature of the natural world. Racism—the need to ascribe bone-deep features to people and then humiliate, reduce, and destroy them—inevitably follows from this inalterable condition. In this way, racism is rendered as the innocent daughter of Mother Nature, and one is left to deplore the Middle Passage or the Trail of Tears the way one deplores an earthquake, a tornado, or any other phenomenon that can be cast as beyond the handiwork of men.[33]

That is why Coates argued that many whites, including courts of justice dominated by whites, fail to discern anything really amiss when the police kill blacks in America's streets. Coates recalled, for example, the murder of Prince Jones, an unarmed college student, shot by a Prince George's County undercover narcotics police corporal on September 1, 2000. The officer fired 16 shots at Jones who was sitting in his Jeep. Eight of the shots hit Jones, five in the back. The *Washington Post* reported "that the Fairfax commonwealth's attorney and the Justice Department declined to file charges against . . . [the officer] or even bring the case before a grand jury, and that Prince George's police said they found no wrongdoing by the officer." Six years later, a civil jury found the officer responsible for wrongful death and awarded damages to the victim's daughter and parents.[34]

Reflecting on that story, Coates mused that "the earthquake cannot be subpoenaed. The typhoon will not bend under indictment. They sent the killer of Prince Jones back to his work, because he was not a killer at all. He was a force of nature, the helpless agent of our world's physical laws."[35]

David Billings, a white man with extraordinary insights into the Myth of Nature's Nation, confirmed the testimony of Walker, Cone, Wright, Morrison, and Coates when he candidly confessed that "as a child, I would notice black people, but from my earliest memories it was as if we occupied two different planes of existence. . . . Somehow I knew I was better. As far as I knew, white superiority was just a fact of life, like twenty-four hours in a day or the earth orbiting the sun."[36]

Conclusions

The Myth of Nature's Nation is rooted squarely in the principles of the American Creed. The Creed proclaims that among all the truths one might encounter in a lifetime, there are certain truths that are simply "self-evident" and require no formal proof. Among those truths are the propositions "that all Men are created equal, that they are endowed by their Creator with certain unalienable Rights, that among these are Life, Liberty, and the Pursuit of Happiness." Those truths are "self-evident," the Creed contends, because they are rooted in "Nature and Nature's God" and therefore reflect the way things are meant to be.

At the very same time, Carl Becker was correct when he argued that those Enlightenment philosophers—including the American Founders—who embraced nature as the standard for civilization "do not know that the 'man in general' they are looking for is just their own image, that the principles they are bound to find are the very ones they start out with." Because the principles they were bound to find were the very ones with which they began, Americans folded into the Myth of Nature's Nation virtually all the significant contents of their culture. From this perspective, white supremacy was fully as natural as democratic self-government and therefore helped define the meaning of the American nation. In subsequent chapters, I shall explore how nineteenth-century Americans also folded into the Myth of Nature's Nation their dominant religion—Protestant Christianity—and their economic system, laissez-faire capitalism.

Notes

1. Perry Miller popularized the label, "Nature's Nation," in a book by that same title, published in 1967, though he used that term in a much broader sense than I do here. See Perry Miller, *Nature's Nation* (Cambridge: The Belknap Press of Harvard University, 1967).

2. Michael Novak, *On Two Wings: Humble Faith and Common Sense at the American Founding* (San Francisco: Encounter Books, 2002), 5–47.

3. Thomas Jefferson to Benjamin Waterhouse, June 26, 1822, in Norman Cousins, ed., *"In God We Trust": The Religious Beliefs and Ideas of the American Founding Fathers* (New York: Harper, 1958), 160–161.

4. Thomas Jefferson to Jared Sparks, November 4, 1820, in Cousins, *"In God We Trust,"* 156.

5. Thomas Jefferson to Mrs. Harrison Smith, August 6, 1816, in Cousins, *"In God We Trust,"* 147.

6. Thomas Jefferson to Miles King, September 26, 1814, in Cousins, *"In God We Trust,"* 144–145.

7. Benjamin Franklin to Ezra Stiles, March 9, 1790, in Cousins, *"In God We Trust,"* 42.

8. Thomas Jefferson to James Smith, December 8, 1822, in Cousins, *"In God We Trust,"* 159.

9. James Madison, "Memorial and Remonstrance," (1785), in Cousins, "In God We Trust," 309.

10. The interpretations in this section are heavily dependent on Sidney E. Mead's two seminal works, *The Lively Experiment: The Shaping of Christianity in America* (New York: Harper and Row, 1963); and *The Nation with the Soul of a Church* (New York: Harper and Row, 1975).

11. John Adams, *A Defense of the Constitutions of the Government of the United States of America*, abridged in *The Political Writings of John Adams: Representative Selections*, ed. George A. Peek (New York: Liberal Arts Press, 1954), 117; and Thomas Paine, *Rights of Man* [1791–1792], in *The Complete Writings of Thomas Paine*, ed. Philip S. Foner (New York: Citadel Press, 1945), 1:376.

12. Carl L. Becker, *The Heavenly City of the Eighteenth-Century Philosophers* (1932; reprint, New Haven: Yale University Press, 1964), 52–53 and 103–104.

13. Carl L. Becker, *The Declaration of Independence: A Study in the History of Political Ideas* (New York: Vintage Books, 1922), 237–238.

14. Albert Beveridge, "The Star of Empire," in *God's New Israel: Religious Interpretations of American Destiny*, ed. Conrad Cherry (1971); (reprint, Chapel Hill: University of North Carolina Press, 1998), 153–154. Beveridge's emphasis.

15. Frederick Buechner, *The Sacred Journey: A Memoir of Early Days* (New York: HarperOne, 1991), 88. Buechner added, "The memory has haunted me ever since and with it the thought of the pathetic but who knows how telling a little blow I might have struck for common decency."

16. For an assessment of this paradox, see John Chester Miller, *The Wolf By the Ears: Thomas Jefferson and Slavery* (New York: The Free Press, 1977).

17. Thomas Jefferson, *Notes on the State of Virginia*, ed. by William Peden (Chapel Hill: University of North Carolina Press for the Institute of Early American History and Culture, 1955), 138–143.

18. Benjamin Franklin, "Observations Concerning the Increase of Mankind," 1751, in *Observations on the Late and Present Conduct of the French* (Boston: William Clarke, 1755), https://founders.archives.gov/documents/Franklin/01-04-02-0080, accessed April 25, 2017.

19. David Walker, *Walker's Appeal . . . to the Colored Citizens of the World*, 2d ed. with corrections, 1830 (Nashville: James C. Winston, 1994), 38–39.

20. Frederick Douglass, "Freedom in the West Indies: An Address Delivered in Poughkeepsie, New York, August 2, 1858," in John Blassingame, ed., *The Frederick Douglass Papers*, vol. 3 (New Haven: Yale University Press, 1985), 224–226.

21. Walker, *Walker's Appeal*, 26.

22. Ibid., 20.

23. Ibid., 20–21.

24. Ibid., 27.

25. Ibid., 27–29.

26. Ibid., 72–73.

27. Ibid., 73.

28. Ibid., 85–86.

29. "A Brief Sketch of the Life and Character of David Walker," in *Walker's Appeal*, vi–vii.

30. James Cone, *My Soul Looks Back* (New York: Orbis, 1985), 18.

31. Richard Wright, *White Man, Listen!* (New York: HarperPerennial, 1957), 26.

32. Toni Morrison, *Song of Solomon*, in Morrison, *Race* (London: Vintage, 2017), 12.

33. Ta-Nehisi Coates, *Between the World and Me* (New York: Spiegel and Grau, 2015), 7.

34. Ruben Castaneda, "Officer Liable in Student's Killing," *Washington Post*, January 20, 2006, http://www.washingtonpost.com/wp-dyn/content/article/2006/01/19/AR2006011902346_pf.html, accessed April 25, 2017.

35. Coates, *Between the World and Me*, 83.

36. David Billings, *Deep Denial: The Persistence of White Supremacy in United States History and Life* (Roselle, N.J.: Crandall, Dostie and Douglass Books, Inc., 2016), 65.

CHAPTER FOUR

The Myth of the Christian Nation
The Early National Period

William G. McLoughlin tells us that when John Adams was president, the United States "concluded a treaty with the Moslem nation of Tripoli (now Libya) in which one article read in part: 'As the government of the United States of America is not, in any sense, founded on the Christian religion.'" McLoughlin further reports, "That treaty was ratified by more than two thirds of the U.S. Senate and signed by John Adams."[1]

McLoughlin's report is not surprising, since the Founders of the United States never intended America to be an explicitly Christian nation. With the Declaration of Independence as a measure of their sentiments, one must conclude that they sought to ground this country on the Deist assumption that God exists and rules the affairs of humankind, that God can best be discerned in the book of nature, and that God has built into nature certain moral standards that are equally accessible to all human beings. These were the beliefs that would stand at the core of the new Republic, and because the Founders viewed these propositions as "self-evident," they imagined that all Americans could affirm them with ease.

At the same time, if Americans wished to belong to specific religious traditions, or wished to affirm other doctrines—the notion of the Trinity, for example, or the doctrine of substitutionary atonement—they were free to do so. But these other doctrines, peculiar to specific sects and denominations, would never occupy the nation's center stage, would never define the nation's legal tradition, and would be irrelevant to the workings of the American government. The Founders sought to guarantee religious liberty by allowing for particular doctrines and creeds but then by pushing those doctrines and creeds off the center stage of the Republic and into the wings.

The Declaration therefore affirmed a minimalist religious sentiment, that is, the religious convictions that most Americans held in common. But the Constitution went far beyond the Declaration and essentially created a secular state. Nowhere does the Constitution mention God or any other religious symbol. And when, finally, the First Amendment to the Constitution speaks of religion for the very first time, it makes perfectly clear that "Congress shall make no law respecting an establishment of religion, or prohibiting the free exercise thereof."

In other words, while the American people would be free to practice any religion, they would also be free to practice no religion at all. And the government had no business injecting itself into religion or religious issues in any form, shape, or fashion. In this sense, America would be a secular state.

The paradox lies in the fact that in spite of the stipulations of the First Amendment, America nonetheless emerged in several respects as a Christian nation.[2] First, even though the Founders resisted the creation of an explicitly Christian nation, the Deism that they espoused is inexplicable apart from biblical faith. Michael Novak documented this fact extensively and has shown how Jewish and Christian presuppositions informed American political institutions.[3] And second, the myth of America as a Christian Nation took on objective truth, especially in the nineteenth century when Protestants succeeded in Christianizing the country through the power of revivalism. From that time through the early twenty-first century, America was a Christian nation of sorts.

The Attempt to Christianize the Republic

While most Americans in the twenty-first century are comfortable with the notion of a secular government, with the separation of church and state, and with a multiplicity of religious traditions, many in the nation's earliest years were not. Outside of Maryland, Rhode Island, and Pennsylvania, there were virtually no significant models of the separation of church and state when the nation was born, either in Europe or in the United States. Many Americans during that period, therefore, could not imagine a viable nation without a legally established church.

Equally important is the fact that during the Revolutionary period and into the nineteenth century, the majority of Americans who claimed the Christian faith were Calvinists of one stripe or another. Roman Catholics were still a distinct minority. The Anglican Church—or the Church of England—still thrived, especially in the South, but had lost considerable credibility, especially since so many Americans associated that church with Britain, not with the United States. Methodism—a distinctly non-Calvinist faith—was growing by leaps and bounds and would soon take the American frontier by storm. Yet, in the early nineteenth century, Calvinists still dominated religious life in the United States.

Calvinism came in many forms. In New England, the Calvinist faith manifested itself especially in Congregationalism, one of the churches that descended directly from New England Puritanism. In the middle colonies, Presbyterians and Dutch Reformed Christians abounded. And Baptists were numerous in the South. Baptists, however, do not play a significant role in this phase of our story since, at that time at least, they did not share with other Reformed Christians the goal of dominating public life.

As people of the Reformed tradition, Congregationalists, Presbyterians, and Dutch Reformed Christians generally looked to John Calvin and the regime he erected in Geneva to understand how religion should inform the public square. Understanding the Christian resistance to America's Founders, therefore, requires some understanding of religion and politics in Geneva in the sixteenth century.

Calvin shared with virtually all European Christians of the sixteenth century the conviction that for one state, there could be only one church, and that church should be legally established and binding on all citizens. To understand the genius of Calvin, however, one must realize that he went far beyond that position. Simply put, Calvin sought to transform Geneva into a model kingdom of God. *Transform* and *transformation*—these are the operative words when discussing Calvin, for Calvin wished to transform every dimension of Geneva's culture—its politics, its art, its education—into a regime controlled by a Christian understanding of reality.

Since that time, Calvin's vision of a godly society has become central to the Calvinist heritage and has flourished wherever Calvinists have lived throughout the world. When Reformed Christians settled in America, therefore, they brought with them this very same understanding of how Christian faith should relate to the state, to the culture, and to the public order. On the basis of this commitment, they determined to transform the colonies, and then the nation, into a model kingdom of God, just as Calvin had transformed Geneva many years before.

In addition to the Calvinists with their theocratic orientation, Christians of almost every stripe during the Revolutionary period were still devoted to the European model of the state church or, at the very least, to the ideal of a state with significant Christian underpinnings. When one considers those two realities, one can understand why so many Christians of that period regarded the Founders with such suspicion. Because the Founders embraced the separation of church and state, many Christians viewed them as the nation's arch-infidels who sought to destroy Christianity and remove religion from the public square.

We find a marvelous example of the struggle over these issues in the presidential election of 1800. In that year, Thomas Jefferson ran for the presidency of the United States. His candidacy created a firestorm of controversy. Because he was a Deist who rejected any effort to establish or coerce religious faith, his opponents assailed him as an infidel and a godless atheist. And because he disavowed a great deal of traditional Christian theology, some claimed that his administration would encourage the grossest kinds of immoralities and would hasten the Republic's early demise.

One clergyman, the Reverend John M. Mason, discovered that Jefferson had written in his *Notes on Virginia* that "the legitimate powers of government extend to such acts only as are injurious to others. But it does me no injury for my neighbor to say there are twenty Gods, or no God. It neither picks my pocket nor breaks my leg." To Mason, Jefferson had preached both "atheism" and "the morality of devils, which would break in an instant every link in the chain of human friendship, and transform the globe into one equal scene of desolation and horror, where fiend would prowl with fiend for plunder and blood."[4]

Another preacher, the Reverend Clement Clarke Moore—author of "'Twas the Night Before Christmas"—also objected to Jefferson's *Notes on Virginia*. He had only recently read them, he wrote, and found himself "surprised that a book which contains so much infidelity, conveyed in so insidious a manner, should have been extensively circulated in a Christian country, for nearly twenty years, without ever having received a formal answer."[5]

Mason and Moore typified the thousands of Christians in the early national period who were still devoted to the ideals of a state church. More to the point, they could not imagine an America that was not fundamentally Christian, even fundamentally Protestant. Jefferson had challenged all that, and for this reason, he emerged as the arch-infidel of his generation.

For all that, the Jeffersonians won that war. They won it when the First Amendment prohibited Congress from making any law "respecting an establishment of religion, or prohibiting the free exercise thereof." They won again when the various states passed their own versions of the First Amendment, striking down religious establishments in state after state. As might be expected, Massachusetts—long dominated by Puritan visions of a Christian commonwealth—was the last state to disestablish, doing so in 1833. Slowly, one indisputable fact became clear even to the most resolute defender of Christian orthodoxy and the state church ideal: America would not be a Christian nation, at least in legal terms.

The Second Great Awakening

Shortly after the nation's birth, Christians throughout the country launched a massive revival designed, in part, to achieve through persuasion what they could no longer achieve through coercion or force of law. Through that revival, they sought to transform the United States into a Christian nation. We remember that revival as the Second Great Awakening. This awakening was the second such revival in American life. The Great Awakening, which I shall consider in the next chapter, had swept through the colonies some seventy-five years earlier.

The Second Great Awakening was not simply a response to the loss of an established church. At a far deeper level, it was a two-pronged attempt to realize the old Calvinist vision of a social order responsive to the sovereign will of God. First, the Second Great Awakening sought to Protestantize the nation. Second, it sought to transform the republic into the Kingdom of God, whose social order would be thoroughly reformed according to biblical principles. In these ways, the United States would become a distinctly Christian nation.

Factors Prompting the Second Great Awakening

Many factors prompted the rise of the Second Great Awakening. First, as I have noted, many Christians of that time were still devoted to the European model of a state church and could not imagine America without the influence of a Christian establishment. Second, many feared that the Constitution, by disallowing any possibility of an established Christian faith, had opened the door to heresy, skepticism, and irreligion. To some degree, developments since the Revolution confirmed those fears. For example, while many of the Founders were moderate-minded Deists, other freethinkers of the period launched scathing attacks on the Bible and the Christian faith, portraying miracle stories as fairy tales and traditional religion as little more than superstition. Through their various publications, Ethan Allen, Elihu Palmer, and Jefferson's friend and ally, Thomas Paine, made themselves especially prominent in this regard.

Third, the French Revolution began in 1789, and the violence it spawned against religion horrified many Americans and especially American Christians. For example, the French king himself lost his head to the guillotine in 1793. In the chaotic months that followed, the new regime executed literally thousands of people. In 1794 the Convention designated Reason the Supreme Being that must be worshipped and transformed Roman Catholic churches into Temples of Reason where citizens now poured libations to statues depicting the goddess of nature.

These events alarmed many American Christians, since the French Revolution was rooted in the same principles that had undergirded the American Revolution: the equal rights of all people, rooted in Nature and Nature's God. In fact, when Jefferson served as ambassador to France, he assisted the marquis de Lafayette in drafting the Declaration of the Rights of Man, a document patterned directly after Jefferson's own Declaration of Independence.

A fourth factor prompting revival was the virtual flood of settlers pouring over the mountains into regions that soon would become the states of Kentucky, Tennessee, Ohio, Indiana, Illinois, Mississippi, and Alabama—a development that had accelerated especially since 1790. Almost as much as Deism and free thought, these western settlements frightened the older, eastern population. From the eastern perspective, settlers in these new western regions lacked civilizing influences altogether. Easterners typically thought that people on the western frontier lacked serious instruction in the Christian faith. As the western population grew, many easterners imagined that the frontier threatened to overwhelm the entire nation with barbarism.

For all these reasons, many felt that a revival of Christian faith and commitment was sorely needed.

Major Developments in the Second Great Awakening

The first major expression of the Second Great Awakening occurred in 1801 when a full-scale revival erupted at Cane Ridge, Bourbon County, Kentucky. News of this revival quickly spread and attracted people from miles in every direction. Historians estimate that the crowd finally totaled between ten thousand and twenty-five thousand people.

The second notable manifestation of the Second Great Awakening also began in 1801, but this time revival erupted far from the Kentucky frontier, in New England. There, Timothy Dwight, president of Yale College and a grandson of Jonathan Edwards, discovered that Yale students generally questioned Christian orthodoxy and admired the skepticism that characterized the French Revolution. Dwight determined to change all that by preaching strong sermons to his students, convincing them of the horrors of "infidelity." Dwight painted the widest possible gulf between authentic Christianity and what he called "infidelity" and suggested that if one placed one's foot on the path that led to "infidelity," there was no stopping point. To Dwight, the natural religion of the Enlightenment led inevitably to "mere Unbelief, then Animalism, then Skepticism, then partial, and then total Atheism."[6] Revival quickly broke out under Dwight's preaching. To some degree, the Yale revival resulted from other New England revivals, and to some degree, it helped spread the revival fire even further.

Charles G. Finney ushered in the third and most notable phase of the Second Great Awakening, the phase of consolidation. Finney served the Second Great Awakening much as George Whitefield had served the first one some seventy-five years before: beginning in the 1820s, he traveled from one community to the next and led revivals in towns and cities throughout the United States. By so doing, he helped to consolidate many local revivals into a great national religious awakening.

Finney was the first person in American history to promote his revivals through what amounted to marketing techniques. These "new measures," as he called them, stood in marked contrast to the revival styles that had characterized the Great Awakening of the previous century. In particular, Finney's techniques demonstrated that the old Calvinist notion of predestination had fallen on hard times. In the Great Awakening of the 1730s and 1740s, no one thought that conversion was the work of the preacher. Instead, everyone believed that conversion was the work of God. If sinners responded to the gospel message, so much the better. If they did not, well then, perhaps they were not among the elect.

By the early nineteenth century, however, the popular passion for individual liberties snuffed out practically every trace of predestination. To a people convinced that liberty was among their "unalienable rights," it made little sense to claim that God, from the foundations of the world, had preselected those who would be saved and those who would be damned.

The Humanitarian Crusade of the Second Great Awakening

Charles Finney not only consolidated the revivals of the early nineteenth century into a national spiritual awakening. He also funneled hundreds and perhaps thousands of Christians into a great moral crusade, designed to alleviate the social ills of the United States. In his revivals, Finney insisted that no one could be a Christian by and for one's self. Genuine Christians, he argued, would seek perfection, not only for themselves but also for the world around them. In this way, Finney lived out the standard Calvinist concern to transform the surrounding culture into the Kingdom of God.

Finney told new converts that they must throw themselves into the transformation of society in some meaningful way. Many of his converts committed themselves to prison reform. Others took up the banner of temperance. Still others sought to uplift society through education. Most of all, Finney's converts worked for the abolition of slavery.

Harriet Beecher Stowe, an active participant in the Second Great Awakening, provides one of the most striking examples of the Christian zeal to abolish slavery during that period. In her book, *Uncle Tom's Cabin*, she sought to portray the horrors of American slavery in ways that might help end that practice. The book won a wide readership and exerted a broad influence, both in the North and in the South.

In addition to their revivals, Protestants also formed national trans-denominational organizations to achieve the purposes of the Second Great Awakening. Before Finney became involved in the Awakening, these organizations sought mainly to extend the influence of Protestantism throughout the nation. The American Bible Society and the American Education Society, both organized in 1816, sought to distribute Bibles and to promote Protestant-oriented education, especially on the western frontier. The American Colonization Society, formed in 1817, sought freedom for enslaved blacks and helped many return to Africa where they established the Republic of Liberia. The American Sunday School Union appeared in 1824 and the American Tract Society in 1825.

The work of the American Colonization Society and the effort to educate and uplift the American frontier were not unrelated. Lyman Beecher, a famous preacher of that period and the father of Harriet Beecher Stowe, explained that relationship. He saw the nation as a pair of scales on which its various populations rested. On one side was the eastern Protestant establishment. On the other were Catholics, western settlers, and blacks. To Beecher, if no effort were made to educate and uplift the western settlements, and if at the same time enslaved people were to win their freedom, those two populations, along with the Catholics, would outweigh the white, Protestant civilization of New England. In that case, Beecher thought, America would be doomed. His solution was to establish schools throughout the western settlements and to return freed blacks to their African homeland. Through those two strategies, Beecher thought, a white, Protestant America would triumph over the forces that threatened civilization.

Then, with the preaching of Finney, the burden shifted from the promotion of Protestant principles throughout the nation to genuine social reform. The American Temperance Society, for example, emerged in 1826, and the American Peace Society in 1828. Finally, northern abolitionists organized in

1833 the American Antislavery Society, an organization founded on explicitly Christian grounds and devoted to the destruction of American slavery. All these organizations had roots in one way or another in the Second Great Awakening.

The Second Great Awakening succeeded fabulously in Christianizing—indeed, in Protestantizing—the American Republic. It ushered in a period of Protestant domination in the United States that lasted for well over a hundred years. In fact, the Second Great Awakening succeeded so well that even the federal government, in various official statements, sometimes referred to the United States as a "Christian nation," even into the twentieth century. The last official statement of this sort came from the Supreme Court of the United States in 1931. Writing for the majority on *United States v. Macintosh*, a case of that year, Justice George Sutherland observed in an offhand way that "We are a Christian people."[7]

A Christian Critique of the Myth of the Christian Nation

I have already argued that when measured by the intentions of America's Founders, the notion that America was a Christian nation is questionable at best. This notion is questionable in a second sense as well. This second sense will become apparent in the answer to the question, "What does it *really* mean to say that America is a Christian nation?"

The Voice of the Sixteenth-Century Anabaptists

One of the aims of this book is to help us listen carefully to dissenting voices, especially the voices of African Americans. In the context of the nineteenth-century drive to transform America into a Protestant nation, it will be useful to hear another dissenting voice—that of the Anabaptists whose American descendants include the Amish, Mennonites, and Hutterites.

Like the Reformed tradition that led the effort to transform the United States into a Christian nation, the Anabaptists also had their roots in the sixteenth-century Reformation. But if the Reformed tradition sought to transform human culture into a Christian civilization, the Anabaptists completely rejected any such option. From their perspective, a Christianized culture was a contradiction in terms, since nations were inevitably full of people who would never conform themselves to the moral discipline of the Christian faith. One might therefore hope for a Christian *church*—a community of voluntary believers—but one could not realistically hope for a Christian *nation*.

Because they took this position, the Anabaptists of the sixteenth century rejected the state-church ideal and established their own churches, completely separate and apart from the established church that was sanctioned by the state. They thereby became the first people in the western world to advocate a notion that most Americans hold dear: the separation of church and state.

In their own time, however, they suffered grievously for taking that position. Reformed and Lutheran leaders, the Roman Catholic hierarchy, kings, and princes sought their extermination. All over Europe, thousands of Anabaptists were hanged, drowned, burned at the stake, or run through by the sword. The price they paid suggests how incredibly radical was the ideal of the separation of church and state in the sixteenth century.

The separation of church and state, as the Anabaptists understood this notion, is an incredibly radical ideal even in modern America, because the Anabaptists took that position not to protect the welfare of the state but to protect the integrity of the church. The Anabaptists understood that in order to Christianize the nation, the church would have to make itself acceptable to the larger public. It would therefore have to accommodate itself to values and perspectives commonly accepted in the larger culture.

The Trade-Off of a Christianized Culture

Christianizing the culture, therefore, involved a trade-off: The culture might absorb bits and pieces of the Christian faith, while the church would absorb many of the values common to the larger society. This is precisely what happened when Christians in the early nineteenth century sought to create an informal Christian establishment in the United States.

Of all the values prevalent in America at that time, none was more important than liberty, that is, freedom for the individual to pursue his or her self-interest. Freedom to pursue self-interest stands diametrically opposed to the Christian understanding of freedom, for the Christian understanding of freedom ultimately means freedom *from* self-interest in order to serve the neighbor. Nonetheless, in order to make itself acceptable to the larger culture, the church would have to lend its support, to one degree or another, to the larger cultural understanding.

There is more: liberty, as Americans understood that term in the early nineteenth century, was grounded in "Nature and Nature's God," not in the Christian faith. Christians had to argue, therefore, that the faith they promoted was fully compatible with "Nature and Nature's God." They had to argue, in effect, that the Christian faith was both reasonable and natural.

This strategy backfired, however, since by understanding their faith as both reasonable and natural, white Christians typically read their own European American experience not only into nature but also into the Christian faith. In this way, they stripped the Christian faith of much of the ability it might otherwise have had to stand in judgment on ethnocentric cultural norms. It therefore became easy to speak of "unalienable rights" for "all men," but to mean by that rhetoric "unalienable rights" for all *white men.*

In this way, white American Christians typically domesticated the Christian faith and robbed it of the radical demands one encounters in the ethical teachings of Jesus. By the time they finished their work, an unbiased observer might have found it difficult to distinguish American Christianity from cultural values common to most Americans at the time. On the other hand, we know that some American Christians did challenge the ethical norms and standards of the larger culture. One thinks, for example, of the humanitarian crusade that I have already explored in the context of the Second Great Awakening.

If some white Christians worked tirelessly for the abolition of slavery, however, others worked just as zealously to free the blacks and return them to Africa, on the grounds that a free black population would corrupt a white society. And many white Christians, especially in the South, had so completely interpreted the Christian faith in the light of cultural values that they could actually make the case that the Christian religion sanctioned the institution of slavery.

While segments of American Christianity did challenge prevailing cultural norms and standards, therefore, many American Christians invoked divine approval in order to sanctify the cultural status quo. That was the problem that stood at the heart of the African American critique of the Myth of the Christian Nation.

An African American Critique of the Myth of the Christian Nation

If whites had a difficult time discerning the contradictions in the Myth of the Christian Nation, blacks did not. If America was really a Christian nation, blacks pointed out, how could the institution of slavery possibly survive? At the very least, one would think that the Christian character of the nation would help to make slavery more humane and less brutal.

Even the churches, however, had abandoned Christian principles, at least on the question of race. Officials at the white-controlled St. George's Methodist Episcopal Church in Philadelphia, for example, enforced racial discrimination in a variety of ways. In 1787, when they pulled black members, engaged in prayer, off their knees, the black members voted with their feet: they left, and established in 1794 the African Methodist Episcopal Church with Richard Allen as pastor and, beginning in 1816, as bishop.

Blacks often complained that American whites were bad enough without their religion, but as Christians, "they are ten times more cruel, avaricious and unmerciful," as David Walker observed.[8] Walker spoke specifically of the Myth of the Christian Nation and ridiculed it. Slavery, he knew, had existed in many other parts of the world. He pointed out that the suffering of enslaved people "in ancient and heathen nations, were, in comparison with ours, under this enlightened and Christian nation, no more than a cypher."[9]

Walker recalled a camp meeting he attended in South Carolina. "To my no ordinary astonishment," he wrote, "our Reverend gentleman got up and told us (coloured people) that slaves must be obedient to their masters—must do their duty to their masters or be whipped." Walker stood amazed. "Here I pause for a moment, to give the world time to consider what was my surprise, to hear such preaching from a minister of my Master, whose very gospel is that of peace and not of blood and whips." Even in Boston, Walker noted, "in the very houses erected to the Lord, they have built little places for the reception of coloured people, where they must sit during meeting, or keep away from the house of God."[10] Walker felt that most white American Christians simply did not take the Christian faith seriously. "Have not the Americans the Bible in their hands?" he asked. "Do they believe it? Surely they do not."[11]

Frederick Douglass, who taught himself to read and then became the country's most powerful voice for the abolition of slavery, concurred with virtually all of Walker's points. In a profoundly eloquent passage in his speech, "What to the Slave Is the Fourth of July?" he mercilessly assailed American Christianity:

> The church of this country is not only indifferent to the wrongs of the slave, it actually takes sides with the oppressors. . . . It is . . . a religion which favors the rich against the poor; which exalts the proud above the humble; which divides mankind into two classes, tyrants and slaves; which says to the man in chains, *stay there*, and to the oppressor, *oppress on*; it is a religion which may be professed and enjoyed by all the robbers and enslavers of mankind; it makes God a respecter of persons, denies his fatherhood of the race, and tramples in the dust the great truth of the brotherhood of man. All this we affirm to be true of the popular church, and the popular worship of our land and nation—a religion, a church, and a worship which, on the authority of inspired wisdom, we pronounce to be an abomination in the sight of God.[12]

In his autobiography, Douglass returned to this theme:

> Revivals of religion and revivals in the slave-trade go hand in hand together. The slave prison and the church stand near each other. The clanking of fetters and the rattling of chains in the prison, and the pious psalm and solemn prayer in the church, may be heard at the same time. The dealers in the bodies and souls of men erect their stand in the presence of the pulpit, and they mutually help each other. The dealer gives his blood-stained gold to support the pulpit, and the pulpit, in return, covers his infernal business with the garb of Christianity.

Fifty years after writing the *Narrative* of his life, Douglass still held that judgment. "There is nothing in the history of savages," he affirmed, "to surpass the blood-chilling horrors and fiendish excesses perpetrated against the coloured people of this country, by the so-called enlightened and Christian people of the South."[13] So no one would think he was speaking of the South alone, he wrote, "Dark and terrible as is this picture, I hold it to be strictly true of the overwhelming mass of professed Christians in America."[14]

At the same time, many nineteenth-century African Americans who criticized American Christianity most severely were extraordinarily devout in their commitment to the Christian faith. In other words, they clearly recognized the difference between the Christianity they read about in the New Testament and the Christianity they saw practiced in the United States.

David Walker and Frederick Douglass provide notable examples of this point. In a particularly scathing passage, Douglass wrote:

> Between the Christianity of this land, and the Christianity of Christ, I recognize the widest possible difference—so wide, that to receive the one as good, pure, and holy, is of necessity to reject the other as bad, corrupt, and wicked. . . . I love the pure, peaceable, and impartial Christianity of Christ: I therefore hate the corrupt, slaveholding, women-whipping, cradle-plundering, partial and hypocritical Christianity of this land. Indeed, I can see no reason, but the most deceitful one, for calling the religion of this land Christianity.[15]

In this passage, Douglass makes it clear that white Americans had absolutized the Myth of the Christian Nation. In its highest form, that myth would call on Americans to live out the moral principles of Jesus, especially his admonition to love one's neighbor as one's self. In its corrupted and absolutized form, however, the Myth of the Christian Nation became a self-serving badge of cultural superiority.

The African American critique of this version of the Christian faith did not diminish in the years following emancipation. Among the most prominent voices in this regard was that of Anna J. Cooper, an activist, scholar, and educator. In a speech delivered at the Friends General Conference held in Asbury Park, New Jersey, in 1902, Cooper described the Negro as "the passive and silent rebuke to the Nation's Christianity, the great gulf between its professions and its practices." Then she satirized what she viewed as the perverted gospel preached by most American churches. "Come unto me all ye *whites* who are heavy laden. The Poor (*whites*) have the Gospel preached unto them. Suffer the little *white* children to come unto Me! For of such is the kingdom of heaven. Love the Lord thy God with all thy heart, soul, and strength and thy *white* neighbor as thyself!"[16]

Some sixty-five years later, at the height of the struggle for civil rights in the American South, Anne Moody recalled the mood of the white churches in Mississippi after the murder of black activist Medgar Evers. The Sunday following Evers's funeral, Moody reported, young blacks visited numerous white churches in the city of Jackson in an attempt to worship God alongside the whites. Moody reported, "At each one they had prepared for our visit with armed policemen, paddy wagons, and dogs—which would be used in case we refused to leave after 'ushers' had read us the prepared resolutions."

The following Sunday, they tried again:

We went first to a Church of Christ, where we were greeted by the regular ushers. After reading us the same resolutions we had heard last week, they offered to give us cab fare to the Negro extension of the church. Just as we had refused and were walking away, an old lady stopped us. "We'll sit with you," she said.

We walked back to the ushers with her and her family. "Please let them in, Mr. Calloway. We'll sit with them," the old lady said.

"Mrs. Dixon, the church has decided what is to be done. A resolution has been passed, and we are to abide by it."

"Who are we to decide such a thing? This is a house of God, and God is to make all of the decisions. He is the judge of us all," the lady said.

The ushers got angrier then and threatened to call the police if we didn't leave. We decided to go.[17]

No single African American was more critical of the white Christian establishment in the American South during the years of the Freedom Movement than Martin Luther King Jr. At the beginning of the freedom movement, he recalled, he fully expected to "have the support of the white church." He found himself bitterly disappointed: "In the midst of blatant injustices inflicted upon the Negro, I have watched white churches stand on the sidelines and merely mouth pious irrelevancies and sanctimonious trivialities. In the midst of a mighty struggle to rid our nation of racial and economic injustice, I have heard so many ministers say, 'Those are social issues with which the gospel has no real concern.'" King found himself completely puzzled by this lack of support:

> On sweltering summer days and crisp autumn mornings I have looked at her [the South's] beautiful churches with their lofty spires pointing heavenward. . . . Over and over again I have found myself asking: "What kind of people worship here? Who is their God? Where were their voices when the lips of Governor Barnett dripped with words of interposition and nullification? Where were they when Governor Wallace gave the clarion call for defiance and hatred? Where were their voices of support when tired, bruised and weary Negro men and women decided to rise from the dark dungeons of complacency to the bright hills of creative protest?"[18]

White supremacy, so widely practiced in America's Christian churches, prompted many blacks to turn their backs on the Christian faith which they viewed, at best, as complicit in the oppression of blacks and, at worst, as responsible for that oppression. Richard Wright offers a case in point. "I was born a black Protestant in that most racist of all the American states: Mississippi," he wrote. "I lived my childhood under a racial code, brutal and bloody, that white men proclaimed was ordained by God, said was made mandatory by the nature of their religion. Naturally, I rejected that religion . . . and . . . I became passionately curious as to why Christians felt it imperative to practice such wholesale denials of humanity."[19]

Likewise, Malcolm X concluded that the Christian religion in the United States "taught the 'Negro' that black was a curse. It taught him to hate everything black, including himself. It taught him that everything white was good, to be admired, respected, and loved. It brainwashed this 'Negro' to think he was superior if his complexion showed more of the white pollution of the slavemaster."[20] Malcolm viewed the Christian religion as a fraud. "The blond-haired, blue-eyed white man has taught [us] to worship a *white* Jesus. . . . The white man has taught us . . . to wait until *death*, for some dreamy heaven-in-the-hereafter, when we're *dead*, while this white man has his milk and honey in the streets paved with golden dollars right here on *this* earth!"[21] Sounding remarkably like Frederick Douglass a century before, Malcolm prophetically asked, "And what is the greatest single reason for this Christian church's failure? It is its failure to combat racism. It is the old 'You sow, you reap' story. The Christian church sowed racism—blasphemously; now it reaps racism."[22] As a result, even though his father, Earl Little, had been a Baptist preacher, Malcolm turned his back on the Christian faith and embraced Islam.

James Baldwin rejected Christianity for similar reasons. "I am called Baldwin because I was either sold by my African tribe or kidnapped out of it into the hands of a white Christian named Baldwin, who forced me to kneel at the foot of the cross," he wrote.[23] Baldwin believed, in fact, that many whites, through their embrace of a racist theology, had transmuted the cross into an instrument of oppression. "I knew that, according to many Christians, I was a descendant of Ham, who had been cursed, and that I was therefore predestined to be a slave. This had nothing to do with anything I was, or contained, or could become; my fate had been sealed forever, from the beginning of time. And it seemed, indeed, when one looked out over Christendom, that this was what Christendom effectively believed. It was certainly the way it behaved."[24]

What loomed especially large for Baldwin was the utter failure of the Christian church in Germany during the Third Reich, which, Baldwin argued, "makes obsolete forever any question of Christian superiority." The Holocaust also made obsolete for Baldwin any viable notion of a Christian America. Given the Myth of White Supremacy that pervaded both American culture and the American churches, "I could not but feel, in those sorrowful years, that this human indifference, concerning which I knew so much already, would be my portion on the day that the United States decided to murder its Negroes systematically, instead of little by little and catch-as-catch-can. I was, of course, authoritatively assured that what had happened to the Jews in Germany could not happen to the Negroes in America, but I thought, bleakly, that the German Jews had probably believed similar counselors."[25]

Baldwin concluded that one who "wishes to become a truly moral human being . . . must first divorce himself from all the prohibitions, crimes, and hypocrisies of the Christian church. If the concept of God has any validity or any use, it can only be to make us larger, freer, and more loving. If God cannot do this, then it is time we got rid of Him."[26]

In a later time, Ta-Nehisi Coates explained that the notion of white supremacy prompted his parents to reject all religious dogmas, Christian and otherwise. "We spurned the [Christian] holidays marketed by the people who wanted to be white. We would not stand for their anthems. We would not kneel before their God. And so I had no sense that any just God was on my side. 'The meek shall inherit the earth' meant nothing to me. The meek were battered in West Baltimore, stomped out at Walbrook Junction, bashed up on Park Heights, and raped in the showers of the city jail." And then in a clear rejection of Martin Luther King's assertion that "the moral arc of the universe bends toward justice," Coates concluded, "My understanding of the universe was physical, and its moral arc bent toward chaos then concluded in a box."[27]

In the twenty-first century, no one has voiced a more scathing criticism of white supremacy in the context of the American church than James M. Cone in his book, *The Cross and the Lynching Tree*. Cone's point is both simple and straightforward. White Christians—people who pledge their allegiance to a *crucified* Savior who was hung on a tree—hung thousands of innocent African Americans on lynching trees between the end of Reconstruction in 1877 and 1950.[28] How does Cone know the perpetrators were Christians? Because the work of lynching took place in "Christian America," especially in the South where Christians dominated the culture, and because a given lynching typically involved thousands of citizens, not just a few. But Cone's fundamental point is this: while the cross was itself a lynching tree, most white, American Christians never discerned the connection between the crucifixion of Jesus and the crucifixion of blacks. As Cone explains,

> The cross and the lynching tree are separated by nearly 2,000 years. One is the universal symbol of Christian faith; the other is the quintessential symbol of black oppression in America. Though both are symbols of death, one represents a message of hope and salvation, while the other signifies the negation of that message by white supremacy. Despite the obvious similarities between Jesus' death on a cross and the death of thousands of black men and women strung up to die on a lamppost or tree, relatively few people, apart from black poets, novelists, and other reality-seeing artists, have explored the symbolic connections. Yet, I believe this is a challenge we must face.[29]

Because most contemporary white Americans have never given a moment's thought to the lynching tree or the horrors of that reality, it is important to quote at length Cone's description of what the lynching tree involved:

> Whites lynched blacks in nearly every state, including New York, Minnesota, and California. Wherever blacks were present in significant numbers, the threat of being lynched was always real. . . . By the 1890s, lynching fever gripped the South, spreading like cholera, as white communities made blacks their primary target, and torture their focus. Burning the black victim slowly for hours was the chief method of torture. Lynching became a white media spectacle, in which prominent newspapers, like the *Atlanta Constitution*, announced to the public the place, date, and time of the expected hanging and burning of black victims. Often as many as ten to twenty thousand men, women, and children attended the event. It was a family affair, a ritual celebration of white supremacy, where women and children were often given the first opportunity to torture black victims—burning black flesh and cutting off genitals, fingers, toes, and ears as

souvenirs. Postcards were made from the photographs taken of black victims with white lynchers and onlookers smiling as they struck a pose for the camera. They were sold for ten to twenty-five cents to members of the crowd, who then mailed them to relatives and friends, often with a note saying something like this: "This is the barbeque we had last night."[30]

Ida B. Wells, part owner and editor from 1889 to 1892 of the *Memphis Free Speech*, a newspaper serving blacks in the Memphis area, crusaded against the practice of lynching. Her reporting on those events corroborates Cone's description. In a speech presented in Boston in 1893, Wells highlighted two particular examples of this practice, one in Texarkana in 1892 and another in Paris, Texas, in 1893. "The Texarkana man, Ed Coy, was charge[d] with assaulting a white woman. A mob pronounced him guilty, strapped him to a tree, chipped the flesh from his body, poured coal oil over him and the woman in the case set fire to him." In the Paris, Texas, burning,

The man [Henry Smith] was drawn through the streets on a float, as the Roman generals used to parade their trophies of war, while the scaffold ten feet high, was being built, and irons were heated in the fire. He was bound on it, and red-hot irons began at his feet and slowly branded his body, while the mob howled with delight at his shrieks. Red hot irons were run down his throat and cooked his tongue; his eyes were burned out, and when he was at last unconscious, cotton seed hulls were placed under him, coal oil poured all over him, and a torch applied to the mass. When the flames burned away the ropes which bound Smith and scorched his flesh, he was brought back to sensibility and burned and maimed and sightless as he was, he rolled off the platform and away from the fire. His half-cooked body was seized and trampled and thrown back into the flames while a mob of twenty thousand persons who came from all over the country howled with delight, and gathered up some buttons and ashes after all was over to preserve for relics.[31]

If Wells puzzled over the fact that "this Christian nation, the flower of the nineteenth century civilization, says it can do nothing to stop this inhuman slaughter,"[32] James Cone puzzled over the fact that "between 1880 to 1940, white Christians lynched nearly five thousand black men and women in a manner with obvious echoes of the Roman crucifixion of Jesus. Yet these 'Christians' did not see the irony or contradiction in their actions." Indeed, Cone continues,

The lynching tree—so strikingly similar to the cross on Golgotha—should have a prominent place in American images of Jesus' death. But it does not. In fact, the lynching tree has no place in American theological reflections about Jesus' cross or in the proclamation of Christian churches about his Passion. The conspicuous absence of the lynching tree in American theological discourse and preaching is profoundly revealing, especially since the crucifixion was clearly a first-century lynching."[33]

Cone leaves us with this massive contradiction—that Christians who believed in an innocent Jesus, lynched for their sins, lynched thousands of innocent blacks while never discerning the contradiction between their faith and their deeds. The only way I know to explain that contradiction is to acknowledge—candidly, honestly, and forthrightly—the extent to which white supremacy defined for many—perhaps even most—white Americans of that time not only the Great American Myths but also the meaning of the Christian faith. Contradictions like this suggest that the Anabaptists of the sixteenth century were likely correct, that any effort to Christianize an entire culture will likely involve a tradeoff: while the culture might absorb bits and pieces of the Christian faith, the church will inevitably absorb huge chunks of the culture's dominant values.

White American Christians and the Quest for Cultural Dominance

But that is a lesson that white American Protestants, for the most part, have never learned—a fact that offers yet another profound contradiction in the relation between religion and culture in the United States. It makes sense that churches during the colonial period—Puritans in New England, Presbyterians in the Middle Colonies, and Anglicans in the South—would have sought to Christianize and control the culture in which they lived; after all, they were, in fact, established churches. But following legal disestablishment, which, by 1833, had come to all the colonies, one might legitimately expect that white American churches would have fully embraced the separation of church and state, along with its implications for the common good, as something beneficial both for the church and for the nation. But that was not to be.

As recently as the twentieth century, white American Protestants—first, the so-called mainline and then the evangelicals—sought to control, Christianize, and dominate American culture. Of the more liberal mainline, Robert Jones writes in his important book, *The End of White Christian America*, "At the beginning of the twentieth century, white mainline Protestants believed that they were on the verge of 'The Christian Century.' In the last hundred years of the millennium, they predicted, Christian principles would finally begin to shape national policy and world events."[34] So powerful did the mainline become that David Hollinger observed that by the mid–twentieth century,

"Persons at least nominally affiliated with these denominations controlled all branches of the federal government and most of the business world, as well as the nation's chief cultural and educational institutions, and countless state and local institutions. If you were in charge of something big before 1960, chances are you grew up in a white Protestant milieu."[35]

Then came the 1960s when the cultural revolution of that period effectively tumbled the mainline out of its seat of power. With that development, white conservative Protestants—fundamentalists and evangelicals alike—saw an opening and mobilized to fill the power vacuum, impose on the United States a conservative Christian agenda, and dominate American culture. As early as 1947, the National Association of Evangelicals had campaigned for a reference to "Jesus of Nazareth" in the United States Constitution. Less than thirty years later, *TIME* magazine proclaimed 1976 the "Year of the Evangelical"—a year when 34 percent of Americans claimed to be "born again" Christians.[36] But early in the twenty-first century, they, too, saw their influence eroding and ebbing away as younger people—even those raised in conservative denominations—increasingly rejected white evangelical Protestantism, many opting for "unaffiliated." By 2015, for example, Southern Baptists, the largest evangelical denomination in the nation, had lost members for eight years in a row, with some 200,000 people abandoning that tradition in 2014 alone.[37]

Important for the thesis of this book is the fact that the precipitous loss of cultural dominance of both Christian traditions—the white mainline in the 1960s and the white fundamentalists/evangelicals in the early twenty-first century—were related to the extent to which both had been mired in the bog of white supremacy and white privilege. The mainline, for example, was complicit in Jim Crow segregation until the 1950s and the rise of the Civil Rights Movement. Even though mainline denominations and agencies supported the Freedom Movement through pronouncements and actions at the official level, that support often failed to make much difference at the grassroots, congregational level. The Episcopal Church offers a case in point. As Robert Jones reports,

> Like other mainline denominations, the Episcopal Church issued strong statements supporting the *Brown* decision in 1954, championing the court's judgment and calling for "interracial fellowship" within the denomination. But it did little else to support the risky task of dismantling segregation on the local level; it even issued an official statement in 1958 saying that any moves toward integration should be slow. Most tellingly, in 1961 the denomination let stand a decision by an all-white Episcopal private school to deny admission to Martin Luther King Jr.'s son because of his race.[38]

By the time the mainline began to deal in a serious way with its legacy of white supremacy, it was too late. An entire generation of younger people had been captivated by the message of the Freedom Movement and abandoned the white, mainline Protestant tradition in droves.

Much the same can be said of the white evangelical tradition. "No segment of White Christian America," writes Jones, "has been more complicit in the nation's fraught racial history than white evangelical Protestants. And no group of white evangelical Protestants bears more responsibility than Southern Baptists, who comprise the overwhelming majority of white evangelicals, particularly in the states of the former Confederacy."[39]

Only four years after the *Brown* decision that mandated racial integration in America's public schools, Jerry Falwell, founder of the Moral Majority, preached a sermon titled, "Segregation or Integration: Which?" He argued in that sermon that "if Chief Justice [Earl] Warren and his associates had known God's word and had desired to do the Lord's will, I am quite confident that the 1954 decision would never have been made. . . . The facilities should be separate. When God has drawn a line of distinction, we should not attempt to cross that line." During the late 1950s and 1960s, white evangelical churches, especially in the South, responded to the *Brown* decision by establishing segregationist "Christian" academies so their children would not have to attend school with blacks. In 1967, Falwell opened his own segregationist school—the Lynchburg Christian Academy, described by the *Lynchburg News* as "a private school for white students."[40]

The resistance of evangelical and fundamentalist Christians to racial equality was part and parcel of their resistance to human equality on many fronts, especially equality for LGBTQ people, and it was that resistance that finally undermined their bid for conservative Christian dominance in the United States. The nation, after all, was moving in the opposite direction—in the direction of the American Creed ("all men are created equal")—and when the Supreme Court legalized same-sex marriage in its *Obergefell v. Hodges* decision of 2015, evangelical leaders like Rod Dreher, author of *The Benedict Option*, understood that their bid to impose on the nation the values of the Christian Right had been lost.[41]

At the same time, a significant core of evangelical leaders, epitomized by Jerry Falwell Jr., persisted in their bid for political power and control, even when it was clear to most observers that the battle for Christian America had been lost. Nothing better symbolized the irony of that effort than their unfailing support for Donald J. Trump in spite of his rejection, apparent in both word and action, of anything remotely resembling the historic values of the Christian faith.

America's Times of Trial

The rise and fall of the white Protestant mainline, on the one hand, and white evangelicalism, on the other, connect with a recurring pattern in American history, a pattern Robert Bellah described in his 1975 book *The Broken Covenant* as America's "three times of trial." "Once in each of the last three centuries," Bellah wrote, "America has faced a time of trial, a time of testing so severe that not only the form but even the existence of our nation have been called into question."[42]

One can scarcely understand those times of trial apart from the collapse of the religious and moral values that always sustain any given society. "It is one of the oldest of sociological generalizations," Bellah explains, "that any coherent and viable society rests on a common set of moral understandings about good and bad, right and wrong, in the realm of individual and social action. It is almost as widely held that these common moral understandings must also in turn rest upon a common set of religious understandings that provide a picture of the universe in terms of which the moral understandings make sense."[43] When those common understandings collapse—when the moral glue that has held a nation together disintegrates—that nation faces possible disintegration as well.

That sort of collapse is precisely what Americans witnessed in the late twentieth and early twenty-first centuries as the white Protestant structures that had always sustained the nation's traditional, mainstream values fell into disarray. Accordingly, the American nation, as I write this text, stands in the midst of a fourth time of trial, fully as severe as the earlier ones. Before inquiring further into that fourth time of trial, it is important to grasp the contours of the previous three.

The First Three Times of Trial

Bellah identified those times of trial as the founding, the Civil War, and the 1960s. Each was a time of trial since during each of those periods, there was precious little agreement about the meaning of the American experiment. And central to the debate over the meaning of the nation during all three times of trial was the question of black/white relations.

Among the most contentious of issues during the American founding— and one of the issues standing at the heart of the meaning of the American experiment from its beginning—was the question of slavery. The Constitution recognized slavery by defining blacks as "three-fifths of all other persons" (Article I, Section 2), a provision aimed at restricting Congressional representation from states that had large numbers of enslaved people; by permitting the slave trade through 1808 and taxation on that trade (Article I, Section 9); and by requiring that enslaved people who had escaped be returned to their original owners (Article IV, Section 2). Those provisions, in turn, virtually guaranteed the "times of trial" that would undermine the meaning of the nation and threaten to tear it apart in years to come.

The single issue that, more than anything else, drove the Civil War was the question, would black people continue to be enslaved or would they be freed? Americans debated that question in light of the American Creed, but Americans also debated that question in light of the Great American Myths. The Civil War came on the heels of the Second Great Awakening that Christianized the nation and moved the Myth of Christian America front and center, along with its implications for human slavery. The question that demanded an answer was this—could the United States remain a Christian nation and continue to enslave millions of human beings?

Two great issues drove America's third time of trial which played itself out from 1954 until roughly 1972, a period often labeled as "the sixties"—the Vietnam War and the question of racial equality which challenged head-on the nation's long-standing commitment to white supremacy.

By the 1960s, the Myth of Christian America, though weakened, still had considerable viability, and most leaders of the Freedom Movement understood that fact. Accordingly, Martin Luther King Jr., while appealing to the American Creed, also appealed time and again both to the biblical text and to the nation's Christian conscience.[44]

The white Protestant mainline responded to those appeals with support at the official level but with lackluster support, at best, from its pews, as noted above. On the other hand, white conservative Christians typically greeted King's appeals to the Christian conscience of the nation with deafening silence, refusing even to engage the conversation. In my own Christian tradition, one could read its white "gospel papers" from 1955—the year Emmett Till was murdered and the Montgomery Bus Boycott was launched—through 1968—the year King was murdered—and never know that a Civil Rights Movement even existed.[45] A comparable silence also dominated larger conservative traditions. Robert Jones reports that "the Southern Baptist Convention—known for passing resolutions on even minor matters of concern—largely ignored the early civil rights movement," and that Martin Luther King Jr. "was barely mentioned" in the pages of the leading evangelical publication, *Christianity Today*. No wonder that King compared these people—and others like them—to Rip Van Winkle who slept through a revolution.[46]

In a 1964 sermon, "Ministers and Marchers," Jerry Falwell articulated the rationale for the silence. Falwell declared, "Preachers are not called to be politicians, but soul winners," effectively denying the social implications of the Christian gospel and restricting the pertinence of the gospel to the "sweet by and by." Large swaths of conservative Christian churches, therefore, sought to defend the Myth of Christian America by ignoring the challenges that black Christians had raised against that myth in such powerful ways. By ignoring those challenges, they also ignored what was emerging as America's "third time of trial."

America's Fourth Time of Trial

America's fourth time of trial had everything to do with race and unfolded in three distinct movements. That time of trial emerged for many whites when the United States elected its first black president, Barack Obama, in 2008. That landmark election placed in question the long-standing assumption that whites were superior to people of color and therefore must occupy the highest ranks of power. Toni Morrison observed in November of 2016,

> White people's conviction of their natural superiority is being lost. Rapidly lost. There are "people of color" everywhere, threatening to erase this long-understood definition of America. And what then? Another black President? A predominantly black Senate? Three black Supreme Court Justices? The threat is frightening.[47]

The response of some whites to this sea-change in racial status and power triggered, in turn, the second wave of the fourth time of trial, a wave that swept over America's black community with mind-numbing power. Ta-Nehisi Coates described that wave in a letter he wrote to his son:

> I write to you in your fifteenth year. I am writing you because this was the year you saw Eric Garner choked to death for selling cigarettes; because you know now that Renisha McBride was shot for seeking help, that John Crawford was shot down for browsing in a department store. And you have seen men in uniform drive by and murder Tamir Rice, a twelve-year-old child whom they were oath-bound to protect. And you have seen men in the same uniforms pummel Marlene Pinnock, someone's grandmother, on the side of a road. And you know now, if you did not before, that the police departments of your country have been endowed with the authority to destroy your body. It does not matter if the destruction is the result of an unfortunate overreaction. It does not matter if it originates in a misunderstanding. It does not matter if the destruction springs

from a foolish policy. Sell cigarettes without the proper authority and your body can be destroyed. Resent the people trying to entrap your body and it can be destroyed. Turn into a dark stairwell and your body can be destroyed. The destroyers will rarely be held accountable. Mostly they will receive pensions.[48]

The killing of Michael Brown in Ferguson, Missouri, on August 9, 2014, and then the announcement on November 24 that a grand jury had determined not to charge the officer who killed him, became a powerful symbol for blacks that, in America, their lives seemed not to matter—a trigger that, in many ways, launched them into the fourth time of trial.

Early in the week of that murder, Coates appeared on a news show, trying to explain why blacks in the United States felt such despair. "At the end of the segment," he recalled, "the host flashed a widely shared picture of an eleven-year-old black boy tearfully hugging a white police officer. Then she asked me about 'hope.' And I knew then that I had failed." Then, in his letter to his son, he said this:

> That was the week you learned that the killers of Michael Brown would go free. The men who had left his body in the street like some awesome declaration of their inviolable power would never be punished. It was not my expectation that anyone would ever be punished. But you were young and still believed. You stayed up till 11 p.m. that night, waiting for the announcement of an indictment, and when instead it was announced that there was none you said, "I've got to go," and you went into your room, and I heard you crying. . . . What I told you is . . . that this is your country, that this is your world, that this is your body, and you must find some way to live within the all of it. I tell you now that the question of how one should live within a black body, within a country lost in the Dream, is the question of my life, and the pursuit of this question, I have found, ultimately answers itself.[49]

If many whites experienced America's fourth time of trial with the election of Barack Obama, and if blacks experienced that time of trial in the racial brutality that followed, many other whites, along with the vast majority of blacks, experienced that time of trial with the election of Donald Trump to the American presidency. Throughout the course of the presidential campaign of 2015 and 2016, many white Americans—along with most people of color—had the sense that an intensified time of trial was near at hand. Late in the evening of November 20, 2016, when Americans finally knew the election results, the fourth time of trial struck the nation like a thunderbolt, destroyed much of the ideological mortar that had held the nation together, and left Americans—both black and white—with no consensus on the meaning of the American nation. In the months that followed, as the president sought to ban Muslims from entering the United States and routinely assaulted fundamental American institutions, including the courts, the Federal Bureau of Investigation, and a free American press, many Americans agreed with *New York Times* editorial writer Charles Blow that "the America that I know and love is hanging by a thread."[50] With that backdrop, the national divide over race, over religion, over the president, and over American ideals and institutions widened into a national abyss.

Times of Fall and Restoration

The nation's first three times of trial typically produced efforts on the part of Christians to recover the moral and religious consensus that had been lost. But recovery was more than recovery. Instead, it was full-blown restoration. Always more than an effort to correct a ship that had sailed off course, the restoration was an effort to leapfrog over a period of history now viewed as fallen and corrupt, and then to resurrect—and fully identify with—a golden age that stood at the beginning of the only time that mattered for those involved.

While the notion of a golden age might point to Eden before the fall as with America's Founders, for many Christians the golden age was the time of Jesus and the Apostles and the beginnings of the Christian religion. For many white American Christians in the twenty-first century, the golden age was the period between the end of World War II and the dawn of the Civil Rights Movement, a time when white Christians dominated American public life. However the golden age might be defined, it makes no sense apart from a disastrous decline and fall. As old as the Puritans who sought to sanctify their "errand into the wilderness" by restoring the primitive church, this way of dealing with loss and decline has been central to the American self-understanding.

Perhaps the best way to grasp the meaning of the restoration vision is to view it in microcosmic form. Two Christian traditions that were born on American soil in the early nineteenth century essentially replicated the restorationist project that was the larger American nation but gave it a different focus. If the nation sought to restore "self-evident truths" embedded in nature from the dawn of time, these new Christian traditions, like the Puritans before them, sought to restore ancient Christian truths that they believed had been lost and obscured over the course of Christian history.

These new Christian traditions were the Latter-day Saints (Mormons) and the Disciples/Churches of Christ. The popularity of these traditions on the American frontier suggests how deeply embedded into the American psyche the restoration vision had become.

Both Mormons and Disciples/Churches of Christ self-consciously defined themselves as "restoration movements." By using that term, they meant to suggest that the church had fallen from its original purity, requiring the faithful to leapfrog over 1,800 years of Christian history in order to restore the purity that characterized the earliest Christians. That commitment implicitly suggested that no one in Christian history, from the close of the founding age to the dawn of the nineteenth century, had maintained the purity of the faith. To one degree or another, then, the entire history of the Christian church was a history of apostasy and corruption.

While Mormons and Disciples/Churches of Christ shared a common commitment to the goal of restoration, they differed significantly in what they hoped to restore.[51] Mormons viewed the ancient faith through the lens of wonder, imagination, and new revelation. They therefore sought to recover a golden age when God communicated directly with humankind, just as he had with Adam, Moses, and Jesus. For 1,800 years, they argued, most Christians had made a terrible mistake when they claimed that, following the days of Jesus and the Apostles, God had spoken to humankind only through a book—the Bible. Accordingly, Mormons contended that God had spoken directly to their prophet, Joseph Smith, who now had the mandate and the blueprint for restoring the ancient church in these latter days.

When we turn to the Disciples/Churches of Christ, the story differs in details but not in the substance of their commitment to the restoration vision. Alexander Campbell led a significant wing of this religious movement from his home in Bethany, Virginia (later West Virginia) for some forty years, beginning in roughly 1820. By 1860 this movement had become the fourth-largest Christian denomination in the country, trailing only Baptists, Methodists, and Presbyterians. After a variety of divisions and subdivisions, the church is represented today by three major American denominations: the Disciples of Christ, the Churches of Christ, and the Independent Christian Churches.

Like the Mormons, the Disciples/Churches of Christ committed themselves completely to the task of restoration but defined that task in very different terms. If Mormons sought to recover divine revelation, contending that God could speak to humankind in the nineteenth century just as he had to prophets and apostles in ancient times, the Disciples/Churches of Christ rejected that claim out of hand. God spoke in their time, they claimed, only through the biblical text. Any effort to restore the ancient church, therefore, must focus on the Bible and especially on the New Testament. Further, Disciples/Churches of Christ read the biblical text through the rational lens of the eighteenth-century Enlightenment. A complete restoration of the primitive church, they argued, would be inconceivable apart from a rational reading of the Bible.

The fact that Mormons and Disciples/Churches of Christ fought over the nature of the primitive church should not obscure, however, the singular commitment they shared in common: the restoration of the golden age of the Christian religion. The dream of restoring a golden age of the past, regardless of how that age might be defined, was central to the American imagination in the early nineteenth century and has remained as a quintessential American strategy, especially in times of trial and disestablishment.

We turn now to explore the process of disestablishment and/or decline, on the one hand, and restoration, on the other, during each of the times of trial identified by Bellah: the Founding, the Civil War, and the 1960s.

The Founding

As the Founders grappled with the question of slavery—a profoundly moral and ethical issue that stood at the heart of the nation's "first time of trial"—they also grappled with the role of the churches, institutions that were central to any debate over moral and ethical issues. The churches that dominated colonial America—Puritans in New England, Presbyterian and Reformed in the Middle Colonies, and Anglicans in the South—were all committed to a Christian establishment. The First Amendment to the Constitution, however, rejected those establishments with these words: "Congress shall make no law respecting an establishment of religion or prohibiting the free exercise thereof." Individual states followed the federal model with their own laws striking down religious establishments, the last to do so being Massachusetts in 1833.

Disestablishment, however, left the nation with a pressing question. Historically, the role of established churches had been, with notable exceptions, to work hand-in-glove with the state, validating the moral legitimacy of state-sponsored decisions and initiatives. In the absence of the established churches, what would guarantee the moral and ethical legitimacy of the new American nation?

The answer to that question can be found in the American propensity for restoration. The intention and net effect of the nation's appeal to "self-evident truths," grounded in "Nature and Nature's God," was to secure wide agreement on the moral legitimacy—and therefore the moral meaning—of the nation, in spite of the obvious moral flaws that attended the founding and the compromises the Founders made to address those flaws. First among those flaws was the institution of slavery. In effect, then, the appeal to "Nature and

Nature's God" constituted the very first appeal in American history to the myth of American innocence, a myth that, during the founding generation, threw a shroud of moral legitimacy over the practice of human bondage.

In the face of constitutional disestablishment, many denominations joined hands to launch a counter-restoration. They designed that movement to restore something they thought vital to the health of the nation, something that had been a defining feature of all the colonies and, for fifteen centuries, a defining feature of all the nations of Europe from whence the colonists had come: a distinctly Christian identity. That counter-restoration emerged as the Second Great Awakening.

With respect to slavery and the doctrine of white supremacy that sustained it, that restoration was a two-edged sword. Over the short term, it contributed mightily to the end of slavery, as noted earlier in this chapter. But it did not eradicate the doctrine of white supremacy, which, by any measure, continued to stand at the heart of American culture. Over the years to come, that doctrine would absorb the Christian identity of the American nation that the Second Great Awakening had worked so hard to create and transform it into a distinctly racial image.

From the Civil War to World War I

Bellah labeled the Civil War America's "second time of trial," precisely because the question of human bondage called into radical question the meaning of the American nation and ripped the nation apart. That second time of trial accelerated a second disestablishment[52] that had actually begun some years before. As Steven K. Green describes the process, "Throughout the first half of the nineteenth century, the idea that Christianity was part of the common law impeded the secularization of the law and the movement toward greater disestablishment. . . . By midcentury, the maxim that Christianity was part of the common law had lost favor, and laws regulating blasphemy, oaths, and Sunday conduct had either been abandoned or transformed to reflect secular rationales."[53]

This "second disestablishment" persisted and deepened for the rest of the nineteenth century as the process of secularization and modernization increasingly marginalized the role of traditional Christian faith in American life. The war, itself, with its unthinkable levels of violence, death, and mechanized, wholesale destruction, severely undermined the spiritual fabric of the nation. Then, following the war, other factors contributed to that marginalization.

First, the Civil War prompted the northern states to invest heavily in industrialization and, following the war, industrialization and commerce became engines driving unprecedented prosperity for the few. The others, including the millions of immigrants who arrived in the United States during that period, became the forgotten poor, doomed to grinding poverty in America's northern cities. Needless to say, these disparities opened the door for labor unrest and violence and urban crime.

Historians describe the period from the Civil War to 1890 as "the Gilded Age" when, as historian Green writes, "Americans witnessed a rapid commercial expansion that placed financial self-interest above concerns for community and fellow citizens."[54] Those priorities, in turn, produced a deep "spiritual crisis"[55] that accelerated disestablishment. For their part, white Protestant churches in northern cities made themselves essentially irrelevant both to the needs of the poor and to the spiritual crisis. Instead of responding with compassion, they responded with the Gospel of Wealth—praise for the rich and damnation for the poor, themes discussed at length in chapter 6.

In addition to the spiritual crisis of the Gilded Age, other factors hastened what Green calls this "second disestablishment." First, Charles Darwin's theory of evolution suggested to the popular imagination that human beings were not created in the image of God but in the image of a monkey, the result not of creation but of natural selection. To the extent that this view of Darwin prevailed in popular culture, it contributed even further to the marginalization of America's churches.

Second, critical theories regarding the origins of the biblical text suggested that the Bible was not always the result of divine inspiration. Instead, biblical critics seemed to suggest that the Bible was simply a human creation. Implicitly drawing on evolutionary theory, the critics argued that the biblical text had evolved over a period of hundreds of years as a variety of editors had rearranged and adapted portions of that text to make its message relevant to the needs of particular epochs.

To the traditional Christian mind, Darwinian evolution and biblical criticism were damaging enough, since they cast serious doubt on the divine origin both of human beings and of the biblical text. But those two suggestions were minor indeed when compared with the third manifestation of secularity. Modern psychology in the early twentieth century—especially under the tutelage of Sigmund Freud—argued that the very idea of God was a myth, a figment of our collective human imagination. Our primitive ancestors, Freud claimed, had created "God" as a way to protect themselves from forces over which they had no control.[56]

How would it be possible to build a Christian civilization when power-ful forces had launched a devastating assault on what many viewed as basic building blocks of a Christian culture? How would it be possible to build a Christian civilization when more and more Americans seemed to doubt that humankind was a creation of God, that scripture was inspired of God, and that the notion of God had any basis in reality?

These developments were all the more disconcerting since efforts to build a Christian America had seemed so successful in the nineteenth century. To many Christians, the future looked incredibly bright as the twentieth century dawned. A thoroughly Christianized America seemed well within their reach.

But now, this.

Little wonder, then, that a large segment of American Christians embarked on the time-honored strategy of restoration. They determined to fight the forces of the modern world, resist the encroachments of secularity, and re-store a Christian America against all odds. They typically identified Darwin's theory of evolution as the chief culprit, and they hammered that doctrine unmercifully. In case they lost this battle, however, they elaborated a theory of the end times according to which Jesus would return, expunge the secular-ists from the face of the earth, and reign with his saints for a thousand years. In this way, those Christians who resisted the march of the modern world were guaranteed final victory, regardless of the outcome of any particular skirmish. We know these Christians today as fundamentalists.

From 1925 through the 1970s, however, fundamentalism fell silent on po-litical issues and, in effect, went underground. This transition occurred after the fundamentalist movement at large suffered national embarrassment in the Scopes "Monkey Trial" in Dayton, Tennessee, in the summer of 1925. In that infamous trial, the noted lawyer Clarence Darrow defended John Scopes, a schoolteacher accused of violating the Tennessee statute that forbade the teaching of evolution in the public schools. William Jennings Bryan, a noted statesman and the acknowledged champion of the fundamentalist cause, prosecuted Scopes on behalf of the state of Tennessee.

Simply put, Darrow made Bryan look foolish and held his fundamentalist religious convictions up to ridicule. And journalists who covered the trial from around the country—especially H. L. Mencken of the *Baltimore Sun*—made it appear that fundamentalists at large were ignorant country bumpkins. After suffering such humiliation, it was little wonder that fundamentalists retreated to their churches and turned their backs on American public life for the next half-century.

For the purposes of this text, it is crucial to note that this second restoration of a Christian nation took place precisely during the time when, as James

Cone has noted, "Lynching fever gripped the South, spreading like cholera, as white communities [throughout the nation] made blacks their primary targets."[57] Yet, unlike those who led the first restoration of a Christian nation, those who led this second restoration seldom challenged the pattern of race relations that dominated the nation in those years, seldom questioned the reigning Myth of White Supremacy, and seldom challenged the practice of lynching, at least not in a public and conspicuous way.

Indeed, this attempt to restore the mythic, pre–Civil War golden age of Christian America aimed, first of all, to restore a white, nineteenth-century version of the Christian religion to its traditional role of power and prestige in the face of a rapidly encroaching secularity. At the very same time, it covered and obscured the racial crimes of the late nineteenth and early twentieth centuries, allowing its proponents to find innocence in a golden age of the past.

The 1960s

Any discussion of the period we call "the 1960s"—a period bounded by 1955, the year of the Montgomery Bus Boycott and the murder of Emmett Till, on the front end, and 1973, the year when the last troops returned from Vietnam, on the back end—must begin with a frank recognition of how revolutionary, pivotal, and defining that period was for American life and history. In the 1960s, virtually everything about traditional America—from race relations to gender roles to gender identity to the use of drugs to sexual ethics to perspectives on war and peace and to attitudes about America, itself—began to change.

That change was all the more pronounced—and for American traditionalists, all the more devastating—against the backdrop of the 1950s, which epitomized for most white Americans a golden age of peace, prosperity, moral rectitude, and religious devotion. The decade of the 1950s predated civil rights. It predated voting rights. It predated women's rights. It predated the vast immigration into the United States of both Asians and Hispanics. It predated a tolerance of—and even the embrace of—religions native to both Asia and the Middle East.[58] It predated environmental concerns. And thanks to the Vietnam War, the 1950s was the last decade when Americans could claim that their nation had never lost a war.

But there is more, for the 1950s was a time when, in the face of the Communist threat, Americans absolutized the Great American Myths, allowing those myths to reign virtually unquestioned in American life.

Most whites during those years never doubted that God had chosen the United States for a special mission in the world. After all, had not this nation saved the world from Nazi tyranny through its pivotal role in World War II? And now, in the 1950s, they understood that the nation's mission was to save the world from the Soviet Union.

Most whites during those years never doubted that the bedrock principles of the United States had been modeled on the natural order of things revealed to the nation by "Nature and Nature's God." And that is why most whites during those years never doubted that, in spite of resistance from tyrannical nations like the Soviet Union, the United States would eventually usher in a golden age of freedom and democracy for the entire world to enjoy.

Likewise, in the 1950s, most whites never doubted that the United States was a Christian nation, standing for truth and right against "godless Communism."

Armed with all those convictions, most whites in the 1950s never doubted that the United States stood innocent among the nations of the world.

In the 1950s, when the nation was engaged in a life and death struggle with Communism, there was no room for doubt or uncertainty regarding the meaning of the American nation. And that is why the decade of the 1960s was particularly devastating to many Americans, for the 1960s replaced certainty over the meaning of the American nation with radical doubt. No wonder Robert Bellah described the 1960s as America's third time of trial.

That time of trial helped trigger the third disestablishment of the nation's dominant religion—white, mainline, Protestant Christianity—a fact we observed earlier in this chapter. But disestablishment occurred in other ways as well, especially among the nation's youth, many of whom came to view the Christian religion as the handmaid of racism and segregation, a willing partner in American imperialism in Southeast Asia, an actor in environmental destruction, and a bastion of prejudice against changing ethical norms. For these reasons and more, many young people abandoned the Christian faith, or at least the version of the faith with which they had been raised, and turned to no faith at all or to a variety of eastern religions that, up to that point, had been foreign to most Americans.

While many conservative Christians worried over all these developments, they also worried over what they perceived as a widespread attempt to evict God from the public square and a consequent breakdown in public morality. They agonized over the Supreme Court ruling of 1962 in *Engel v. Vitale*, striking down prayer in America's public schools, and the *Roe v. Wade* decision of 1973 in which the Court legalized abortion on demand.

These conservative Christians—chiefly evangelicals and fundamentalists—responded in the time-honored, American way of coping with moral and religious decline. They sought to restore the moral and religious glories of what they regarded as a golden age of the past—in this case, the 1950s—and to make the Myth of Christian America a reality once again. Stephen Mansfield put it starkly: "It was time to restore what had been lost."[59]

Pat Robertson, an ordained Baptist minister and a highly influential evangelical leader based in Virginia, was among the first to build Christian institutions specifically designed to recover a Christian America. In 1961 Robertson started a single television station in Norfolk Virginia (WYAH-TV), and then built that station into the Christian Broadcasting Network. In 1966 he launched a Christian talk show, the *700 Club*. In 1977 he established Regent University. And in 1989 he created the Christian Coalition, an organization designed to encourage Christian participation in the political process. All these organizations were crucial to Robertson's goal of reestablishing the United States on a Christian foundation.

Robertson stated his vision for a Christianized America, if not for a Christianized world, in his 1991 book, *The New World Order*:

> There will never be world peace until God's house and God's people are given their rightful place of leadership at the top of the world. How can there be peace when drunkards, drug dealers, communists, atheists, New Age worshipers of Satan, secular humanists, oppressive dictators, greedy moneychangers, revolutionary assassins, adulterers, and homosexuals are on top? Under their leadership the world will never, I repeat never, experience lasting peace. Peace will only come when its source is flowing from the benign influence of Almighty God, through the people given to His service who comprise "His house." As long as the cynical politicians and equally cynical media continue to deny God's people their rightful place in God's order for the world, they are condemning their world to violence, turmoil, oppression, and war.[60]

Jerry Falwell, founder of Liberty University in 1971, emerged as another significant leader in the Christian America crusade when he issued a summons to fundamentalists throughout the country to return to political life in order to reclaim America as a Christian nation. Playing on Richard Nixon's contention that there was in the United States a "silent majority" of people who supported his policies, Falwell claimed that there existed in America a "moral majority" who would support, once again, his vision for a Christian America. In 1979, therefore, Falwell created a Christian political organization that he called, appropriately enough, the Moral Majority. The organization supported conservative candidates for political office throughout the 1980s, supported both prayer and the teaching of creationism in the public schools, and opposed the Equal Rights Amendment, gay rights, abortion rights, and the U.S.-Soviet SALT treaties. In 1989, the Moral Majority was dissolved.

That attempt to restore the golden age of the 1950s was more than an appeal to turn the clock back on religious and cultural diversity; on civil rights; on voting rights; on women's rights; and on gay and lesbian rights. It was also an attempt to absolutize the Great American Myths in the face of radical change in American life. What belied those myths in the 1950s, however, was the nation's persistent addiction to the Myth of White Supremacy. Indeed, the 1950s was for America's blacks a time of Jim Crow segregation, intense harassment, and even persecution. It was a time when whites could brutally murder Emmett Till and be acquitted by an all-white jury who was told by the defense attorney, "I know that every last Anglo-Saxon one of you has the courage to set these men free."[61] It was a time when school districts throughout the nation resisted to the teeth an order from the Supreme Court of the United States to integrate their schools. It was a time when many white churches looked upon Martin Luther King Jr. and the Freedom Movement with deep suspicion, rightly suspecting that it might upset their way of life. And it was a time when white churches throughout the South established "Christian" segregationist academies so that white children would not have to attend school with black children. Any appeal, therefore, to recover a "golden age" of the 1950s was, at heart, a racist appeal, rooted—perhaps unconsciously on the part of some and without discernment on the part of virtually all—in the Myth of White Supremacy.

This was not, however, a one-time shot at restoration that might be abandoned if it failed. This restoration, instead, grew into a decades-long attempt to reverse what liberals viewed as the social gains of the 1960s and to reinstate a more conservative, more traditional—and needless to say, more "Christian"—way of life that had found its clearest expression, its advocates believed, in the America of the late 1940s and early 1950s.

For fifty years and more, following the civil rights revolution of the 1960s, legions of conservative, privileged whites—including many white Christians—engaged in a concerted effort to turn the clock back on the achievements that defined that period—to undermine voting rights, for example; to resegregate America's public schools[62] or, failing that, to abandon public schools altogether; to make those schools the domain of poor people of color while whites with the means to do so could send their children to private academies; and through the provisions of America's "War on Drugs," to decimate black lives and families, to place black people behind bars in staggering numbers, and essentially to subject black life to the same sorts of constraints that prevailed before the 1960s.

These developments bear heavily on the question of American innocence, for those Americans who have sought to reverse the racial reforms won since the 1960s have said, in effect, that there was no guilt in the racial patterns that defined the United States prior to the Civil Rights Movement. That is why the election of Barack Obama was such an affront to so many whites, for his election took the nation further and further away from what so many perceived as the "golden age" of the 1950s. Indeed, as the nation's first black president, Obama became a symbol for the cultural changes, rooted in the 1960s, that so many found so problematic—racial equality, to be sure, but also gender equality and LGBTQ equality. The backlash to Obama's presidency, therefore, was part and parcel of the long-standing backlash to the cultural revolution of the 1960s.

Donald J. Trump, the Fall, and the Restoration

Those who drove this restoration agenda finally achieved their objectives with the election in 2016 of Donald J. Trump as president of the United States. In fact, had there been no President Obama, there would never have been a President Trump. Ta-Nehisi Coates put it starkly: "Trump truly is something new—the first president whose entire political existence hinges on the fact of a black president."[63]

What is crucial here is that Trump, himself, capitalized on the decades-long attempt of evangelicals and other conservatives to restore the golden age of the 1950s when he placed a restorationist agenda at the center of his presidential campaign. He not only would "make America great again," but he would "take the country back."[64] Most black Americans understood those commitments to mean that he would "make America great again" by taking the country back for white dominance and control. David Duke, former Grand Wizard of the Ku Klux Klan, validated that interpretation when, at a white nationalist "Unite the Right" rally in Charlottesville, Virginia, on August 12, 2017, he proclaimed, "We're going to fulfill the promises of Donald Trump. That's what we believed in. That's why we voted for Donald Trump, because he said he's going to take our country back—and that's what we've got to do."[65]

Trump deepened his commitment to restore the golden age of the 1950s when he promised to "protect Christianity" which, he claimed, was "under siege."[66] The Christianity he vowed to protect, however, was hardly mainline or liberal Christianity, but American Evangelicalism. To be sure, evangelical Christians found themselves badly out of step with moral and ethical trends that transformed the nation in the wake of the 1960s, including racial, gender, and religious equality. They therefore portrayed themselves as "persecuted" and "under siege" and longed to recover "the good old days" of the 1950s when their version of Christian morality was dominant.[67] In that context, Donald

Trump became their savior. It made no difference to them that his speech and lifestyle routinely flew in the face of traditional Christian values since, as some evangelical leaders noted, the Bible recorded that God had often used corrupt and evil rulers to achieve his ends. One evangelical magazine, for example, compared Trump to the ancient Persian King Cyrus who freed the Jews from Babylonian captivity and restored them to their homeland in Jerusalem.[68] As Robert Jones explained, "Trump's promise to restore a mythical past golden age—where factory jobs paid the bills and white Protestant churches were the dominant cultural hubs—powerfully tapped evangelical anxieties about an uncertain future."[69]

Indeed, 81 percent of white, evangelical Christians who voted for president in 2016 voted for Donald Trump[70]—a fact that stunned many Americans since Trump's personal values struck many as completely at odds with the historic values of the Christian faith. Historian Randall Balmer wondered, "How can a movement ostensibly concerned about 'family values' support a twice-divorced, thrice-married man who said that his 'personal Vietnam' was avoiding sexually transmitted diseases? How could evangelicals vote for someone who flaunted his infidelities and who boasted about his tawdry behavior toward women?"

The answer, Balmer concluded, could be found precisely in the Myth of White Supremacy that, since the early twentieth century, had driven large swaths of the American evangelical movement, both its leadership and its rank and file.[71] In fact, according to Balmer, their allegiance to the Myth of White Supremacy played a defining role in the rise of the Moral Majority in 1979, which summoned white evangelical Christians out of their religious isolation and onto the battlefield of American politics.[72]

When Donald Trump ran for president of the United States, he placed that myth at the center of his campaign. He complained that Mexican immigrants were rapists, that Muslims were often terrorists, and that a federal judge of Mexican descent was incapable of impartiality. He promised to ban all Muslim immigration into the United States, to build along the southern border of the United States a massive wall that would keep illegal immigrants out of this country, and to deport millions of Latino immigrants who had come to the United States illegally, regardless of their contributions to the American economy and culture. Those proposals clearly appealed to the racist underbelly of the United States.[73]

Once in office, Trump went even further and appointed to his cabinet people whose priorities seemed designed to restrict, not expand, equality and opportunity for America's blacks, and indeed, for the poor and all people of color. He appointed as attorney general of the United States, for example,

Senator Jefferson Beauregard Sessions (R-Ala.), a man whom Congress had refused to confirm for a federal judgeship some thirty years earlier precisely because of his record on civil rights.

After Sessions was nominated for that position in 1986, Coretta Scott King, widow of Martin Luther King Jr., submitted a letter of opposition to the Senate Judiciary Committee. Regarding his previous service as U.S. attorney for the Southern District of Alabama, a position he held from 1981 to 1983, Ms. King wrote that "Mr. Sessions has used the awesome power of his office to chill the free exercise of the vote by black citizens in the district he now seeks to serve as a federal judge."[74] In the confirmation hearing for Sessions to become Attorney General of the United States in 2017, another senator—Senator Cory Booker (D-N.J.)—argued that "Sessions has not demonstrated a commitment to a central requisite of the job—to aggressively pursue the congressional mandate of civil rights and justice for all of our citizens. In fact, at numerous times in his career, he has demonstrated a hostility toward these convictions."[75] When the Supreme Court, for example, gutted the Voting Rights Act of 1965, Sessions applauded, calling that decision "good news for the South."[76]

In many respects, the fact that Sessions occupied the office of attorney general of the United States during the second decade of the twenty-first century serves as a powerful symbol of Trump's determination to eclipse the civil rights gains of the 1960s and restore the nation to the "golden age" of the 1950s. The extent to which Sessions symbolized that restoration impulse becomes all the more apparent when one compares his record on civil rights with that of Robert F. Kennedy, attorney general of the United States during the early 1960s. Kennedy used the power of his office to secure safe passage for Freedom Riders who challenged the southern tradition of segregated interstate buses; to enforce a court order allowing James Meredith to become the first African American to enroll in the University of Mississippi; and to work with two presidents—John F. Kennedy and Lyndon B. Johnson—to create the Civil Rights Act of 1964, the act whose gutting Attorney General Sessions cheered.

Trump also appointed as Secretary of Education Betsy DeVos, a woman who, in her home state of Michigan, actively supported charter schools and voucher programs at the expense of public schools, when public schools were typically the only option for the vast majority of black children in the United States.[77]

Those appointments, however, seemed not to phase America's evangelical Christians whose support for Trump, when news of these appointments became public, continued unabated.

Seven months into his presidency, when neo-Nazis and avowed white supremacists marched in Charlottesville, Virginia, bearing torches and chanting, "Jews will not replace us," the president placed white supremacists and those who protested white supremacy on the same moral plane.[78] But even that equation failed to dislodge evangelical support for Trump. When most evangelical leaders refused to question the president's moral equivocation, historian Balmer wrote, "In the 19th and early 20th centuries, evangelicals took the part of those on the margins of society—women, the poor, workers, people of color. The 2016 election, coupled with the religious right's anemic response to racism and white supremacy, suggests that this once proud and noble tradition is morally bankrupt."[79]

The charge of moral bankruptcy is, of course, a generalization to which there are significant exceptions. Russell Moore, president of the Ethics and Religious Liberty Commission of the Southern Baptist Convention, spoke out strongly against both white supremacy and then-candidate Trump's proposed Muslim ban,[80] though he faced a serious backlash from his own denomination.[81] *Sojourners* magazine has routinely resisted white supremacy, and its editor, Jim Wallis, called the nation to account in his book, *America's Original Sin: Racism, White Privilege, and the Bridge to a New America*.[82] *Christianity Today*, the flagship evangelical magazine, has resisted racism as well.[83] So have scores of evangelical colleges and universities,[84] the Council for Christian Colleges and Universities, the National Association of Evangelicals, numerous evangelical relief agencies, and many local evangelical churches.

Still and all, the 81 percent of America's white evangelical Christians who voted for Donald J. Trump for president represents a stunning majority of American evangelicals who, at the very least, saw no conflict between the faith they professed and Trump's attacks on minorities of every kind. If they did discern a conflict, it apparently made no difference. So when a historian of the stature of Randall Balmer—a Dartmouth professor who has spent an entire career exploring the history and character of American evangelicalism[85]—calls that tradition "morally bankrupt," we are forced to pay attention. In particular, we must ask what the moral decline of the evangelical tradition means for the life and health of the American nation, on the one hand, and the life and health of the Myth of Christian America, on the other.

With respect to the nation itself, it must be said that when a religious tradition that served as the nation's conscience in the nineteenth century and, in many respects, even in the twentieth century, finally experiences a moral decline that results in significant levels of moral bankruptcy, the nation suffers in grievous ways. George Washington voiced that principle when he said in his "Farewell Address" of 1796, "Of all the dispositions and habits which lead to political prosperity, religion and morality are indispensable supports."[86]

As if to illustrate the shadow side of Washington's counsel, America's evangelical tradition was already in steep decline by the 1960s, a fact that contributed in important ways to America's third time of trial. By the second decade of the twenty-first century, the moral breakdown of the evangelical tradition contributed to the nation's fourth time of trial in even more powerful ways and left the evangelical tradition essentially helpless to effect a national change of course.

The ethical failures of the evangelical tradition also held vast implications for the viability of the Myth of Christian America. On the one hand, a shrinking minority of Americans were willing to identify the United States as a Christian nation. At the same time, the Myth of Christian America was far from dead. If anything, it grew in strength as the reality of Christian America declined.

One way to understand the accelerated vitality of the myth of Christian America is to place it within the context of the work of Mircea Eliade who wrote perceptively of "the myth of the eternal return."[87] Traditional people, Eliade wrote, sought to make profane (ordinary) time both bearable and meaningful by living symbolically and mythically in a sacred time, the time of the founding of their world. Likewise, many traditional Americans, finding the secular world of rapid change virtually unbearable, have sought to escape that secular world with appeals to a golden age when Christian America was alive and well and have lived in the hope of its restoration. In the United States, the restoration vision has been reenacted with such regularity that it has become an American version of "the myth of the eternal return."

In *The Courage to Be*, Paul Tillich described "the mass neuroses which usually appear at the end of an era" and which "make the average man a fanatical defender of the established order."[88] That is precisely what Americans witnessed in the early years of the twenty-first century, and especially in the age of Trump, as large numbers of Americans professed their allegiance to the Myth of Christian America even as the reality of Christian America was collapsing around them.

What Might We Make of the Disconnect between Christian Belief and Practice?

The disconnect between what evangelicals claimed to believe and their behavior in the public square was not lost on black Christians. Yolanda Pierce, a professor of African American religion at Princeton Theological Seminary, offered a case in point. Pierce taught and lectured for years in evangelical churches and schools, many of them white or predominantly white, in her "quest to be a bridge-builder within the body of Christ." And then came the news that 81 percent of America's white evangelicals voted for Trump—a fact that she found almost impossible to process. Just days after the election she wrote,

> Last week I watched as 81 percent of white evangelicals and born-again Christians voted for someone who, on tape, mocked a journalist with disabilities . . . [and] admitted to sexually assaulting women. . . . I watched as 81 percent of white evangelicals and born-again Christians dismissed his affairs, adultery, multiple marriages, participation in porn subculture, refusals to release his tax returns, failure to donate to charities to which he promised money, . . . participation in racist lies about President Obama, of African Americans, Mexican Americans and Muslims—and still voted for him.

Pierce concluded that "something has been broken for me," namely, "a fragile hope that the work of racial and gender justice will be embraced by the larger church."[89]

How can one explain such a radical disconnect between the stated values of a religious culture and the behavior that culture either promotes or tolerates in the public square? Frederick Douglass made no attempt to answer that question, but only made it more acute when he made this astounding claim in 1845:

> I assert most unhesitatingly, that the religion of the south is a mere covering for the most horrid crimes. . . . Were I to be again reduced to the chains of slavery, next to that enslavement, I should regard being the slave of a religious master the greatest calamity that could befall me. For of all the slaveholders with whom I have ever met, religious slaveholders are the worst. I have ever found them the meanest and basest, the most cruel and cowardly, of all others.[90]

James Cone, with his observation that Christians lynched blacks and never discerned the connection between the innocent blacks they lynched and the innocent Christ they worshipped, raised to almost unbearable levels the question that begs for an answer, "How can we understand such a radical disconnect between religion and life, between biblical ethics and lived behavior?"

From all these assessments and more, it seems obvious that the slippage between Christian belief and practice in the United States owes much to the Myth of White Supremacy and the role it played in shaping Christianity in the United States.

In one sense, however, even that answer begs the question, for why have Christians been so susceptible to the power of white supremacy in American life? With respect to evangelicals, at least, I wish to offer several suggestions.

As noted earlier in this chapter, evangelical Christians paid serious attention to social issues prior to the Civil War. Following the War, however, they increasingly turned their backs on the broad, social implications of the Christian religion and defined their commitments in highly individualistic terms. That pattern persists today. Moreover, they typically focus their convictions on the world to come with little attention to the real world where real people suffer from poverty, oppression, and wars. People who embrace a religion that is both individualistic and otherworldly can easily view as irrelevant to the Christian message the abhorrent behavior which Yolanda Pierce, James Cone, and Frederick Douglass describe with such passion.

Second, in 1979, when the Moral Majority sought to mobilize conservative Christians to seize the reins of political power in the United States, who would have guessed that, over the next thirty-five years, their commitment to political power would trump their commitment to the values of the Christian faith embedded in the biblical text? As disconcerting as that premise may be, it is one plausible answer to the question, "How can we understand such a radical disconnect between religion and life, between biblical ethics and lived behavior?"

Finally, part of the answer lies in the power of myth to transform reality into a dream, to transform a period of profound moral breakdown—a period like the 1950s, for example—into a golden age of the past. And that sort of transformation has happened in Christian America time and time again.

Conclusions

America has always been a Christian nation in certain important respects. The notion of Christian America is rooted, first, in the aspirations of the New England Puritans. Second, the Founders grounded their program in a worldview defined by the moral principles of Judaism and Christianity. And third, thanks largely to the work of the Second Great Awakening, the notion of America as a predominantly Christian nation did become a reality in the nineteenth century. But over the course of American history, at least on the part of whites, the meaning of "Christian" was always shaped—to greater or lesser degrees—by the Myth of White Supremacy.

That reality helped trigger America's four times of trial, even as it contributed to the end of white Christian America—a fact documented extensively by Robert Jones. It also helped trigger the four restorations that served as one of the Christian responses to the four times of trial. Especially striking was the fact that, by the early twenty-first century, *the Myth* of Christian America gained greater and greater strength, even as *the reality* of Christian America suffered systematic decline.

In the next chapter, I shall explore the fourth of America's myths—the Myth of the Millennial Nation—and show how all the myths I have considered converged and reinforced one another to sustain America's doctrine of manifest destiny.

Notes

1. William G. McLoughlin, *Soul Liberty: The Baptists' Struggle in New England, 1630–1833* (Hanover: Brown University Press, 1991), 249.

2. On the United States as a Christian nation, see Martin E. Marty, *Righteous Empire: The Protestant Experience in America* (New York: Dial Press, 1970); Robert T. Handy, *A Christian America: Protestant Hopes and Historical Realities*, 2d ed. (New York: Oxford University Press, 1984); John Fea, *Was America Founded as a Christian Nation? A Historical Introduction* (Philadelphia: Westminster John Knox Press, 2011); Steven K. Green, *Inventing a Christian America: The Myth of the Religious Founding* (Oxford: Oxford University Press, 2015); Kevin M. Kruse, *One Nation under God: How Corporate America Invented Christian America* (New York: Basic Books, 2015); and Richard T. Hughes, *Christian America and the Kingdom of God* (Urbana: University of Illinois Press, 2009).

3. Michael Novak, *On Two Wings: Humble Faith and Common Sense at the American Founding* (San Francisco: Encounter Books, 2002), 5–47.

4. John M. Mason, *The Voice of Warning, to Christians, on the Ensuing Election of a President of the United States* (New York, 1800), 20, cited in G. Adolf Kock, *Religion of the American Enlightenment* (New York: Thomas Y. Crowell Co., 1968; orig. pub. 1933), 271.

5. Clement Clarke Moore, *Observations upon Certain Passages in Mr. Jefferson's Notes on Virginia, Which Appear to Have a Tendency to Subvert Religion, and Establish a False Philosophy* (New York, 1804), 5, cited in Kock, *Religion of the American Enlightenment*, 271–272.

6. Timothy Dwight, "A Discourse on Some Events of the Last Century," delivered January 7, 1801, in *American Christianity: An Historical Interpretation with Representative Documents*, ed. H. Shelton Smith, Robert T. Handy, and Lefferts A. Loetscher, vol. I (New York: Scribner's, 1960), 533, 537–538.

7. "United States v. Macintosh," in Robert T. Miller and Ronald B. Flowers, eds., *Toward Benevolent Neutrality: Church, State, and the Supreme Court* (Waco: Baylor University Press, 1977), 161.

8. David Walker, *Walker's Appeal . . . to the Coloured Citizens of the World*, 2d ed. (1830; Nashville: James C. Winston, 1994), 28.

9. Ibid., 11; see also 17 and 19.

10. Ibid., 50–52.

11. Ibid., 49.

12. Frederick Douglass, "What, to the Slave, Is the Fourth of July?" 1852, in Philip S. Foner and Robert James Branham, eds., *Lift Every Voice: African American Oratory, 1787–1900* (Tuscaloosa: University of Alabama Press, 1998), 262–263.

13. Frederick Douglass, *Why Is the Negro Lynched?* (Bridgewater: John Whitby and Sons, 1895; repr. London: Forgotten Books, 2012), 3.

14. Frederick Douglass, *Narrative of the Life of Frederick Douglass, An American Slave, Written by Himself*, orig. pub. 1845 (New York: Signet Books, 1968), 121 and 123.

15. Ibid., 120.

16. Anna J. Cooper, "The Ethics of the Negro Question," address delivered at the biennial session of the Friends General Conference, Asbury Park, N.J., September 5, 1902, in Anna J. Cooper Papers, Manuscript Division, Moorland-Spingard Research Center, Howard University. Text reproduced in Marcia Y. Riggs, *Can I Get a Witness: Prophetic Religious Voices of African American Women: An Anthology* (Maryknoll, N.Y.: Orbis, 1997), 133 and 143.

17. Anne Moody, *Coming of Age in Mississippi* (New York: Dell, 1968), 283–284.

18. Martin Luther King Jr., "Letter from Birmingham City Jail," in James Melvin Washington, ed., *A Testament of Hope: The Essential Writings and Speeches of Martin Luther King, Jr.* (San Francisco: HarperSanFrancisco, 1986), 299.

19. Richard Wright, *White Man, Listen!* (New York: HarperPerennial, 1957), 55.

20. Malcolm X as told to Alex Haley, *The Autobiography of Malcolm X* (New York: Ballantine Books, 1973), 166.

21. *Autobiography of Malcolm X*, 224.

22. Ibid., 377.

23. James Baldwin, *The Fire Next Time*, in Toni Morrison, ed., *Baldwin: Collected Essays* (New York: Library Classics of the United States, 1998), 335.

24. Ibid., 307–308.

25. Ibid., 317.

26. Ibid., 314.

27. Ta-Nehisi Coates, *Between the World and Me* (New York: Spiegel and Grau, 2015), 28.

28. Numerous studies on lynching of blacks in America have appeared in recent years. See especially *Lynching in America: Confronting the Legacy of Racial Terror* (Montgomery: Equal Justice Initiative, 2017), which reports nearly 5,000 lynchings during this period (p. 4); and *Lynching in America: Targeting Black Veterans* (Montgomery: Equal Justice Initiative, 2016). James Allen, Hilton Als, Congressman John Lewis, and Leon F. Litwack, *Without Sanctuary: Lynching Photography in America* (Santa Fe, N.M.: Twin Palms Publishers, 2004) offers a particularly graphic verbal and pictorial description of lynching in America. And Angela Sims, in *Lynched: The Power of Memory in a Culture of Terror* (Waco: Baylor University Press, 2016), offers the results of her oral history project in which she interviewed over fifty older black Americans who remember the lynching time with clarity.

29. James M. Cone, *The Cross and the Lynching Tree* (Maryknoll, N.Y.: Orbis Books, 2012), xiii.

30. Ibid., 8–9.

31. Wells, "Lynch Law in All its Phases," 1893, in Shirley Wilson Logan, *With Pen*

and Voice: A Critical Anthology of Nineteenth-Century African-American Women (Carbondale: Southern Illinois University Press, 1995), 92–93.

32. Ibid., 94.

33. Cone, *The Cross and the Lynching Tree*, 30–31.

34. Robert Jones, *The End of White Christian America* (New York: Simon and Schuster, 2016), 34.

35. David A. Hollinger, "After Cloven Tongues of Fire: Ecumenical Protestantism and the Modern American Encounter with Diversity," *Journal of American History* (June, 2011): 23.

36. Jones, *The End of White Christian America*, 262, n. 27.

37. Ibid., 52–55.

38. Ibid., 178.

39. Ibid., 167.

40. Max Blumenthal, "Agent of Intolerance," *The Nation* (May 28, 2007), https://www.thenation.com/article/agent-intolerance/, accessed June 18, 2017.

41. See, for example, Rod Dreher, *The Benedict Option: A Strategy for Christians in a Post-Christian Nation* (New York: Sentinel, 2017), 2, where he called on Christian conservatives to embrace a kind of Christian monasticism, "[to] no longer live business-as-usual lives in America, . . . to develop creative, communal solutions to help us hold on to our faith and our values in a world growing ever most hostile to them." See also Russell Moore who called on conservative Christians to accept their status as strangers in a hostile culture: *Onward: Engaging the Culture without Losing the Gospel* (Nashville: B&H Books, 2015).

42. Robert Bellah, *The Broken Covenant: American Civil Religion in Time of Trial* (New York: Seabury, 1975), 1.

43. Ibid., xvi.

44. Gary Selby, *Martin Luther King and the Narrative of Freedom: The Exodus Narrative in America's Struggle for Civil Rights* (Waco: Baylor University Press, 2008), where Selby argues that the biblical story of the Exodus was the driving narrative for the Freedom Movement.

45. Richard T. Hughes, *Reviving the Ancient Faith: The Story of Churches of Christ in America* (Grand Rapids: Eerdmans, 1996; repr. Abilene: ACU Press, 2008), 295–296.

46. Martin Luther King Jr., "Remaining Awake through a Great Revolution," 1968, in James M. Washington, ed., *The Essential Writings and Speeches of Martin Luther King, Jr.* (San Francisco: HarperSanFrancisco, 1986), 268–269.

47. Toni Morrison, "Making America White Again," *The New Yorker*, November 21, 2016, http://www.newyorker.com/magazine/2016/11/21/making-america-white-again, accessed July 23, 2017.

48. Coates, *Between the World and Me*, 9.

49. Ibid., 10–12.

50. Charles Blow, "Scions and Scoundrels," *New York Times*, July 13, 2017, https://www.nytimes.com/2017/07/13/opinion/donald-trump-jr-emails.html?ref=opinion, accessed July 16, 2017.

51. For an impressive comparison of the restorationist agendas of Alexander Campbell and Joseph Smith, see RoseAnn Benson, *Alexander Campbell and Joseph Smith: Nineteenth-Century Restorationists* (Provo: Brigham Young University in cooperation with Abilene Christian University Press, 2017). See also Richard T. Hughes, "Tanner Lecture: Two Restoration Traditions: Mormons and Churches of Christ in the Nineteenth Century," *Journal of Mormon History* 19 (Spring 1993): 34–51.

52. Several scholars have argued for multiple disestablishments over the course of American history. See, for example, Steven K. Green, *The Second Disestablishment: Church and State in Nineteenth-Century America* (Oxford: Oxford University Press, 2010); Phillip E. Hammond, *Religion and Personal Autonomy: The Third Disestablishment in America* (Columbia: University of South Carolina Press, 1992); Robert T. Handy, *A Christian America: Protestant Hopes and Historical Realities* (Oxford: Oxford University Press, 1971); and C. Leonard Allen, *Things Unseen: Churches of Christ in (and after) the Modern Age* (Abilene: Leafwood Publishers, 2004).

53. Green, *The Second Disestablishment*, 150.

54. Ibid., 331.

55. See, for example, Paul Leroy Carter, *The Spiritual Crisis of the Gilded Age* (DeKalb: Northern Illinois University Press, 1971).

56. Freud made this point in his classic book, *The Future of an Illusion*, where he argued that God and religion are fundamentally illusory. Originally in German, an English edition of this book was published in the United States in 1928.

57. Cone, *The Cross and the Lynching Tree*, 9.

58. On this point, see Diana L. Eck, *A New Religious America: How a "Christian Country" Has Become the World's Most Religiously Diverse Nation* (San Francisco: HarperSanFrancisco, 2001).

59. Stephen Mansfield, *Choosing Donald Trump: God, Anger, Hope, and Why Christian Conservatives Supported Him* (Grand Rapids: Baker Books, 2017), 14.

60. Pat Robertson, *The New World Order* (Dallas: Word Publishing Co., 1991), 227.

61. Douglas O. Linder, "The Emmett Till Murder Trial: An Account," 2012, http://law2.umkc.edu/faculty/projects/ftrials/till/tillaccount.html, accessed January 21, 2017.

62. See, e.g., Beverly Daniel Tatum, *Can We Talk about Race? And Other Conversations in an Era of School Resegregation* (Boston: Beacon Press, 2008).

63. Ta-Nehisi Coates, "The First White President," *The Atlantic*, October, 2017, https://www.theatlantic.com/magazine/archive/2017/10/the-first-white-president-ta-nehisi-coates/537909/, accessed October 4, 2017.

64. "Trump: We're Going to Take the Country Back," *Fox News Insider*, July 12, 2015, http://insider.foxnews.com/2015/07/12/donald-trump-phoenix-speech-were-going-take-country-back, accessed January 15, 2017.

65. Libby Nelson, "'Why We Voted for Donald Trump': David Duke Explains the White Supremacist Charlottesville Protests," *Vox*, April 12, 2017, https://www.vox.com/2017/8/12/16138358/charlottesville-protests-david-duke-kkk, accessed August 13, 2017.

66. Jessica Taylor, "Citing 'Two Corinthians,' Trump Struggles to Make the Sale to Evangelicals," NPR, http://www.npr.org/2016/01/18/463528847/citing-two-corinthians-trump-struggles-to-make-the-sale-to-evangelicals, accessed July 4, 2017.

67. Alan Noble, "The Evangelical Persecution Complex," *The Atlantic*, August 4, 2014, https://www.theatlantic.com/national/archive/2014/08/the-evangelical-persecution-complex/375506/, accessed August 26, 2016.

68. Michael Brown, "Is Donald Trump a Modern Cyrus?" *CharismaNews* (March 10, 2016), http://www.charismanews.com/opinion/in-the-line-of-fire/55754-is-donald-trump-a-modern-day-cyrus, accessed July 15, 2017.

69. Robert P. Jones, "Trump Can't Reverse the Decline of White Christian America," *The Atlantic*, https://www.theatlantic.com/politics/archive/2017/07/robert-jones-white-christian-america/532587/, accessed July 4, 2017.

70. http://www.pewresearch.org/fact-tank/2016/11/09/how-the-faithful-voted-a-preliminary-2016-analysis/, accessed July 31, 2017.

71. Randall Balmer, "Under Trump, Evangelicals Show Their True Racist Colors," *Los Angeles Times*, August 23, 2017, http://www.latimes.com/opinion/op-ed/la-oe-balmer-evangelical-trump-racism-20170823-story.html, accessed August 26, 2017.

72. Randall Balmer, *Thy Kingdom Come: An Evangelical's Lament: How the Religious Right Distorts the Faith and Threatens America* (New York: Basic Books, 2006), 13–17.

73. David Leonhardt and Ian Prasad Philbrick, "Donald Trump's Racism: The Definitive List," *New York Times*, January 15, 2018, https://www.nytimes.com/interactive/2018/01/15/opinion/leonhardt-trump-racist.html, accessed January 15, 2018.

74. "Statement of Coretta Scott King on the Nomination of Jefferson Beauregard Sessions for the United States District Court, Southern District of Alabama," March 13, 1986, https://www.washingtonpost.com/news/powerpost/wp/2017/01/10/read-the-letter-coretta-scott-king-wrote-opposing-sessionss-1986-federal-nomination/?utm_term=.f7c334b5a4dc, accessed August 26, 2017.

75. Matt Zapotosky, "Corey Booker Breaks with Tradition, Says Fellow Senator Jeff Sessions Should Not Be Attorney General," *Washington Post*, January 11, 2017, https://www.washingtonpost.com/world/national-security/jeff-sessions-has-made-his-case-to-be-the-attorney-general-now-the-senate-will-hear-from-supporters-and-detractors/2017/01/10/5683ce24-d796-11e6-9a36-1d296534b31e_story.html?utm_term=.dcd7837bd01a, accessed August 26, 2017.

76. Ari Berman, "Jeff Sessions Has Spent His Whole Career Opposing Voting Rights," *The Nation*, January 10, 2017, https://www.thenation.com/article/jeff-sessions-has-spent-his-whole-career-opposing-voting-rights/, accessed August 27, 2017.

77. See, e.g., Rebecca Mead, "Betsy DeVos and the Plan to Break Public Schools," *The New Yorker*, December 14, 2016, http://www.newyorker.com/news/daily-comment/betsy-devos-and-the-plan-to-break-public-schools, accessed August 26, 2017.

78. Colleen Shalby, "From Blaming 'Many Sides' to 'Racism Is Evil' and Back Again, What Trump Has Said So Far on Charlottesville," *Los Angeles Times*, August 15, 2017, http://www.latimes.com/politics/washington/la-na-essential-washington-updates

-how-trump-s-responded-to-violence-in-1502831078-htmlstory.html, accessed August 26, 2017.

79. Balmer, "Under Trump."

80. Russell Moore, "Russell Moore: Why Christians Must Speak Out against Donald Trump's Muslim Remarks," *Washington Post*, December 8, 2015, at https://www.washingtonpost.com/news/acts-of-faith/wp/2015/12/07/russell-moore-people-who-care-an-iota-about-religious-liberty-should-denounce-donald-trump/?utm_term=.9b1c95a3fc99, accessed August 30, 2017; and Brandon Showalter, "White Supremacy and Racism Are 'Anti-Christ,' Russell Moore Tells Southern Baptists," *The Christian Post*, June 15, 2017, http://www.christianpost.com/news/white-supremacy-and-racism-are-anti-christ-russell-moore-tells-southern-baptists-188087/, accessed August 30, 2017.

81. Tom Gjelten, "Evangelical Leader under Attack for Criticizing Trump Supporters," NPR, December 20, 2016, at http://www.npr.org/2016/12/20/506248119/anti-trump-evangelical-faces-backlash, accessed August 30, 2017.

82. Grand Rapids: Brazos Press, 2017.

83. See, for example, D. L. Mayfield, "Facing Our legacy of Lynching," *Christianity Today*, August 18, 2017, http://www.christianitytoday.com/ct/2017/september/legacy-lynching-america-christians-repentance.html, accessed on August 29, 2017.

84. Messiah College in Grantham, Pennsylvania, is a case in point. When I taught there from 2006 to 2015, Messiah made anti-racism work central to its core first-year curriculum.

85. See, e.g., Randall Balmer, *Mine Eyes Have Seen the Glory: A Journey into the Evangelical Subculture in America* (Oxford: Oxford University Press, 1989); *Blessed Assurance: A History of Evangelicalism in America* (Boston: Beacon Press, 1999); *Thy Kingdom Come* and *The Making of Evangelicalism: From Revivalism to Politics and Beyond* (Waco: Baylor University Press, 2010).

86. George Washington, "Washington's Farewell Address," 1796, Lillian Goldman Law Library, Yale University Law School, http://avalon.law.yale.edu/18th_century/washing.asp, accessed August 27, 2017.

87. Mircea Eliade, *Cosmos and History: The Myth of the Eternal Return* (New York: Harper Torchbooks, 1959).

88. Paul Tillich, *The Courage to Be* (New Haven: Yale University Press, 2000), 70.

89. Yolanda Pierce, "Watching 81% of My White Brothers and Sisters Vote for Trump Has Broken Something in Me," *Religion Dispatches*, November 15, 2016, http://religiondispatches.org/watching-8fs1-of-my-white-brothers-and-sisters-vote-for-trump-has-broken-something-in-me/, accessed November 18, 2016.

90. Douglass, *Narrative*, 86–87.

CHAPTER FIVE

The Myth of the Millennial Nation
The Early National Period

The Myth of Nature's Nation dominated the Revolutionary period and quickly became a staple in the American imagination. This myth held up for emulation the virtues and perfections of a golden age that nature embodied and that stood at the beginning of time.

In the early national period, another myth—equally ahistorical—captured the American imagination. This was the Myth of the Millennial Nation.[1] These two visions—Nature's Nation and the Millennial Nation—connected with one another in powerful ways, since they effectively placed brackets around human history. One looked back toward the beginning of time. The other looked forward to its end. If the Myth of Nature's Nation suggested that the United States embodied themes built into nature from the time of the Creation, the Myth of the Millennial Nation pointed in the opposite direction. This second myth suggested that the United States would illumine the globe with truth, justice, goodness, and democratic self-government and would thereby usher in a final golden age for all humankind.

In this chapter, I want to accomplish several objectives. First, I want to explore the backgrounds to the Myth of the Millennial Nation, both in the ancient world and in the American colonies. Second, I want to explore how this myth worked in the early national period. Third, I want to explore how the Myth of the Millennial Nation combined with all the other myths I have considered to this point to produce the doctrine of manifest destiny. And finally, I want to explore the ways in which the Myth of the Millennial Nation intersected with the Myth of White Supremacy.

Background

The Ancient World

The notion of a Millennial Nation ultimately derives from Jewish and Christian understandings of the end of time. Ancient Judaism nurtured a vision of a messiah who would someday appear and usher in a time when peace, justice, and righteousness would prevail. There is perhaps no biblical passage more descriptive of the messiah and the messianic age than Isaiah 11:2–6 (NIV).

> The Spirit of the Lord will rest on him—
> the Spirit of wisdom and of understanding,
> the Spirit of counsel and of power,
> the Spirit of knowledge and of the fear of the Lord—
> and he will delight in the fear of the Lord.
>
> He will not judge by what he sees with his eyes,
> or decide by what he hears with his ears;
> but with righteousness he will judge the needy,
> with justice he will give decisions for the poor of the earth.
> He will strike the earth with the rod of his mouth;
> with the breath of his lips he will slay the wicked.
> Righteousness will be his belt
> and faithfulness the sash around his waist.
>
> The wolf will live with the lamb,
> the leopard will lie down with the goat,
> the calf and the lion and the yearling together;
> and a little child will lead them.

Christians believed that in Jesus Christ, the Messiah had appeared. It was, nevertheless, apparent that the advent of Jesus Christ had not transformed the world in ways that the messianic vision had predicted. Christians therefore began to apply that vision to the earth's final age, when Christ would reign triumphant.

Only one passage in the entire New Testament fleshes out that vision with any detail—Revelation 20:1–3. The book of Revelation falls into the category of apocalyptic literature, that is, literature that deals with the end time. It is filled with visions and images that often make little sense to the modern reader. To ancient Christian believers, however, it made all the sense in the world. It explained how Christian believers, harassed and persecuted by the Roman Empire, would finally reign victorious with God.

Though much of the book of Revelation focused on final victory in an afterlife, many Christians found in one particular passage a prediction that righteousness would someday reign triumphant even on this earth. That passage was Revelation 20:1–3 (NIV): "And I saw an angel coming down out of heaven, having the key to the Abyss and holding in his hand a great chain. He seized the dragon, that ancient serpent, who is the devil, or Satan, and bound him for a thousand years. He threw him into the Abyss, and locked and sealed it over him, to keep him from deceiving the nations anymore until the thousand years were ended. After that, he must be set free for a short time."

The imagery here seems clear. Satan, as the source of all evil, would be bound and locked away for a thousand years. During that period he could tempt no one. Many Christians interpreted that passage to mean that if the devil would someday be bound for a thousand years, they could therefore expect a thousand-year period, sometime in the future, when peace, justice, and righteousness would prevail over all the earth.

This is the basis for the vision of a millennial age, since the word *millennium* literally means "thousand years." Some believed that the millennium would be a period of a literal thousand years. Others understood the thousand years to be symbolic of a golden age of undetermined duration. In any event, the expectation of a final, golden age of peace, justice, and righteousness has been a powerful theme throughout Christian history.

Premillennialism and Postmillennialism

Christians have differed over the means by which this golden age would become reality. Many Christians believed that the golden age could appear only at the second coming. People who held to this position believed that human beings were powerless to create a golden age on their own. The advent of the golden age, therefore, depended entirely on God's power and initiative. At the second coming, therefore, Jesus would set up his throne and rule the earth for a thousand years. The term for this vision is *premillennialism*, since it emphasizes the conviction that Jesus's second coming would be *pre-*, or prior to, the dawn of the millennium.

To the extent that western Christians concerned themselves with any version of millennial speculation prior to the eighteenth century, they usually embraced premillennial sentiments. After all, for centuries human beings had been subject to plagues, diseases, natural disasters, and short life spans. What could they possibly do to counteract those devastating forces? They could only live—and die—with these disasters. For all those centuries, therefore, no one really thought that human beings could transform their world into a paradise of goodness, peace, and tranquility.

The Enlightenment of the eighteenth century, however, completely transformed the way Europeans envisioned their future. Suddenly, science opened up the possibility that human beings might control far more of their destiny than anyone had ever dreamed. Perhaps, to a degree, they could conquer fate. Perhaps they could conquer disease. Perhaps by taking a rational and scientific approach to life, they could even put an end to wars and bring about an era of peace and justice. And if all this were to occur, what would that era be, if not the golden age so long expected by their forebears?

During the eighteenth century, therefore, the prevalent Christian understanding of the millennium shifted from *premillennialism* to *postmillennialism*.[2] Once again, the prefix had reference to the second coming of Christ. In this case, however, Christ's second coming would occur *post-*, or after, the millennium. What means, then, would make the golden age a reality? The answer was human initiative, especially science, rational thought, and education. If Christ wished to return to the earth, that was his business. But he was not needed to launch a golden age. Human beings would do that.

Postmillennial thinking emerged in the American colonies early in the eighteenth century. In the American context, it is interesting that the shift in millennial thinking had more to do with religion than it did with science or education.

Decline in New England

When the Puritans first came to America, they sought to create a society dominated by the church and by Christian ideals. They assumed that every citizen would be a faithful member of a Puritan congregation. By and large, the first generation successfully implemented that vision. In the second and third generations, however, that vision slowly dimmed.

By the 1660s, a variety of developments revealed that the spiritual vision that drove the Founders had fallen on hard times. Many Puritans now grew discouraged, suspecting that New England was rapidly violating the covenant they had struck with God. In 1679, therefore, the Puritans convened a Reforming Synod that sought to correct this collapse of religious zeal. The document issued by that Synod reveals the problems they sought to address.

In the first place, commerce, not religion, increasingly seized the imaginations of the children and grandchildren of the original immigrants. As the synod observed, "Farms and Merchandising" were "preferred before the things of God." This passion for the things of the world also manifested itself in fashionable clothing—and the lack thereof. The synod complained of the "Laying out of Hair, Borders, naked Necks and Arms, or, which is more abominable, naked Breasts."

Second, even though the Puritans made every effort to ensure religious uniformity in New England, they found they could not successfully fence out other kinds of Christians, especially Presbyterians, Baptists, and Quakers. Their impotence in this regard became especially apparent by the 1680s when the British revoked the original Bay Colony charter, dispatched a royal governor to the colony, and built an Anglican chapel in the heart of Boston.

Third, church membership declined in comparison to the general population, and many in the second and third generations showed little interest in fulfilling the requirements that would make them full-fledged members of the church. According to Puritan theory, only the elect—that is, those chosen by God for salvation—could be admitted fully into the church. To verify one's election, one had to relate an experience of saving grace and demonstrate the results of that grace in holy living. Without these signs, no one could be fully admitted into the church, even though one had been baptized as an infant.

The first generation of Puritan immigrants never dreamed that their children would fail to seek these signs, but many among the second and third generations were content to continue as "half-way" members of the church. They had been baptized as infants, and that was sufficient.

Problems emerged when these halfway church members of the second and third generations requested baptism for their own children. This request was highly irregular, since Puritan theology held that children were eligible for baptism only if their parents were among the elect and were therefore full-fledged members of the church. Now a generation that claimed neither election nor complete church membership sought baptism for their children.

This request placed the leadership of the Puritan churches in a serious quandary. If they agreed to the request that had been presented, they implicitly would abandon their insistence that the church be composed only of the elect. Soon, it seemed, the church would be filled with members who cared more for the world than for the kingdom of God. On the other hand, if the leadership rejected the request, they would virtually kill the church by denying baptism—and therefore any level of church membership—to a whole generation of children. From the 1640s into the 1660s, this issue festered. Because neither horn of the dilemma was acceptable, the leadership found it could not arrive at a resolution.

Finally, in 1662, a synod convened, determined to resolve the question. A bitter debate ensued, but when the dust finally settled, the liberals had won the day. The synod—thereafter known as the Half-Way Synod—rendered the decision that infants may be baptized, even if their parents were only half-way members who had not demonstrated the signs of their own election. True to the conservatives' predictions, the church continued its spiraling decline for the remainder of the century.

Capping all these concerns, a whole series of disasters beset New England, beginning in the 1660s. These included droughts, famines, Indian wars, fires, and finally the hysteria over alleged witchcraft that seized Salem Village in 1692. True to their covenant theology, the Puritans saw in these disasters the wrath of God, now poured out upon his covenant-breaking people.

As a result, Puritan preaching took on a new form as early as the 1660s. Instead of preaching traditional sermons that reinforced Puritan theology, Puritan ministers now wept for the sins of New England and warned the people to repent before God eradicated them from the land. This form of preaching is called the *jeremiad*, a term that recalls the Old Testament prophet Jeremiah, who wept over the sins of ancient Israel. In keeping with their concern that New England Christians had broken their covenant with God, the Reforming Synod asked why God would "have kindled such devouring Fires, and made such fearful Desolations in the Earth, if he had not been angry."

The decline of religious zeal that I have described here was not unique to New England. It characterized virtually all the colonies by the close of the seventeenth century. In the context of the covenant that the Puritans believed God had made with them, the righteous leaders of New England found the decline especially devastating.

The Great Awakening

The Puritan lamentations persisted from roughly 1660 for the remainder of the century and into the next. Finally, in the 1720s, a revival began to stir. It began in small ways when a Dutchman, Theodore Frelinghuysen, arrived in New Brunswick, New Jersey, to pastor four Dutch Reformed congregations. Frelinghuysen stressed genuine conversion and his preaching produced startling results. Soon a neighboring Presbyterian preacher, Gilbert Tennent, adopted similar strategies that ignited the revival fires in his congregation. From those small beginnings, the revival spread into other colonies. In 1734, revival broke out in a Puritan congregation pastored by Jonathan Edwards in Northhampton, Massachusetts.

Not until 1739, however, did these isolated revivals converge into a general spiritual awakening that swept the colonies from New England to Georgia. More than anyone else, an English revivalist named George Whitefield helped ignite those revival fires. Whitefield had been actively involved in a British revival that helped produce the Methodist movement there in the 1730s. Now, in 1739, he brought his immense oratorical and persuasive powers to the colonies.

Whitefield made several contributions to the Great Awakening. First, his persuasive, oratorical powers were nothing short of astounding. Second, by traveling from one end of the colonies to the other, taking reports of the revival from one town to the next, Whitefield served as an important source of news for the colonies. By themselves, Whitefield's reports helped to spread the revival wherever he went, but when he coupled his reports with stirring revivalistic preaching, the impact was even greater. In this way, Whitefield provided the spark that helped to turn a few isolated revivals into a Great Awakening that deluged the colonies with religious fervor.

The Emergence of the Millennial Nation

The extent and power of the Great Awakening grew so impressive that many wondered whether perhaps this was not the beginning of the millennial age foretold in scripture. Jonathan Edwards, widely recognized as the leading theologian in the colonies, typified this viewpoint. In 1742 he wrote a treatise called "Some Thoughts Concerning the Present Revival of Religion in New England." There he made a bold prediction. "It is not unlikely," he wrote, "that this work of God's Spirit [i.e., the Awakening], so extraordinary and wonderful, is the dawning, or at least a prelude of that glorious work of God, so often foretold in scripture, which, in the progress and issue of it, shall renew the world of mankind." Indeed, Edwards argued, "We cannot reasonably think otherwise."

In part, Edwards made this case because of another theme he found in the book of Revelation. In addition to a coming golden age, Revelation seemed to predict a cosmic Battle of Armageddon (Rev. 16:16) in which the forces of Christ would finally vanquish the forces of the Antichrist. Many thought that it was through this battle that Satan would be bound, thereby inaugurating the golden age. To Edwards, and to many of that generation, the Great Awakening was just such a cosmic battle. Through the power of revival, the colonists had joined hands with God to deal Satan his final defeat.

In addition to the extraordinary power of the Great Awakening, there were several other factors that led Edwards to his conclusion. First, he thought he found in Isaiah 60:9 a prediction that the millennium would begin "in some very remote part of the world." Edwards could not imagine that "any thing else can be here intended but America."

Second, Edwards viewed America as a "new world" in contrast to the "old world" back in Europe. In fact, Edwards thought that "this new world is probably now discovered, that the new and most glorious state of God's church on earth might commence there; that God might in it begin a new world in a spiritual respect, when he creates the *new heavens and new earth.*"

Third, Edwards considered America a "new world" in another respect as well. "The other continent," he declared, "hath slain Christ, and has from age to age shed the blood of the saints and martyrs of Jesus, and has often been as it were, deluged with the church's blood.—God has, therefore, probably reserved the honour of building the glorious temple to the daughter that has not shed so much blood." For this reason, Europeans "shall not have the honour of communicating religion in its most glorious state to us, but we to them."

Though Edwards thought God had chosen the "new world" for the birth of the golden age, he especially thought of New England in these terms: "If we may suppose that this glorious work of God shall begin in any part of America, I think, if we consider the circumstances of the settlement of New England, it must needs appear the most likely, of all American colonies, to be the place whence this work shall principally take its rise." For all these reasons, Edwards believed that the revival "now seen in America, and especially in New England, may prove the dawn of that glorious day."

In the early 1740s, as the revival reached its crescendo, sentiments like these grew increasingly common. Then, in 1743, the revival ran out of steam and came to a grinding halt. Strikingly, the world had not changed. Evil and injustice still prevailed. In spite of the colonists' fondest hopes, it was obvious that the millennium was still a distant dream.

In 1754 something happened that once again stirred the millennial vision. England and France went to war in order to determine which colonial power would play what role in the North American wilderness. The conflict soon became known as the French and Indian War. In the course of the conflict, British colonists refocused their millennial vision.[3] It is easy to understand why. As Protestants, British colonists imagined themselves the agents of Christ and Catholic France the agent of Antichrist. The French and Indian War, therefore, appeared to many as a second front in the great Battle of Armageddon.

By 1759 it was apparent that the British had won the war that officially concluded in 1763 with the signing of the Peace of Paris. It also was apparent that the millennium still had not dawned. Nevertheless, the colonists continued to hope. Over the course of the eighteenth century, too many people had invested too many dreams and too much effort into the realization of a golden age for that vision to dissipate and die.

Then, in 1776, America declared its independence from Britain. The American Revolution rapidly ensued and concluded with an American victory, ratified by the Peace of Paris, signed by all parties in 1783. By 1788 the colonies had agreed to a constitution and thereby became a new nation: the United States of America.

The point for us to grasp is this: The Revolution and the birth of the nation fanned the millennial imagination of Americans as nothing had before. Moreover, in this case the millennial vision did not fade as it had following both the Great Awakening and the French and Indian War. Instead, the vision grew stronger and stronger. Many Americans were convinced that the nation's birth had launched the golden age. If not, they believed that at the very least, they were standing on its threshold.

What was it about the new nation that stimulated such exuberant millennial excitement on the part of so many American citizens? We should mention several factors. First, the land itself struck many as a virtual Garden of Eden. It was no polluted, overcrowded landscape. Instead, here was a virgin land that seemed to have come fresh from the hand of God. As the British philosopher John Locke observed in his *Second Treatise on Government*, "In the beginning, all the world was America."

Second, the new nation guaranteed to its white citizens a variety of freedoms virtually unknown in the countries from which they had come. Here, they could think as they wished to think, believe as they wished to believe, worship as they wished to worship, and speak as they wished to speak, without fear of reprisals from the government. White male citizens could even choose the president of the country and those who would represent them in the new corridors of power. Even though suffrage was limited, these developments must have seemed absolutely revolutionary to many white Americans of that time. The fact that the nation excluded blacks from these privileges suggests the extent to which the Myth of White Supremacy, at this early period in the nation's history, had defined the Myth of the Millennial Nation.

It is hardly surprising, then, that among white Americans, millennial excitement abounded. It even found its way onto the Great Seal of the United States. There, an unfinished pyramid grows from arid desert sands. Inscribed on the pyramid's base is that notable date, 1776. Clearly, the pyramid represents the new nation. The barren desert terrain, above which the pyramid towers and from which it seems to grow, signifies all human history prior to 1776. For all their glories and achievements, past civilizations were essentially barren compared to the glories that would mark the new American state. The pyramid is unfinished since the American experiment remained incomplete. Above this scene, the eye of God looks down with obvious pleasure, and the

Latin inscription records His response: "annuit coeptis," or, "he (God) has favored our undertakings." Beneath this picture stands the most relevant phrase of all: "novus ordo seclorum," or, "a new of the ages."

Many Americans living in the late eighteenth and early nineteenth centuries believed their nation to be precisely that. For them, America was no ordinary nation, corrupted by time and tradition. Instead it was radically new, a nation that would bless all the nations of the world with the glories of the long-anticipated millennial age.

One finds stirrings of this vision even before the Revolution. John Adams, for example, confided to his diary in 1765, "I always consider the settlement of America with reverence and wonder, as the opening of a grand scene and design in Providence for the illumination of the ignorant, and the emancipation of the slavish part of mankind all over the earth."[4]

After the Revolution, this vision grew more and more common. Ezra Stiles, president of Yale University, preaching before the General Assembly of the State of Connecticut in 1783, offered this:

> This great American revolution, this recent political phenomenon of a new sovereignty arising among the sovereign powers of the earth, will be attended to and contemplated by all nations. . . . That prophecy of Daniel is now literally fulfilling—there shall be an universal traveling "to and fro, and knowledge shall be increased." This knowledge will be brought home and treasured up in America: and being here digested and carried to the highest perfection, may reblaze back from America to Europe, Asia and Africa, and illumine the world with TRUTH and LIBERTY. . . . Light spreads from the day-spring in the west; and may it shine more and more until the perfect day.[5]

By the 1830s, Lyman Beecher expressed in almost classic terms the vision of the "millennial nation" that would renovate the world. Reflecting on Jonathan Edwards's claim that the millennium would begin in America, Beecher wrote, "When I first encountered this opinion, I thought it chimerical; but all providential developments since, and all the existing signs of the times, lend corroboration to it."[6]

Any millennial vision presupposes that the moral structure of the world has deteriorated from its original perfection at the time of creation. Accordingly, in a speech he delivered in 1827, Beecher argued that "the history of the world is the history of human nature in ruins." We should not despair, he counseled, for a text from the Bible "throws light upon this dark destiny of our race. It is a voice from heaven announcing the approach of help from above: 'He that sitteth upon the throne saith, Behold, I make all things new.' [Rev. 21:5]."

In Beecher's vision, one of the primary means through which God would "make all things new" was the American nation. For the world to be made free, "a great example is required. . . . But where could such a nation be found?" Before the American Revolution, he thought, "it had no existence upon the earth." Now, "Behold what God hath wrought." God had brought forth a nation radically new in the history of the world, a nation whose laws "recognize the equal rights of man" and whose institutions "give the soil to the cultivator, and self government and the rights of conscience to the people."[7] The United States would therefore lead the world until "the world's hope is secure. The government of force will cease, and that of intelligence and virtue will take its place; and nation after nation cheered by our example, will follow in our footsteps, till the whole earth is free."[8]

When Beecher described the process by which America would renovate the world, he grew almost euphoric. The light that America will send into the world, he said,

> will throw its beams beyond the waves; it will shine into darkness there and be comprehended; it will awaken desire and hope and effort, and produce revolutions and overturnings, until the world is free. . . . Then will the trumpet of Jubilee sound, and earth's debased millions will leap from the dust, and shake off their chains, and cry, "Hosanna to the Son of David." [9]

The notion that "earth's debased millions" would ultimately cry "Hosanna to the Son of David" is important, since to Beecher, the work of renovating the world was also the work of Christianizing the world. To be sure, Beecher based his hope that America would renovate the world on his belief that America was Nature's Nation. But he also based that hope on the power of the Second Great Awakening and the extent to which that revival was Christianizing the United States. "The revivals of religion which prevail in our land among Christians of all denominations," he confidently proclaimed, "are without parallel in the history of the world and are constituting an era of moral power entirely new. . . . These revivals . . . seem to declare the purpose of God to employ this nation in the glorious work of renovating the earth."[10]

Beecher's vision was not unique to the early nineteenth century. Time and again since Beecher's day, Americans have predicted that Nature's Nation would launch the millennial dawn. In 1990, for example, when Communism finally collapsed in both Eastern Europe and the Soviet Union, the American people were euphoric. The Cold War had come to an end, and Soviet-style communism no longer threatened the United States. Americans celebrated, however, not only the collapse of Communism. They also celebrated what they viewed as the inevitable triumph of key American values in those far-off lands. Commentators, politicians, newscasters, and other Americans confidently predicted that nations once dominated by communism would now embrace democracy, capitalism, and other aspects of the American way of life.

In this context, President George Herbert Walker Bush proclaimed that a "New World Order" was emerging. In part, the new world order would be a world "in which major powers worked together to ensure peace; to settle their disputes through cooperation, not confrontation." It also would be a world inspired by democratic ideals. "Today," he told the American people, "a transformed Europe stands closer than ever before to its free and democratic destiny." To a great extent, Bush explained, this new world order reflected the power of the American example: "This order gains its mission and shape not just from shared interests, but from shared ideals. And the ideals that have spawned new freedoms throughout the world have received their boldest and clearest expression in our great country the United States. Never before has the world looked more to the American example. Never before have so many millions drawn hope from the American idea."[11]

Why would Americans assume that the values of this country would fill the void where communism had reigned supreme? Why would an American president suggest that democracy was the "destiny" of these nations? And why would he proclaim the emergence of a new world order at all?

The myths of Nature's Nation and the Millennial Nation help explain why, in the popular imagination, America is a new world order. On the one hand, it reflects the values of the natural order, built into creation by God Himself. On the other, it heralds the dawn of a coming golden age. It heralds a golden age precisely because its values are essentially natural, conforming to the golden age at the beginning of time, uncontaminated by history or tradition. George Bush's new world order, therefore, was an idea as old as America itself.

Finally, what changed and what remained constant in the transition from the Great Awakening to the Revolutionary era and the early national period? What remained constant was the expectation that a millennial age would shortly dawn. What changed was the way Americans conceptualized that age. During the Great Awakening, most thought of the millennium in terms of the sovereignty of God. That was only natural, since the majority of Christians in the colonies stood in the Reformed tradition. For centuries, Calvinists had nurtured the hope that some day, God would rule over all the earth, a vision Calvin himself sought to realize in Geneva. Now in the American colonies, two hundred years later, Calvinists still nurtured that dream. They therefore hailed the Great Awakening as the dawn of the millennial age, since it seemed to promise that soon God would reign triumphant, first over America and then over all the world.

During the period of the French and Indian War, that vision changed dramatically. Now the colonists hoped not so much for the sovereignty of God as for the sovereignty of one particular expression of the Christian faith—Protestantism.

By the Revolutionary era, the colonists had invested the millennial vision with yet another meaning: "unalienable rights." They defined the golden age not so much in terms of God's sovereignty or even in terms of Protestant dominance. Instead, the golden age would be a time when all human beings would exercise their "unalienable rights" to "life, liberty, and the pursuit of happiness." Put another way, in the Revolutionary era, an affirmation of human rights largely displaced the expectation of the rule of God.

The transition from the sovereignty of God to the sovereignty of the people with their unalienable rights marked a radical shift in the thinking of the American populace. Most of all, it tells us that the old Puritan dream of a distinctly Christian state no longer controlled American expectations. In its place stood a new vision of liberty and democratic self-government, a vision generated not by Puritanism but by the Enlightenment.

But the dream of a Christian nation was by no means dead. Instead, Christian proponents of the Millennial Nation ideal argued that Christianity and the nation's "unalienable rights" were handmaidens to each other. On the one hand, they claimed, there would be no "unalienable rights" in the United States were it not for the Christian faith. On the other hand, Christianity depended on the extension of civil liberties for its own propagation. In this way, these Christian visionaries collapsed the Myth of Nature's Nation and the Myth of the Christian Nation into a single, unified ideal.

America's Manifest Destiny

By the mid-1840s, the United States had developed a full-blown civic faith, informed by all the myths considered to this point. Nothing more effectively marks the triumph of that faith than the doctrine of manifest destiny.[12]

The doctrine of manifest destiny meets all the requirements for the notion of myth that I laid out in chapter 1. Yet I choose not to treat manifest destiny as a foundational myth of the United States for one fundamental reason. The myths under consideration in this book are myths that have continued to define the American character since they first emerged at some particular point in American history. In contrast, the doctrine of manifest destiny served a very specific purpose—the goal of westward expansion—and therefore flourished for a short time, namely, the second half of the nineteenth century.

It is pertinent that manifest destiny drew on all the myths I have considered to this point and represents the absolutizing of all those myths, especially the Myth of the Millennial Nation.

The term *manifest destiny* appeared for the first time in an unsigned article in the July–August 1845 issue of the *Democratic Review*, edited by John L. O'Sullivan. In the context of exploring the annexation of Texas to the United States, the article spoke of "our manifest destiny to overspread the continent allotted by Providence for the free development of our yearly multiplying millions."[13]

In using that term, the article merely gave voice to a notion that had been widely held in the United States for several years. The War of 1812 had enabled whites to seize strategic Indian lands west of the Appalachian Mountains, and in the aftermath of that war, the westward movement began in earnest. Between 1810 and 1820, the white population west of the mountains more than doubled. When one adds to that the fact that so many white Americans of that period believed so strongly in the United States as a divinely Chosen Nation, as Nature's Nation, as a Millennial Nation, and as a Christian Nation, a clear statement of the doctrine of manifest destiny was inevitable. Indeed, the doctrine of manifest destiny was writ large on the hearts and minds of white Americans long before that term appeared in print.

In December 1845, in another of his papers, *The New York Morning News*, O'Sullivan himself defended American acquisition of the Oregon Territory on the same premise. He dismissed treaties and international law and argued America's claim to the Oregon territory squarely on religious grounds: "Away, away with all these cobweb tissues of rights of discovery, exploration, settlement, contiguity, etc. To state the truth at once in its naked simplicity, . . . our claim to Oregon . . . is by the right of our manifest destiny to overspread and to possess the whole of the continent which Providence has given us for the development of the great experiment of liberty and federative self-government entrusted to us." O'Sullivan concluded that editorial with the ringing affirmation that "the God of nature and of nations has marked it [the Oregon territory] for our own; and with His blessing we will firmly maintain the incontestable rights He has given, and fearlessly perform the high duties He has imposed."[14]

This classic statement reflects the extent to which the Myth of White Supremacy underpinned both the Myth of the Millennial Nation and the notion of manifest destiny, for manifest destiny was a vision of white dominance and control of the North American continent. Natives would be dispossessed and blacks would be excluded.

The Great Transition: From Millennial Nation to Manifest Destiny

In the transition from the vision of a Millennial Nation to the doctrine of manifest destiny, a significant change occurred in the way Americans understood their calling in the world. The significance of that change is almost impossible to overstate.

In the early nineteenth century, those who contended for America's millennial role in the world typically argued that America would perform that role solely through the power of example. Lyman Beecher was a case in point. "The government of force will cease," he predicted, "and nation after nation cheered by our example, will follow in our footsteps, till the whole earth is free." The Great Seal of the United States implicitly proclaimed the same vision. The pyramid that represents the United States would be complete when other nations, moved by the power of the American example, would throw off their chains and claim freedom and democratic self-government as their own inheritance.

On the other hand, those who subscribed to the doctrine of manifest destiny typically embraced a very different view of things. God, they believed, chose America not so much to exercise moral responsibility in the world as to embrace a destiny—a destiny that was "manifest" or self-evident. That destiny was "manifest" because America was both a Christian Nation, faithful to the mandates of God, and Nature's Nation, reflecting the natural order of the way things were meant to be.

Completely faithful to "the laws of Nature and Nature's God," therefore, and completely unique in the history of the world, such a nation had every right to extend its influence not only by example, but also by force—first throughout the North American continent, and then around the world. The transition from the notion of a Millennial Nation to the doctrine of manifest destiny, then, was also a transition from the belief in the power of moral example to the belief in the legitimacy of raw force to achieve America's objectives. In this way, the doctrine of manifest destiny absolutized the myth of America as the Millennial Nation.

Two examples will suffice. In the midst of the Mexican War (1845–1848), when the doctrine of manifest destiny was the very air that Americans breathed, Senator H. V. Johnson described his belief in that doctrine not in terms of moral example but in terms of military might. "War has its evils," Johnson said of that war and he confessed that "in all ages it has been the minister of wholesale death and appalling desolation." Nonetheless, he maintained, "however inscrutable to us, it has also been made, by the Allwise Dispenser of events, the instrumentality of accomplishing the great end of human elevation and human happiness. . . . It is in this view, that I subscribe to the doctrine of 'manifest destiny.'"

A second example comes from the period of the Spanish-American War, when America's military involvement in the Philippines struck many as unveiled, unabashed imperialism. "Did we need their [Filipinos'] consent to perform a great act for humanity?" President William McKinley asked in defense of the government's policies. "We had it in every aspiration of their minds, in every hope of their hearts."[15] McKinley could make that claim in spite of the fact that for more than two years, Emilio Aguinaldo, a Filipino freedom fighter, led a bloody, popular revolution against what he viewed as American domination of his country. By the time the United States finally defeated this resistance movement, one-fifth of the entire Filipino population had died from war or disease.[16]

I wish now to explore three questions. First, I want to ask how the myths we have considered in this book helped to shape the doctrine of manifest destiny. Second, I want to ask how the notion of the Millennial Nation and the corresponding doctrine of manifest destiny affected America's minority peoples, especially its Native American population. Finally, I want to ask how these minority peoples evaluated and responded to those themes.

Clearly, the American claim to be both a Christian Nation and a Millennial Nation undergirded the doctrine of manifest destiny in very important ways. This entire chapter has sought to demonstrate the ways in which manifest destiny found its grounding in the Myth of the Millennial Nation.

As far as the idea of the Christian Nation was concerned, apologists for manifest destiny occasionally appealed to that ideal as well. Josiah Strong, for example, argued that manifest destiny rested upon America's civil liberties and "a pure spiritual Christianity." When President McKinley sought to justify America's involvement in the Philippines, he explained that the United States had sought "to educate the Filipinos, and uplift and civilize and Christianize them, and by God's grace do the very best we could by them, as our fellow-men for whom Christ also died." And Senator Albert Beveridge argued that an American retreat from the Philippines would be "a crime against Christian civilization."[17]

The most fundamental rationale for the doctrine of manifest destiny was so widely assumed that it seldom required a defense. That, of course, was the Myth of White Supremacy. Still and all, when supporters of manifest destiny sought to work out a cogent defense of that doctrine, they turned time and again to the myths of the Chosen Nation and Nature's Nation. For this reason, I will confine the analysis that follows to those two motifs.

Manifest Destiny and the
Myth of the Chosen Nation

From the wording of O'Sullivan's editorials, it is clear that the doctrine of manifest destiny rested squarely on the Myth of the Chosen Nation. "Providence," he claimed, had granted the North American continent to Euro-Americans "for the development of the great experiment of liberty and federative self-government."

The notion of chosenness at work in mid-nineteenth-century America differed profoundly from the Puritan understanding of that same theme. For the most part, the Puritans adopted a biblical understanding of chosenness, while European Americans in the mid–nineteenth century embraced a notion of chosenness that had no serious connection with the Bible.

There are two ways to understand the difference between the Puritan understanding of chosenness and the American understanding of that theme in the mid–nineteenth century.

First, the Bible never claimed that God chose Israel as his covenant people because of Israel's innate goodness. Rather, God chose Israel for reasons altogether hidden to human reason. The most that one could say is that God chose Israel to manifest his own love and grace. But why Israel and not some other people? The answer to that question was hidden in the divine will.

The Puritan conviction that God had made them a chosen people reflected similar understandings. It is certainly true that Puritans claimed virtual perfection for their churches. Still, Puritans seldom made their righteousness the basis for their election. Rather, God chose them for reasons known only to himself.

By the mid–nineteenth century, however, the reasons for America's chosenness were hardly mysterious. To the contrary, the reasons were *manifest*. And because the reasons were manifest, America's destiny was manifest as well. God chose America, O'Sullivan claimed, because America stood for "liberty and federative self-government."

We can state this difference between seventeenth- and nineteenth-century understandings of chosenness in yet another way. Seventeenth-century Puritans understood that chosenness was due entirely to God's will and initiative. It was *his* call. By the nineteenth century, however, God had become a puppet in the hands of the American people who had placed on God an indisputable claim. The assumption seemed to be that God could hardly refuse to choose America, since the nation so *manifestly* exemplified God's will.

The second fundamental difference between the Puritan and the nineteenth-century understandings of chosenness is similar to the first and involved the idea of covenant. In Puritan New England, the notion of covenant duties always accompanied the notion of chosenness. This means that the blessings of the Almighty were always contingent on the extent to which God's people remained faithful to him. I noted in chapter 2, for example, that John Winthrop, the first governor of Massachusetts Bay Colony, spelled out the terms of the covenant to the Puritan immigrants before they even disembarked from the *Arbella*. He explained that "we are entered into a Covenant with him [God] for this work. . . . Now if the Lord shall please to hear us, and bring us in peace to the place we desire, then hath he ratified this Covenant and sealed our Commission"

Winthrop also explained that if the Puritans failed to conform to the terms of the covenant, they would suffer the wrath of God. If, he declared, we seek "great things for our selves and our posterity, the Lord will surely break out in wrath against us, be revenged of such a perjured people and make us know the price of the breach of such a Covenant."

Winthrop went on to explain that covenant-keeping involved, among other things, compassion and concern for one another. "The only way to avoid this shipwreck," he argued, is "to do justly, to love mercy, to walk humbly with our God. For this end, . . . we must entertain each other in brotherly affection, . . . we must delight in each other, make others conditions our own, rejoice together, mourn together, labor and suffer together."[18]

By the mid–nineteenth century, however, almost no trace of covenant remained. Because of the nature of the American experiment, most European Americans believed that God had chosen the United States for a special destiny in the world, and that was that. The sense of responsibility to others had given way to privilege and divine right.

Manifest Destiny and the Myth of Nature's Nation

While the doctrine of manifest destiny partly rested on assumptions of American chosenness, it rested even more profoundly on the Myth of Nature's Nation. By any measure, this myth was a two-edged sword. On the one hand, it argued that "unalienable rights" belonged to "all men" and grounded those rights in "Nature and Nature's God." On the other hand, it implicitly claimed that some men were more natural than others and therefore especially entitled to those unalienable rights.

How could this be? When Americans of that period tried to define nature, they generally sought to extract from the whole of human history certain universal principles that they thought were pertinent to all human beings in all times and places. Inevitably, however, they read into nature their own experience, their own biases, and their own points of view. How could it have been otherwise? I noted in chapter 3 Carl Becker's judgment that these people were "deceiving themselves" for "they do not know that the 'man in general' they are looking for is just their own image, that the principles they are bound to find are the very ones they start out with. That is the trick they play on the dead."[19] This also was the trick they played on America's minorities, for "nature" in virtually every instance acquired a European coloration. Whoever, therefore, did not conform to European norms and standards was by definition unnatural.

The egocentric understanding of nature bore especially unfortunate consequences for America's Native American population. Native American cultures were radically different from European civilizations and European explorers almost always measured Native-American cultures by European norms and found the native civilizations lacking. Worst of all, early European explorers often stereotyped all Native American populations on the basis of the worst examples they encountered.

For example, in his *Mundus Novus*, published early in the sixteenth century, Amerigo Vespucci flatly portrayed the natives of Brazil as savages and cannibals. "They eat one another," he wrote, "the victors the vanquished, and among other kinds of meat human flesh is a common article of diet with them." Vespucci told of meeting a man "who was reputed to have eaten more than three hundred human bodies." He recalled "a certain city where I saw salted human flesh suspended from beams between the houses, just as with us it is the custom to hang bacon and pork."[20] Vespucci's pamphlet circulated widely and helped create an image of Native American peoples as fundamentally unnatural.

In another report published in 1550, Juan Gines de Sepulveda described the native peoples whom Christopher Columbus encountered in the island occupied today by Haiti and the Dominican Republic. He took pains to portray these people not only as unnatural, but as fundamentally inhuman: "Now compare their [the Spanish] gifts of prudence, talent, magnanimity, temperance, humanity, and religion with those little men [homunculus] in whom you will scarcely find traces of humanity; who not only lack culture but do not even know how to write, who keep no records of their history except certain obscure and vague reminiscences of some things put down in certain pictures, and who do not have written laws but only barbarous institutions and customs."[21]

The English portrayed Native American populations precisely as had the Italians and the Spanish before them. I have already noted that white settlers in New England generally regarded Native Americans as agents of Satan. The same was true further south. After native populations wreaked vengeance on English settlements in Virginia in 1622, for example, one poet urged Europeans to

> consider what those Creatures are,
> (I cannot call them men) no Character
> of God in them: Soules drown'd in flesh and blood;
> Rooted in Evill, and oppos'd in Good;
> Errors of nature, of inhumane Birth,
> The very dregs, garbage, and spanne of Earth;
> Who ne're (I think) were mention'd with those creatures
> ADAM gave names to in their several natures;
> But such as coming of a later Brood,
> (Not sav'd in th' Arke) but since the generall Flood
> Sprung up like vermine of an earthy slime,
> And so have held b' intrusion to this time.[22]

Roger Williams explained in 1643 that when English colonists spoke of Native American populations, they routinely described them with names like "*Natives, Salvages, Indians, Wild-men, . . . Abergeny men, Pagans, Barbarians, Heathen.*"[23]

By the time of the American Revolution and the founding of the United States, these images still held. Most whites still thought of the natural order in terms of European civilizations. The natural order therefore meant settled communities, roads, schools, books, parliaments, factories, and the Christian religion. Typically, Native American cultures had none of these. Most whites therefore continued to view native populations as fundamentally unnatural and less than human. Further, because of their presence on the land, Native Americans blocked the path to American "progress."

Accordingly, even Thomas Jefferson—the man who claimed that according to "Nature and Nature's God, . . . all men are created equal"—even Jefferson argued that the American government should "pursue [the Indians] to extermination, or drive them to new seats beyond our reach." In fact, after a careful reading of Jefferson's works, one historian concluded that his "writings on Indians are filled with the straightforward assertion that the natives are to be given a simple choice—to be 'extirpate[d] from the earth' or to remove themselves out of the Americans' way."[24]

Why should this be surprising if, according to the popular sentiment of that age, Native Americans were neither natural nor fully human? Here, in Jefferson's Indian policy, therefore, one finds perhaps the most poignant example of the clash between an absolutized American myth, on the one hand, and the American Creed, on the other.

In the early nineteenth century, two characteristics of the supposed "natural order" dominated the thinking of American whites. First, whites routinely ascribed to the natural order a characteristic that one historian describes as "geographical predestination." In other words, European Americans believed that God had placed natural boundaries for all the nations of the earth. It became America's duty and destiny, therefore, to extend its domain until its borders coincided with the divinely placed natural boundaries.

Representative David Trimble argued for the acquisition of Texas on just these grounds. Speaking of the Rio Grande and the mountains to the west, Trimble declared, "The great Engineer of the Universe has fixed the natural limits of our country. . . . To that boundary we shall go; 'peaceably if we can, forcibly if we must.'"[25] In time, European Americans employed the same argument to justify the march of their civilization to the Pacific Ocean.

Often, European Americans combined the argument based on "natural" use of the land with the argument based on "natural boundaries" and thereby made what they regarded as an irrefutable claim to North American lands. For example, an 1829 editorial in the *Nashville Republican* explained why the Rio Grande "seems to be marked out for a boundary": "On this side of the Rio Grande, the country is seasonable, fertile, and every way desirable to the people of the United States. On the other side the lands are unproductive, crops cannot be matured without irrigation; in short they are entirely calculated for a lazy, pastoral, mining people like the Mexicans."[26]

Second, whites routinely argued that settlement, cultivation, and improvement of the land stood at the very heart of the natural order. They justified this conviction on the grounds that God, at the creation itself, had given humanity the charge, "Fill the earth and subdue it" (Gen. 1:28). From the white perspective, that was precisely what Native American populations had never done.

In 1845, the year that O'Sullivan proclaimed his doctrine of manifest destiny, a writer in O'Sullivan's paper, *The New York Morning News*, made this point crystal clear. "There is in fact," he wrote, "no such thing as title to the wild lands of the new world, except that which actual possession gives. They belong to whoever will redeem them from the Indian and the desert, and subjugate them to the use of man."[27] One must note in this statement not only the appeal to possession and redemption of the land, but also the implicit judgment that Native Americans were not men. That, of course, was precisely the assumption that many white Americans made.

Throughout the century, many whites took up the refrain that those who subdued the earth were entitled to own the land. Senator Thomas Hart Benton of Missouri, for example, argued that the claim that white settlers placed on the land was far superior to all other claims since whites "used it according to the intentions of the CREATOR." Likewise, William Henry Harrison, noted Indian fighter, governor of the Indiana territory, and finally president of the United States (1841), pointedly asked, "Is one of the fairest portions of the globe to remain in a state of nature, the haunt of a few wretched savages, when it seems destined by the Creator to give support to a large population and to be the seat of civilization, of science, and of true religion?"[28] Horace Greeley concurred and in 1859 decreed extinction for Native Americans precisely on this ground:

> As I passed over those magnificent bottoms of the Kansas which form reservations of the Delawares, Potawatamies, etc., constituting the very best corn lands on earth, and saw their owners sitting round the floors of their lodges in the height of the planting season, and in as good, bright planting weather as sun and soil ever made, I could not help saying, "These people must die out—there is no help for them. God has given this earth to those who will subdue and cultivate it, and it is vain to struggle against His righteous decree."[29]

And die they did.

Fruits of the Doctrine of Manifest Destiny

Manifest destiny ultimately meant the virtual extermination of Native American peoples, and no one contributed more to that process than Andrew Jackson, president of the United States from 1829 to 1837. Long before he became president, Jackson had made a name for himself as an Indian fighter.

In the Battle of Horseshoe Bend in 1814, Jackson's troops killed eight hundred Creeks. According to historian David E. Stannard, Jackson personally "supervised the mutilation of [their] corpses—the bodies of men, women, and children that he and his men had massacred—cutting off their noses to count and preserve a record of the dead, slicing long strips of flesh from their bodies to tan and turn into bridle reins."[30] Another historian, Howard Zinn, reports that Jackson then "got himself appointed treaty commissioner and dictated a treaty which took away half the land of the Creek nation."[31] Then, in 1818, Jackson's troops inflicted a devastating defeat on the Seminoles (Creek refugees), thereby preparing the way for Florida to become a territory of the United States in 1821.

Once in the presidency, Jackson announced a virtual war on Native Americans everywhere, and Congress immediately approved the Indian Removal Act. Under Jackson's leadership, the United States entered into some ninety-four removal treaties with various tribes. By 1835, Jackson announced that Indian removal was well under way and, in many instances, practically complete.

When he learned of Jackson's policy of Indian removal, an aged Creek named Speckled Snake responded: "Our great father . . . said much; but it all meant nothing, but 'move a little farther; you are too near me.' I have heard a great many talks from our great father, and they all begun and ended the same."[32]

It must be granted that all of this occurred several years before John L. O'Sullivan gave the doctrine of manifest destiny a quasi-official status through his editorials in the *New York Morning News* and the *Democratic Review*. Yet, because the myths we have discussed in this book were so powerful in the early nineteenth century, and because westward expansion seemed so inevitable, the doctrine of manifest destiny was written on the hearts of most white Americans long before O'Sullivan put that doctrine into words.

In that context, two clashes between whites and Native Americans are especially noteworthy. The first such clash, the Black Hawk War, occurred in the state of Illinois and the Wisconsin territory. Shortly after the War of 1812, white settlers flooded into those regions. Many Sauk and Fox fled west, but one Native American leader, Chief Black Hawk, refused to run. In time, he established alliances with other tribes and, together, they waged war on the expanding white settlements. The tribes who joined Black Hawk in this effort included the Winnebagos, the Potawatomis, and the Kickapoos.

When Andrew Jackson and the United States Congress sought to drive these tribes from their lands in the early 1830s, they naturally resisted. The resulting Black Hawk War raged from April to August 1832. When finally they were unable to continue their resistance, the Indians fled into Wisconsin territory with the U.S. Army in hot pursuit. When the Indians attempted to cross the Mississippi River, the army massacred warriors, women, and children, thereby ending the Black Hawk War.

Another important clash occurred between whites and the Cherokee nation in Georgia and North Carolina. The Cherokees believed that if they adopted the ways of the whites, their homes would be safe. Accordingly, they built settlements that resembled towns of white people, adopted ownership of private property, became artisans and craftspersons, invented a written language, adopted a written constitution, established a formal government that resembled that of the whites, welcomed Christian missionaries, and published a newspaper called the *Cherokee Phoenix*. They even adopted the practice of enslaving blacks, thereby confirming the lament of Black Hawk that "we were becoming like them [the whites]" in ways that Native Americans would later regret.

When gold was discovered on Cherokee lands, none of their efforts made any difference. Perhaps 40,000 white settlers initially swarmed over Cherokee lands.[33] They confiscated farms and killed the game. Soon the Cherokees faced mass starvation. Still, the Cherokees determined to resist. They appealed to a 1791 treaty with the United States, placing the Cherokees under the protection of the federal government and stipulating that whites would never hunt on their lands or even enter their country without a passport. For all practical purposes, they claimed, theirs was an independent nation whose rights were being violated.

President Jackson responded in his "Message to Congress on Indian Removal" in 1830 by pointing out to the Cherokees the advantages of their removal to western lands. For whites, he said, their removal "will place a dense and civilized population in large tracts of country now occupied by a few savage hunters." For the Cherokees, it will "perhaps cause them, gradually, under the protection of the Government and through the influence of good counsels, to cast off their savage habits and become an interesting, civilized, and Christian community."[34] Here was the doctrine of manifest destiny, couched in religious language and articulated long before John L. O'Sullivan made that term a household word.

The truth is, in an effort to dispossess the Cherokees, the government had encouraged white settlers and gold diggers to squat on Cherokee lands. Soon the state of Georgia passed its own laws, severely restricting the Cherokee people. The law provided for confiscation of Cherokee lands, put an end to the independent government the Cherokees had created, barred any Cherokee from testifying in court against any white person, and prohibited the Cherokees from mining any gold found on their own land.

When three white Christian missionaries took the side of the Cherokees and protested plans for their removal, state troops arrested them. The missionaries appealed their case to the Supreme Court of the United States. The Court, led by Chief Justice John Marshall, ruled that Georgia laws violated the Cherokees' treaty with the United States. When Andrew Jackson learned of the Court's ruling, he remarked, "John Marshall has made his decision, now let him enforce it."[35] Obviously, the Court had no power to enforce its own decisions. In effect, President Jackson had granted whites the right to continue their illegal incursion into Cherokee lands.

The federal government then drew up a treaty. Federal officials knew that none of the Cherokee leaders would sign a treaty that would virtually give away their lands. So they arrested tribal leaders and held them in jail while negotiating with a small group of compliant Cherokees.

Finally, the "Trail of Tears" began, a trail that led to Indian Territory in what would eventually become the state of Oklahoma. General Winfield Scott directed the operation. James Mooney later interviewed participants in that operation and wrote the following description:

> Under Scott's orders the troops were disposed at various points throughout the Cherokee country, where stockade forts were erected for gathering in and holding the Indians preparatory to removal. From these, squads of troops were sent to search out with rifle and bayonet every small cabin hidden away in the coves or by the sides of mountain streams, to seize and bring in as prisoners all the occupants, however or wherever they might be found. Families at dinner were startled by the sudden gleam of bayonets in the doorway and rose up to be driven with blows and oaths along the weary miles of trail that led to the stockade. Men were seized in their fields or going along the road, women were taken from their wheels and children from their play. In many cases, on turning for one last look as they crossed the ridge, they saw their homes in flames, fired by the lawless rabble that followed on the heels of the soldiers to loot and pillage. . . . A Georgia volunteer, afterward a colonel in the Confederate service, said: "I fought through the civil war and have seen men shot to pieces and slaughtered by thousands, but the Cherokee removal was the cruelest work I ever knew."[36]

David Stannard describes in numerical terms the results of the assault on the Cherokee civilization:

> All told, by the time it was over, more than 8000 Cherokee men, women, and children died as a result of their expulsion from their homeland. That is, about half of what then remained of the Cherokee nation was liquidated under Presidential directive, a death rate similar to that of other southeastern peoples who had undergone the same process—the Creeks and the Seminoles in particular.

... And all these massacres of Indians took place, of course, only after many years of preliminary slaughter, from disease and military assault, that already had reduced these peoples' populations down to a fragment of what they had been prior to the coming of the Europeans.[37]

Andrew Jackson's Indian Removal Act of 1830 was only the beginning of the organized assault on Native American populations, informed by the premises of manifest destiny. In 1861 General James Carleton finally subdued the Navajos of the American Southwest. Reflecting on their removal, Carleton gloated,

> The exodus of this whole people from the land of their fathers is not only an interesting but a touching sight. They have fought us gallantly for years on years; they have defended their mountains and their stupendous canyons with a heroism which any people might be proud to emulate; but when at length, they found it was their destiny, too, as it had been that of their brethren, tribe after tribe, away back toward the rising of the sun, to give way to the insatiable progress of our race, they threw down their arms, and, as brave men entitled to our admiration and respect, have come to us with confidence in our magnanimity.[38]

Systematic attempts to subdue Native American populations continued throughout the nineteenth century. Finally, in 1890, at Wounded Knee, South Dakota, a tragedy occurred that marked their final defeat. A young Paiute named Wovoka, living in western Nevada, announced in 1888 a new religion that focused on a special ritual called the Ghost Dance. According to Wovoka, if Indians danced the Ghost Dance long enough and hard enough, the Messiah would come, whites would die, Indian ancestors would rise from their graves, and the land would be as it was before the whites ever arrived.

Nothing in the Ghost Dance religion suggested violence. In fact, proponents of this new faith taught just the opposite. The dance made guns, knives, and weapons of all kinds superfluous. Further, Wovoka taught that if the dancers wore certain sacred garments, they would be protected from all harm, including the bullets fired from the guns of the whites.

Nonetheless, government officials saw the Ghost Dance as a major threat, especially when Ghost Dance fever seized the imaginations of Native Americans throughout the west, especially the Sioux. The government therefore dispatched soldiers to disarm the Indians and to put a stop to the dance.

They arrested Big Foot, a Sioux suspected of promoting interest in the dance and disturbing the peace. They took Big Foot, along with 120 men and 230 women and children, to a cavalry tent camp on Wounded Knee Creek. There they began to disarm the Indians. When one of the Sioux accidentally fired his rifle, nervous soldiers repeatedly fired into the crowd of Indians, killing 350 Sioux men, women, and children. Many died instantly. Others died from their wounds only later.

The soldiers took the bodies of the dead and the wounded to an Episcopal mission. As Dee Brown tells the story, "It was the fourth day after Christmas in the Year of Our Lord 1890. When the first torn and bleeding bodies were carried into the candlelit church, those who were conscious could see Christmas greenery hanging from the open rafters. Across the chancel from above the pulpit was strung a crudely lettered banner: PEACE ON EARTH, GOOD WILL TO MEN."[39]

A Native American Critique

Black Elk, a Sioux who witnessed these events, later reflected on what his people had lost:

> You have noticed that everything an Indian does is in a circle, and that is because the Power of the World always works in circles, and everything tries to be round. In the old days when we were a strong and happy people, all our power came to us from the sacred hoop of the nation, and so long as the hoop was unbroken, the people flourished. . . . But the Wasichus (whites) have put us in these square boxes. Our power is gone and we are dying, for the power is not in us any more.
>
> I did not know then how much was ended. When I look back now from this high hill of my old age, I can still see the butchered women and children lying heaped and scattered all along the crooked gulch as plain as when I saw them with eyes still young. And I can see that something else died there in the bloody mud, and was buried in the blizzard. A people's dream died there. It was a beautiful dream . . . the nation's hoop is broken and scattered. There is no center any longer, and the sacred tree is dead.[40]

Other Native Americans reflected on comparable events. After federal troops had subdued the Native American alliance in the Black Hawk War, Chief Black Hawk made a speech. He spoke of the "last sun that shone on Black Hawk":

> He is now a prisoner to the white men. . . . He has done nothing for which an Indian ought to be ashamed. He has fought for his countrymen, the squaws and papooses, against white men, who came, year after year, to cheat them and take away their lands. You know the cause of our making war. It is known to all white men. They ought to be ashamed of it. The white men despise the Indians, and drive them from their homes. But the Indians are not deceitful. The white men speak bad of the Indian and look at him spitefully. But the Indian does not tell lies; Indians do not steal.

An Indian, who is as bad as the white men, could not live in our nation; he would be put to death, and eat up by the wolves. The white men . . . deal in false actions. . . . We told them to let us alone, and keep away from us; but they followed on, and beset our paths, and they coiled themselves among us, like the snake. They poisoned us by their touch. We were not safe. We lived in danger. We were becoming like them, hypocrites and liars, adulterers, lazy drones, all talkers, and no workers. . . .

The white men do not scalp the head; but they do worse—they poison the heart. . . . Farewell, my nation! Black-hawk tried to save you. . . . He can do no more. He is near his end. His sun is setting, and he will rise no more. Farewell to Black Hawk.[41]

In 1854 a Mahican named John Quinney addressed the citizens of Reidsville, New York, in a speech reminiscent of Frederick Douglass's oration, "What, to the Slave, Is the Fourth of July?" delivered two years earlier. "It may appear . . . a singular taste for me, an Indian," Quinney began,

to take an interest in the triumphal days of a people who occupy, by conquest or have usurped, the possessions of my fathers and have laid and carefully preserved a train of terrible miseries to end when my race ceased to exist. . . .

It is curious, the history of my tribe, in its decline, in the last two centuries and a half. Nothing that deserved the name of purchase was made. . . .

The Indians were informed, in many instances, that they were selling one piece of land when they were conveying another and much larger limits. Should a particular band, for purposes of hunting or fishing, for a time leave its usual place of residence, the land was said to be abandoned, and the Indian claim extinguished. To legalize and confirm titles thus acquitted, laws and edicts were subsequently passed, and these laws were said then to be, and are now called, justice.

Oh, what mockery to confound justice with law! . . .

Let it not surprise you, my friends, when I say that the spot upon which I stand has never been rightly purchased or obtained. . . .

My friends, your Holy Book, the Bible, teaches us that individual offenses are punished in an existence—when time shall be no more—and the annals of the earth are equally instructive that national wrongs are avenged, and national crimes atoned for in this world to which alone the conformation of existence adapts them.

For myself and for my tribe I ask for justice—I believe it will sooner or later occur, and may the Great Spirit enable me to die in hope.[42]

An African American Critique

It is telling that many African Americans made common cause with Native Americans in their struggle against America's manifest destiny. After all, having been denied their "unalienable rights" for so many years, blacks were uniquely situated to unmask the "myths American lives by" and the doctrine of manifest destiny that those myths had helped produce.

After the Sioux and their Cheyenne allies completely annihilated Colonel George A. Custer and his men at the Battle of Little Big Horn on June 25, 1876, few blacks in the country felt remorse. Only three weeks after that event, black Christians gathered at Bethel Church in Philadelphia and heard the Reverend B. T. Tanner rebuke not only Custer but also the United States government. "By the sacred obligation of treaty," Tanner began, "no white man had any right or business to the Black Hill country. It belongs to the Sioux, and is guaranteed him by the nation." As a result, Tanner thought, making war on the Sioux made no sense at all. "The thing to do is not to fight him, but to secure him his rights."

Regarding Custer, Tanner said,

> Of all our military captains, [he] was the one who took pleasure in the sword. He was the *beau sabreur* of our Army and with joy did he unsheathe it to strike down the "red nagurs" of the Far West—the "red nagurs," as the men of his command felt free to call the Indians in his presence. Custer hated the Indians, as he hated any man of color. . . .
>
> Of course, we gathered here today do not feel as the nation feels, nor can we—nor can any Negro. Does one say he does? He is either a fool or hypocrite. . . . Have we tears to shed—and we have—we shed them for the scores and hundreds of our people who die violently every day in the South. Have we a heart to bleed, it is rather for our brothers cowardly assaulted and more cowardly riddled with Southern bullets. It cannot be that all the blood shedding is to be on one side.[43]

Twenty-three years later, another African American reflected on another military campaign prompted in large part by the doctrine of manifest destiny: the Spanish American War. African Americans were able to expose the myths that sustained that engagement just as they had exposed the myths that sustained the policy of Indian removal.

In an address delivered in 1899 to the New England Conference of the African Methodist Episcopal Church, D. P. Brown roundly criticized America's involvement in the war. The United States fought this war, he said, "not so much in the interest of humanity as . . . for territorial expansion—a war to open up to this country greater commercial interest and advantages." Brown thought it hard to believe "that a government which had shown so little concern for the lives and liberties of ten millions of its most loyal citizens should so suddenly become interested in and imbued with a love of liberty for our brothers in black in another country."

Then Brown issued a call for resistance:

Let us speak out, in no uncertain language, and enter our protest against this further murdering of an inoffensive people in the Philippines, struggling for their independence. Let us protest against this sham of taking to these people the Christian religion and civilization, with the Bible in one hand, and the bayonet and torch in the other. Until this government shall have demonstrated its ability or willingness to protect the humblest of its citizens at home, in all the enjoyment of all his rights under the law, it is the duty of every black man to protest, even with his vote, against any further expansion or extending its weakness over other black people beyond the seas.[44]

The American Dream

By the early twentieth century, white Americans found a fresh way of describing the Myth of the Millennial Nation. They called it "the American Dream."

If the doctrine of manifest destiny had turned the millennial vision outward, inspiring the acquisition of both land and opportunity for economic investment abroad, the American Dream turned the millennial vision inward, inspiring never-before-imagined visions of opportunity for American citizens within the borders of the United States. These two visions—manifest destiny and the American Dream—were closely related, for the opportunities available to American citizens at home depended in part on economic expansion abroad—a point considered in the next chapter on American capitalism.

In 1931, historian James Truslow Adams popularized the phrase, *American Dream*, which he defined as "a dream of a social order in which each man and each woman shall be able to attain to the fullest stature of which they are innately capable . . . regardless of the fortuitous circumstances of birth or position." Adams recognized that the American Dream had been a dream of material plenty. But, he wrote, "it has been much more than that. . . . It has been a dream of being able to grow to fullest development as man and woman . . ., unrepressed by social orders which had developed for the benefit of classes rather than for the simple human being of any and every class."[45]

It goes without saying that in 1931, when Adams wrote those words, the American Dream was a white dream with little or no relevance to people of color. By 1957, some blacks worried that whites might be willing to sacrifice the lives of billions of people—especially people of color—in order to protect their Dream. "What I dread," wrote Richard Wright,

is that the Western white man, confronted with an implacably militant Communism on the one hand, and with a billion and a half colored people gripped by surging tides of nationalist fanaticism on the other, will feel that only a vengeful unleashing of atom and hydrogen bombs can make him feel secure. I dread that there will be an attempt at burning up millions of people to make the world safe for the "white man's" conception of existence.[46]

It is true that Martin Luther King Jr. believed that when young blacks—people he called the "disinherited children of God"—engaged in lunch-counter sit-ins, "they were in reality standing up for the best in the American dream." What was best in that dream, King believed, was equal opportunity.[47]

But by 2015, after scores of police killings of unarmed blacks in America's streets, Ta-Nehisi Coates reflected on what the American Dream might mean for African Americans in the early years of the twenty-first century. "I have seen that dream all my life," Coates wrote:

It is Memorial Day cookouts, block associations, and driveways. The Dream is treehouses and the Cub Scouts. The Dream smells like peppermint but tastes like strawberry shortcake. And for so long I have wanted to escape into the Dream to fold my country over my head like a blanket. But this has never been an option because the Dream rests on our backs, the bedding made from our bodies.[48]

Indeed, Coates called American whites "the Dreamers"—people who lived in "that other world . . . [which was] suburban and endless, organized around pot roasts, blueberry pies, fireworks, ice cream sundaes, immaculate bathrooms, and small toy trucks that were loosed in wooded backyards with streams and glens."

Coates's notion of whites as "Dreamers" picks up on a major theme of this chapter—the American sense of historylessness. As I have noted repeatedly in this book, white Americans have always believed that the United States stands with one foot planted firmly in the golden age of creation and the other planted firmly in the golden age to come. For that reason, history becomes irrelevant, becomes water under the great American bridge. And divorced from a sense of history, the only world in which white Americans can possibly live is a world shaped by dreams and not by the realities of human avarice, greed, and suffering.

Coates understood this well and spoke of the American way of forgetting. "The forgetting is habit," he wrote, "is yet another necessary component of the Dream":

They have forgotten the scale of theft that enriched them in slavery; the terror that allowed them, for a century, to pilfer the vote; the segregationist policy that gave them their suburbs. They have forgotten, because to remember would tumble them out of the beautiful Dream and force them to live down here with us, down here in the world. . . . To awaken them is to reveal that they are an empire of humans and, like all empires of humans, are built on the destruction of the body.[49]

Coates believed "that the Dreamers, at least the Dreamers of today, would rather live white than live free."[50] And because the Dreamers committed themselves to that Dream above all else and because they built that Dream on the backs of people of color, Coates counseled his son to join the struggle that had defined American blacks from the time the slave ships first arrived on American shores. "But do not struggle for the Dreamers," he wrote. "Hope for them. Pray for them, if you are so moved. But do not pin your struggle on their conversion."

Then, in words that echo Richard Wright's fear, expressed during the Cold War and noted above, that whites might "attempt at burning up millions of people to make the world safe for . . . [their] conception of existence," Coates added, "The Dreamers will have to learn to struggle themselves, to understand that the field for their Dream, the stage where they have painted themselves white, is the deathbed of us all."[51] In this scenario, the American Dream has become a global nightmare, and instead of a golden age, the Millennial Nation has unleashed Armageddon.

Conclusions

This chapter began with a consideration of the fourth American myth—the Myth of the Millennial Nation. It is clear that apart from the other myths I have considered in this book, the notion of America as a millennial nation had no meaning at all. Put another way, the myths of America as Chosen Nation, Nature's Nation, and Christian Nation gave to the millennial vision whatever content it had. The millennium, therefore, would be a time when God's chosen people would liberate and enlighten all the peoples of the earth, when Protestant Christianity would reign supreme, and when all things would be conformed to the standards of "Nature and Nature's God."

Though Americans imagined it a universal vision, they nonetheless understood it in distinctly white and Eurocentric terms. The whiteness that colored that vision colored as well the nineteenth-century doctrine of Manifest Destiny and the twentieth-century notion of the American Dream. And because the Dreamers dreamed in white and not in color, they built a nation that, for the most part, excluded people of color from the bounty that dream envisioned.

I turn next to the myths that surround the free enterprise system in the United States.

Notes

1. The standard account of the millennial role of the United States is Ernest Lee Tuveson, *Redeemer Nation: The Idea of America's Millennial Role* (Chicago: University of Chicago Press, 1968).

2. Both before and after the eighteenth century, many Christians embraced an *amillennial* understanding of end times, that is, a view of the end that has no place for the millennium at all.

3. Nathan O. Hatch, *The Sacred Cause of Liberty: Republican Thought and the Millennium in Revolutionary New England* (New Haven: Yale University Press, 1977), 29–54.

4. Quoted in Tuveson, *Redeemer Nation*, 25.

5. Ezra Stiles, "The United States Elevated to Glory and Honour," 1783, in Conrad Cherry, ed., *God's New Israel: Religious Interpretations of American Destiny*, rev. ed. (Chapel Hill: University of North Carolina Press, 1998), 90.

6. Lyman Beecher, "A Plea for the West," 1835, in Cherry, *God's New Israel*, 123.

7. Beecher, "The Memory of Our Fathers," a sermon delivered at Plymouth, Massachusetts, December 22, 1827, in Winthrop Hudson, ed., *Nationalism and Religion in America* (New York: Harper and Row, 1970), 99, 101–102.

8. Beecher, "A Plea for the West," 1835, in *God's New Israel*, 122–123, 130.

9. Beecher, "Memory of Our Fathers," 104–105.

10. Ibid.

11. George Bush, "The Possibility of a New World Order," in *Vital Speeches of the Day* 57 (May 15, 1991): 450–452.

12. On manifest destiny, see Albert K. Weinberg, *Manifest Destiny: A Study of Nationalist Expansion in American History* (1935; reprint, Chicago: Quadrangle Books, 1963); Frederick Merk, *Manifest Destiny and Mission in American History* (New York: Alfred A. Knopf, 1963); and Anders Stephanson, *Manifest Destiny: American Expansion and the Empire of Right* (New York: Hill and Wang, 1995).

13. "Annexation," *Democratic Review* (New York), July-August 1845, 5.

14. John L. O'Sullivan, quoted in *New York Morning News*, December 27, 1845.

15. H. V. Johnson, *The Congressional Globe*, 30th Congress, 1st sess. (Washington, D.C.: Blair and Rives, 1848), Appendix, 379; and William McKinley in *Congressional Record*, 55th Congress, 3d session, 2518, cited in Weinberg, *Manifest Destiny*, 294.

16. Emily S. Rosenberg, *Spreading the American Dream: American Economic and Cultural Expansion, 1890–1945* (New York: Hill and Wang, 1982), 44.

17. Josiah Strong cited in Conrad Cherry, ed., *God's New Israel*, 119; Charles S. Olcott, *The Life of William McKinley* (Boston: Houghton Mifflin, 1916), 2:109–111; and Albert Beveridge, "For the Greater Republic, Not for Imperialism," an address given February 15, 1899, in Hudson, *Nationalism and Religion in America*, 117–119.

18. John Winthrop, "A Modell of Christian Charity" (1630), in Cherry, *God's New Israel*, 37–41.

19. Carl L. Becker, *The Heavenly City of the Eighteenth-Century Philosophers* (New Haven: Yale University Press, 1932), 103–104.

20. George T. Northrup, trans., *Vespucci Reprints, Texts, and Studies*, vol. 5 (Princeton: Princeton University Press, 1916).

21. Cited in Lewis Hanke, *All Mankind Is One: A Study of the Disputation between Bartolome de Las Casas and Juan Gines de Sepulveda in 1550 on the Intellectual and Religious Capacity of the American Indians* (DeKalb: Northern Illinois Press, 1974), 85.

22. Christopher Brooke, *A Poem on the Late Massacre in Virginia, With Particular Mention of Those Men of Note That Suffered in That Disaster* (London, 1622), 22–23.

23. Roger Williams, *A Key into the Language of America* (1643), ed. John Teunissen and Evelyn J. Hinz (Detroit: Wayne State University Press, 1973), 84–85.

24. David Stannard, *American Holocaust: Columbus and the Conquest of the New World* (New York: Oxford University Press, 1992), 120.

25. David Trimble in *The Debates and Proceedings in the Congress of the United States*, 16th Congress, 1st sess. (Washington, D.C.: Gales and Seaton, 1855), col. 1768.

26. *Nashville Republican and State Gazette*, cited in Albert Weinberg, *Manifest Destiny*, 58.

27. *The New York Morning News*, November 15, 1845.

28. For Benton, see *Congressional Globe*, 27th Congress, 3d session, App., 74; for Harrison, see John F. Cade, "Western Opinion and the War of 1812," *Ohio Archaeological and Historical Society Publications* 33 (1924): 435–436, cited in Weinberg, *Manifest Destiny*, 79.

29. Horace Greeley, letter in *New York Tribune*, June 1859, in James Parton, *Life of Andrew Jackson* (New York: Mason Brothers, 1861), 1:401n.

30. Stannard, *American Holocaust*, 121.

31. Howard Zinn, *A People's History of the United States* (New York: Harper Colophon Books, 1980), 127.

32. Speckled Snake (Cherokee), "Response to a Message from President Andrew Jackson Concerning Indian Removal," 1830, in Wayne Moquin with Charles Van Doren, eds., *Great Documents in American Indian History* (New York: Praeger Publishers, 1973), 149.

33. Stannard, *American Holocaust*, 122.

34. President Andrew Jackson, "Message to Congress on Indian Removal," 1830, https://www.ourdocuments.gov/print_friendly.php?flash=false&page=transcript&doc=25&title=Transcript+of+President+Andrew+Jacksons+Message+to+Congress+On+Indian+Removal+%281830%29, accessed July 27, 2017.

35. Cited in Stannard, *American Holocaust*, 122.

36. Ibid., 123.

37. Ibid., 124–125.

38. Cited in Dee Brown, *Bury My Heart at Wounded Knee: An Indian History of the American West* (New York: Bantam Books, 1972), 31.

39. Ibid., 418.

40. John G. Neihardt, *Black Elk Speaks* (New York: Washington Square Press, 1932), 230.

41. Black Hawk (Sac-Potawatomi), "Farewell Speech at Prairie Du Chien, Wisconsin, at the End of the Black Hawk War," August, 1835, in Moquin with Van Doren, eds., *Great Documents in American Indian History*, 154–155.

42. John Quinney (Mahican), "Fourth of July Address at Reidsville, New York," 1854, in Moquin with Van Doren, eds., *Great Documents in American Indian History*, 166–170.

43. B. T. Tanner, "The Sioux's Revenge," 1876, in Philip S. Foner and Robert James Branham, eds., *Lift Every Voice: African American Oratory, 1787–1900* (Tuscaloosa: University of Alabama Press, 1998), 577–578.

44. D. P. Brown, "The State of the Country from a Black Man's Point of View," 1899, in Foner and Branham, eds., *Lift Every Voice*, 891, 896.

45. James Truslow Adams, *Epic of America* (New York: Blue Ribbon Books, 1931), 404–405.

46. Richard Wright, *White Man, Listen!* (New York: HarperPerennial, 1957), 42–43.

47. Martin Luther King Jr., "Letter from a Birmingham Jail," 1963, in *I Have a Dream: Writings and Speeches That Changed the World* (San Francisco: HarperSanFrancisco, 1986), 100.

48. Ta-Nehisi, Coates, *Between the World and Me* (New York: Spiegel and Grau, 2015), 11.

49. Ibid., 143.

50. Ibid., 143.

51. Ibid., 151.

CHAPTER SIX

The Mythic Dimensions of American Capitalism

The Gilded Age

Like the doctrine of manifest destiny, capitalism is not one of the foundational myths under consideration in this text. Yet, as capitalism entrenched itself in American life, it drew its legitimacy from most of the myths considered in this book. White Americans imagined that capitalism was God-ordained, that it reflected the natural order of things, and that it would finally bring about a golden age of peace and prosperity for all humankind.

Capitalism in the United States, however, is unthinkable apart from the myth of White Supremacy, for its inception, growth, and development were built on stolen land and stolen people. As Harvard professor Walter Johnson notes, "The history of capitalism makes no sense separate from the history of the slave trade and its aftermath." If we "begin with the most basic distinction in political economy: the distinction between capital and labor," we quickly realize that "enslaved people were both." Their value on the eve of the Civil War "was equal to all of the capital invested in American railroads, manufacturing, and agricultural land combined."[1] Likewise, capitalism makes no sense apart from vast tracts of land on the North American continent, stolen from their original owners, which became the ground upon which enslaved people toiled.

Later in this chapter we will explore in some detail what capitalism has meant for America's blacks over the course of American history, but first we must explore the evolution of American capitalism in the context of the other Great American Myths.

Capitalism and Nature's Nation

Americans who benefited from the capitalist system could hardly imagine viable alternatives. Because it seemed so natural, so thoroughly in keeping with "the way things were meant to be," it was easy to imagine that the capitalist system was rooted squarely in the self-evident patterns of "Nature and Nature's God." The Myth of Nature's Nation, therefore, probably did more to legitimate American capitalism than any other single factor.

In line with that assumption, D. S. Gregory affirmed in a popular ethics textbook of the 1880s, "The Moral Governor has placed the power of acquisitiveness in man for a good and noble purpose." William Lawrence, the Episcopal bishop of Massachusetts, also placed capitalism in the context of "Nature and Nature's God." "To seek for and earn wealth is a sign of a natural, vigorous, and strong character," he proclaimed. "The search for material wealth is therefore as natural and necessary to the man as is the pushing out of its roots for more moisture and food to the oak." And Charles Conant, the leading economic advisor to the State Department during that same period, judged as fundamentally natural the "irresistible tendency to expansion" that was part and parcel of the capitalist ethos. "Seeking new outlets for American capital and new opportunities for American enterprise," he wrote, was simply "a natural law of economic and race development."[2]

Here one finds a classic example of Carl Becker's claim—noted often in this book—that those who appealed to "Nature and Nature's God" typically found in nature precisely what they wished to find. In the first place, the myth of Nature's Nation was so pervasive and so powerful that virtually every key element of American culture seemed to reflect some self-evident truth. There is more, for the late nineteenth century was the period of the "barons of industry" who engaged in unrestrained and unregulated laissez-faire capitalism and thereby accumulated immense fortunes, often at the expense of their workers. It is little wonder that these barons of industry and those who admired them grounded their defense of capitalism in "Nature and Nature's God."

The Myth of Nature's Nation sustained American capitalism in other ways as well, and I shall return to this theme later in this chapter. But for now, I must explore the myth under which American capitalism first took shelter.

Capitalism and the Chosen Nation

In the years immediately following the American Civil War, American capitalism found its justification in the Myth of the Chosen Nation that had struck a covenant relationship with its God. The context for this development was the Civil War itself.

Backgrounds

Both North and South entered the Civil War convinced that it was God's chosen people, standing in covenant relationship with the Almighty. If its cause was just—and each side believed that it was—then God would surely grant the victory. When the war was over, the North had won the war. Even more important for the purposes of this book, the war had brought to the northern states burgeoning cities, humming factories, and enormous wealth. On the other hand, it brought to the South not only defeat but also grinding poverty that would haunt the South for years to come. In the context of the national covenant, many northerners interpreted both victory and material prosperity as blessings that God had bestowed upon the North, confirming the righteousness of their cause.

At the very same time, two other developments were occurring that have an enormous bearing on this story. First, a few Americans took advantage of the growing industrialization and wealth of the North and amassed immense fortunes—men like J. Pierpont Morgan, Andrew Carnegie, John D. Rockefeller, Cornelius Vanderbilt, Leland Stanford, and Henry Huntington. We know these men—and others like them—as the "barons of industry," the men who formed the vanguard of the Gilded Age.

Second, between the Civil War and 1900, 13.5 million impoverished immigrants came to these shores, where they often faced desperate economic conditions. In order to earn any livelihood at all, they typically accepted factory positions in which they worked long hours for subsistence wages under extraordinarily poor working conditions. Often, the factories were owned by one of the barons of industry. There was developing in America during this period, then, a great disparity between the few who were extraordinarily wealthy and the masses who were extremely poor and who found themselves dependent on the rich for their very existence.

The Gospel of Wealth

If many northerners viewed the wealth of the northern states as God's reward for national righteousness, it was a very short step to apply that understanding to the wealth of individuals. Many, therefore, came to view the wealth of the barons of industry as God's reward for individual righteousness. Likewise, if many viewed southern poverty as God's curse on the South for the institution of slavery, they also came to view the poverty of the masses in northern cities as God's curse for laziness and immorality.

Put another way, an ideology was rapidly developing in the northern states that equated wealth with righteousness and poverty with sin. In the context of the national myths described in this book, how could it have been otherwise? If America offered everyone an equal opportunity, as was widely believed, and if capitalism was ordained of God and rooted in nature, then those who failed to excel in this system had only themselves to blame. This ideology formed the substance of the Gospel of Wealth that dominated the thinking of privileged people in the northern states from the close of the Civil War to roughly 1900.

Of the thousands of examples that might be offered depicting that sort of thinking, none is more pointedly clear than a sermon preached in 1901 by the Reverend William Lawrence, the Episcopal bishop of Massachusetts. There, Lawrence made this judgment:

> In the long run, it is only to the man of morality that wealth comes. . . . Put two men in adjoining fields, one man strong and normal, the other weak and listless. One picks up his spade, turns over the earth, and works till sunset. The other turns over a few clods, gets a drink from the spring, takes a nap, and loafs back to his work. In a few years one will be rich for his needs, and the other a pauper dependent on the first, and growling at his prosperity.
>
> Put ten thousand immoral men to live and work in one fertile valley and ten thousand moral men to live and work in the next valley, and the question is soon answered as to who wins the material wealth. Godliness is in league with riches.[3]

Other ministers made the same judgment. Russell Conwell, a prominent Baptist preacher from Philadelphia, delivered his classic sermon, "Acres of Diamonds," more than five thousand times throughout the country and saw it issued in print time and again. Among the best-known apologists for the Gospel of Wealth, Conwell advised his listeners, "I say that you ought to get rich, and it is your duty to get rich. How many of my pious brethren say to me, 'Do you, a Christian minister, spend your time going up and down the country advising young people to get rich, to get money?' 'Yes, of Course I do.' They say, 'Isn't that awful! Why don't you preach the gospel instead of preaching about man's making money?' 'Because to make money honestly is to preach the gospel.' That is the reason." Conwell then concluded with a line that reflected the very essence of the Gospel of Wealth: "The men who get rich may be the most honest men you find in the community."[4]

Only five years after the Civil War, the noted preacher Henry Ward Beecher—son of the famed Lyman Beecher and the man whom Sidney E.

Mead described as "that magnificent weathervane of respectable opinion"[5]—preached a sermon that turned the traditional Christian message upside down. Many Christians believe, Beecher affirmed, that virtue requires having and using little. "Far from it. As you go toward the savage state, you go away from complexity, from multitudinous power, down toward simplicity, and when you come to the lowest state—to the simplicity of men that wear skins and leather apparel, and live in huts and caves—you come to the fool's ideal of prosperity."

In Beecher's judgment, the creation of wealth was not incompatible with genuine Christianity; to the contrary, the two went hand in hand: "I affirm that the preaching of the Gospel to the heathen will be invalid and void if it does not make them active workmen, and teach them how to make money. And although the evidences of the conversion of the individual are not that he knows how to make money; yet in a nation no religion is a good religion that does not teach industry, and the thrift which comes from industry." The Myth of White Supremacy implicitly resided in the counsel Beecher offered his white audience who, Beecher claimed, must liberate "the heathen" from "huts and caves," teach them to become "active workmen," and encourage them to practice "industry" and "thrift." Beecher therefore offered this advice:

> So then, I am not afraid to rejoice. Get rich, if you can. . . . And when you shall have amassed wealth, it will be God's power, if you are wise to use it, by which you can make your home happier, the community more refined, and the whole land more civilized.
>
> And, on the whole, the general tendency of wealth is such as to lead me today to thank God for the increasing wealth of America. May it ever be sanctified. May it ever learn nobler uses, and aspire higher and higher, until the symbolism of the heavenly state, where the very streets are paved with gold, shall be reproduced in the realities and actualities of our life here on earth.[6]

Beecher summed up his philosophy, and that of thousands of his peers, with this simple judgment: "The general truth will stand, that no man in this land suffers from poverty unless it be more than his fault—unless it be his sin."[7]

All these passages reflect the same fundamental assumption: the righteousness of a single individual would win God's favor in the form of material blessings, while poverty was a divine curse that a person brought on himself by his laziness, drunkenness, and immorality.

One finds here a significant transformation of the Myth of the Chosen Nation. The older myth spoke of covenant for the *entire nation*. The newer myth spoke of covenant for the *individual*. The older myth persisted, to be sure, but was now supplemented by a radically individualized understanding. In the context of capitalism and the accumulation of wealth, therefore, we can rightly speak of the Myth of Chosen People as opposed to the Myth of the Chosen Nation.

Social Darwinism

The myth of Chosen People underwent another modification as well, this time in the context of Darwin's theory of evolution. Darwin published his *Origin of Species* in 1859, arguing that nature operates on the principle of the survival of the fittest. Fascinated by this idea, an Englishman named Herbert Spencer became "the greatest popularizer of Darwinian notions in both Britain and America."[8]

For my purposes, it is important to understand that as Spencer popularized Darwin's theory of evolution, he did so with an important twist. If Darwin had advocated *biological* evolution, Spencer advocated *social* evolution, or what commentators often call *social Darwinism*. Just like biological organisms, Spencer said, society also passes through the process of natural selection. And the principle of "the survival of the fittest" applies to cultures and classes of people just as it applies to biological entities.

No one in America took over the theme of social Darwinism more effectively than did Andrew Carnegie, a man who had risen from the post of bobbin boy to become one of the most powerful of all the barons of industry in the late nineteenth century. In 1889 Carnegie published in the *North American Review* an important article that he entitled simply "Wealth." There he employed the Spencerian theme of "survival of the fittest" to justify "great inequality of environment [and] the concentration of business in the hands of a few."

Carnegie's essay was influential, to be sure, but to a large extent, his essay only reflected and put into words a set of perspectives already assumed by many in the privileged classes in the United States. For this reason, we should hear him at length:

> It is . . . essential for the progress of the race, that the houses of some should be homes for all that is highest and best in literature and the arts, and for all the refinements of civilization, rather than that none should be so. . . .
>
> While the law [of competition] may be sometimes hard for the individual, it is best for the race, because it insures the survival of the fittest in every department. We accept and welcome, therefore, as conditions to which we must accommodate ourselves, great inequality of environment [and] the concentration of business in the hands of a few. . . .

The Socialist or Anarchist who seeks to overturn present conditions is to be regarded as attacking the foundation upon which civilization itself rests. . . . One who studies this subject will soon be brought face to face with the conclusion that upon the sacredness of property civilization itself depends. . . .

Individualism will continue, but the millionaire will be but a trustee for the poor; intrusted for a season with a great part of the increased wealth of the community, but administering it for the community far better than it could or would have done for itself. . . .

Such, in my opinion, is the true Gospel concerning Wealth, obedience to which is destined some day to solve the problem of the Rich and the Poor, and to bring "Peace on earth, among men Good Will."[9]

Central to Carnegie's analysis was his contention regarding the "sacredness of property"—clearly a way of claiming that capitalism was divinely ordained. Beyond this, he grounded his assessment in a number of the myths I have already considered in this book. First, the Myth of Chosen People is obviously at work here, since, as Carnegie put it, "it is . . . essential for the progress of the race, that the houses of some should be homes . . . for all the refinements of civilization, rather than that none should be so."

Second, the Myth of Nature's Nation is fundamental to Carnegie's assessment on two counts. First, he speaks of capitalism as if it were grounded in an immutable law of nature that he calls the "law of competition." At this point, his analysis of this law of competition is worth hearing: "The price which society pays for the law of competition, like the price it pays for cheap comforts and luxuries, is . . . great; but the advantages of this law are also greater still, for it is to this law that we owe our wonderful material development, which brings improved conditions in its train. But, whether the law be benign or not, we must say of it: It is here; we cannot evade it; no substitutes for it have been found."

The Myth of Nature's Nation is fundamental to Carnegie's analysis in another way as well, for he speaks of the doctrine of the "survival of the fittest" as if it also were an immutable law of nature. Indeed, Carnegie collapsed the Myth of Nature's Nation into the Myth of the Chosen People, since those chosen by wealth were chosen not only by God but also by nature, that is, by the process of natural selection and the principle of the survival of the fittest.

Third, Carnegie's assessment reaches deeply into the long-standing notion of America as a Millennial Nation, although Carnegie's statement contains an important modification of that myth.

During the Great Awakening, as noted in the previous chapter, the emergence of the millennial age depended on faithfulness to the sovereignty of

God. During the French and Indian War, it depended to a very great extent on the sovereignty of Protestantism. During the Revolutionary period, it depended on the sovereignty of the people with their "unalienable rights." Now, in the period of the Gospel of Wealth, it depended on the principle of competition that stood at the heart of the capitalist system, on "the survival of the fittest in every department," and on "the concentration of business in the hands of a few."

Obedience to these principles, Carnegie believed, would "solve the problem of the Rich and the Poor" and "bring 'Peace on earth, among men Good Will.'" It is clear that Carnegie anticipated a millennium or a golden age yet to come. The millennium he anticipated, however, was a secular millennium, now divorced from the Christian faith and completely dependent instead on sound business strategies.

Carnegie's statement, then, expresses the full meaning of the Gospel of Wealth as it emerged in the late nineteenth century. The rich were chosen for privilege and for wealth, and they were chosen twice, not once: God had chosen them because they were virtuous, while nature had chosen them because they were fit. At the same time, the poor received a double curse: God had cursed them for their immorality while nature had cursed them because of their inability to compete in the arena of American capitalism.

Manifest Destiny in the Thought of Josiah Strong

This understanding of the Gospel of Wealth also held great implications for the doctrine of manifest destiny. The Gospel of Wealth, interpreted through the lens of social Darwinism, now served to justify American expansion around the globe at the expense of the smaller and less well-developed nations of the earth.

No one articulated this vision more cogently than Josiah Strong in his best-selling text *Our Country*, published in 1885:

> The unoccupied arable lands of the earth are limited and will soon be taken. . . . Then will the world enter upon a new stage of its history—*the final competition of races, for which the Anglo-Saxon is being schooled.* . . . Then this race of unequaled energy, with all the majesty of numbers and the might of wealth behind it—the representative, let us hope, of the largest liberty, the purest Christianity, the highest civilization—having developed peculiarly aggressive traits calculated to impress its institutions upon mankind will spread itself over the earth. . . . Can anyone doubt that the result of this competition of races will . . . be "the survival of the fittest"? . . . Nothing can save the inferior race but a steady and pliant assimilation. . . . The contest is not one of arms, but of vitality and

civilization. . . . Is there reasonable room for doubt that this race . . . is destined to dispossess many weaker races, assimilate others, and mold the remainder, until in a very true and important sense it has Anglo-Saxonized mankind?[10]

While Strong in this passage affirms the major premise of manifest destiny, he also affirms the major premise of the Myth of White Supremacy. He tells us that the Anglo-Saxon heritage—and by implication, white America as the bearer of that heritage—embodies "the largest liberty, the purest Christianity, [and] the highest civilization." For this reason, it will soon "impress its institutions upon mankind" and "spread itself over the earth."

This is not the doctrine of manifest destiny as John L. O'Sullivan might have defined it forty years before. Rather, now in 1885, in the light of the evolutionary theories of Darwin and Spencer, Strong has grounded the doctrine of manifest destiny squarely in his convictions on the survival of the fittest. "Can anyone doubt," he asks, "that the result of this competition [of races] will . . . be 'the survival of the fittest'?" And because he believes so strongly in "the survival of the fittest," he is able to affirm his belief in the inevitable destiny of the Anglo-Saxon people. "Is there reasonable room for doubt that this race . . . is destined to dispossess many weaker races, assimilate others, and mold the remainder, until in a very true and important sense it has Anglo-Saxonized mankind?"

Shortly, I shall explore the very concrete ways in which this vision played itself out beyond the borders of the United States. But in the interest of clarity, I must now summarize what I have attempted to say thus far about the mythic dimensions of American capitalism.

In the late nineteenth century, capitalism became shrouded in myth and linked to other mythical dimensions of American culture. First, Americans imagined capitalism ordained of God and grounded squarely in the natural order of things. Second, because of their virtue, God had chosen some to succeed on the capitalist playing field, and because of their sinfulness, He had chosen others to fail. Third, because they were fit, nature had decreed that some would survive in the context of capitalist competition, and because they were "weak and listless," as William Lawrence put it, nature had decreed that others would simply die away. Finally, fidelity to the principle of competition that stood at the heart of the capitalist system would usher in the final golden age and bring peace on earth, good will to men.

This constellation of myths provided privileged and wealthy Americans of the late nineteenth century a virtual mandate to extend their power not only throughout the lands that belonged to the United States, but also throughout the world.

International American Business

During the closing years of the nineteenth century, America fought the Spanish-American War, ostensibly designed to liberate Cuba and the Philippines from the cruel tyranny of the Spanish. Senator James Henderson Berry, however, charged on the floor of the Senate that America had fought the war "on the pretense, it may be, of humanity and Christianity, but behind it all . . . is the desire for trade and commerce."[11]

If anything, Berry understated his case. A desire for trade and commerce was fully evident in American life, to be sure. There was also a growing desire on the part of many Americans to dominate the world economically. Senator Albert Beveridge, for example, proclaimed that "we are enlisted in the cause of American supremacy, which will never end until American commerce has made the conquest of the world." Likewise, J. G. Kitchell observed in his book *American Supremacy* (1901), "Commercially we are breaking into every market in the world. It is a part of our economic development. We are marching fast to the economic supremacy of the world."[12]

When one considers that Beveridge and Kitchell made these statements at a time when Jim Crow segregation ruled the United States, it is clear that "American supremacy" and "economic supremacy" translated seamlessly into the Myth of White Supremacy. Still, this kind of talk sounded singularly un-American, especially in light of the Myth of American Innocence, the theme of the following chapter. In addition, how could Americans speak of "the conquest of the world" and remain faithful to the American Creed? How could they speak of "American supremacy" and affirm at the very same time the equality and unalienable rights that nature had bestowed on *all* human beings?

Americans clearly needed a policy that would promote global expansion and, at the very same time, allow Americans to believe that they were not imperialists but rather the benefactors of all humankind. The truth is that strategy was close at hand.

Indeed, it was part and parcel of the kind of expansion Americans had in mind: economic expansion. An economic conquest of the world depended upon the private sector, not upon government or the military. Government would facilitate commercial expansion by providing financial assistance, by negotiating a reduction of foreign restrictions, and by making it clear to all parties that the American military stood ready to intervene if its business interests should be threatened. America could always defend a military action of this kind as defensive rather than aggressive.[13] In all these ways, the private sector became the vehicle by which the doctrine of manifest destiny was implemented beyond the borders of the United States.

We should not imagine, however, that Americans of that period thought themselves duplicitous in any sense at all. On the one hand, circumstances seemed to demand this sort of economic expansion. As State Department Advisor Charles Conant put it in 1900, "The United States have actually reached, or are approaching, the economic state where . . . outlets are required outside their own boundaries, in order to prevent business depression, idleness, and suffering at home."[14]

On the other hand, the myths that dominated American culture in that period also seemed to justify this sort of expansion. Those myths were implicit both in the doctrine of manifest destiny and in the mandates of American capitalism. Thus, if God had singled out America as his chosen instrument among all the nations of the earth, then America had every right to engage in economic expansion. If God blessed the righteous with wealth and cursed sinners with poverty, then it stood to reason that God *required* economic expansion. If capitalism was rooted in the natural order of things, then American economic expansion partook of the natural order as well. If America was a Christian nation, then the work of economic expansion was an act of Christian charity. If part of the American mission was to hasten the redemption of the world and the final golden age, then economic expansion was, in all likelihood, a significant part of the redemptive process. And driving all these assumptions was the Myth of White Supremacy which both mandated and legitimated America's economic conquest of the world.

Driven by circumstance and justified by myth, therefore, America threw its full weight behind a massive economic expansion that relied almost entirely on the private sector for implementation. As Emily Rosenberg has pointed out,

> Singer produced a huge plant in Scotland, producing machines there for Europe, and set up smaller branches in Canada and Australia. American Tobacco moved into Australia, Japan and Germany to avoid being shut out by tariffs. Western Electric manufactured equipment in Japan after the termination of the unequal treaties in 1899 and the adoption of a protective tariff in 1911. General Electric established associates or subsidiaries in Europe, South Africa, Canada, and Mexico. Westinghouse built huge plants in Russia and Western Europe. Food companies and meat packers such as J. F. Heinz, Armour, Swift, and American Tobacco increasingly processed abroad—closer to potential markets. . . . [And] Parke Davis and other drug companies established plants abroad in order to supply foreign markets unhampered by domestic regulation.

Rosenberg goes on to note that "from 1897 to 1914, American direct investments abroad more than quadrupled, rising from an estimated $634 million to $2.6 billion."[15] In this way, America did precisely what Albert Beveridge had predicted. It embarked upon the economic conquest of the world.

Voices of Protest and Dissent

In the late nineteenth century, therefore, unregulated, laissez-faire capitalism stood at the center of two powerful forces in American life. By virtue of the Gospel of Wealth, Americans sought to justify concentration of both business and riches in the hands of a few. By virtue of the doctrine of manifest destiny, Americans embarked upon the economic conquest of the world. Americans who led lives of privilege typically supported both these developments as well as the capitalist system upon which they fed. On the fringes of that support, however, significant voices of dissent began to be heard.

A Labor Critique

As early as 1840, the New England social crusader Orestes A. Brownson lamented the inequalities that industrial capitalism had brought to American life. In his judgment, "the injustices of capitalism now exceeded those of slavery." For this reason, Brownson worried about the possibility of the "most dreaded of all wars, the war of the poor against the rich."[16]

Had Brownson lived another half-century, he would have witnessed the war that he so much feared. In 1886, the American Federation of Labor called on workers to strike throughout the United States against any company that refused to grant the eight-hour workday. Some 350,000 workers in 11,562 business concerns responded and essentially shut down the country.

The proposal for an eight-hour day was not new. The previous year, in 1885, Albert Parsons and August Spies, anarchist leaders of the Central Labor Union, expressed their frustration with the capitalists who had systematically refused to accommodate labor on this point and called for revolution. "Be it resolved," they wrote, "that we urgently call upon the wage earning class to arm itself in order to be able to put forth against their exploiters such an argument which alone can be effective: Violence. . . . Our war-cry is 'Death to the foes of the human race.'"

In May 1886 police fired into a crowd of strikers who were manning the picket lines at McCormick Harvester Works. The next day, some 3,000 working men and women gathered at Chicago's Haymarket Square. Before the meeting ended, 180 policemen arrived and commanded the crowd to disperse. Suddenly, a bomb exploded. Sixty-six policemen were wounded. Of that number, seven died. With no evidence except their literature and their spoken ideas, the police arrested eight anarchists, four of whom were hanged.[17]

The year 1886—the year of the McCormick Harvester strikes and the Haymarket riots—was a signal year in the history of labor-capital relations in the United States. The 1,400 strikes that occurred that year presented "the signs of a great movement by the class of the unskilled, which had finally risen in rebellion. . . . The movement bore in every way the aspect of a social war."[18]

The next several years witnessed what did, indeed, amount to a bloody war between labor and capital in the United States, involving perhaps millions of workers in thousands of strikes, including the strike at the Carnegie Steel plant at Homestead, Pennsylvania, in 1892 and the strike against the Pullman Palace Car Company just outside Chicago in 1894.

These events speak to us today more loudly than any statement we might invoke from any of the working people of that period. The depth and breadth of those strikes clearly proclaimed that, from the perspective of working people, the "law of competition" was neither sacred nor grounded in the natural order. Far from "solving the problem of the rich and the poor" and bringing in a golden age of peace and justice, unregulated capitalism had created for these workers extraordinary suffering and deprivation.

Many working people especially objected to the "sacredness of private property"—a slogan that Andrew Carnegie had invoked in "Wealth." The workers leveled this objection, not so much in principle, but rather when the capitalists seemed to place property rights above human rights.

In a speech that Jack White made to the judge in a San Diego courtroom in 1912, one can practically feel the pent-up frustration over the issue. A member of the Industrial Workers of the World, White was involved in a free-speech fight and was subsequently arrested. The judge sentenced him to six months in jail on a bread-and-water diet. When the judge asked White if he wished to address the court, White said this:

> The prosecuting attorney, in his plea to the jury, accused me of saying on a public platform at a public meeting, "To hell with the courts, we know what justice is." He told a great truth when he lied, for if he had searched the innermost recesses of my mind he could have found that thought, never expressed by me before, but which I express now, "To hell with your courts, I know what justice is," for I have sat in your court room day after day and have seen members of my class pass before this, the so-called bar of justice. I have seen you, Judge Sloane, and others of your kind, send them to prison because they dared to infringe upon the sacred rights of property. You have become blind and deaf to the rights of man to pursue life and happiness, and you have crushed those

rights so that the sacred right of property shall be preserved. Then you tell me to respect the law. I do not. I did violate the law, as I will violate every one of your laws and still come before you and say, "To hell with the courts". . . .

The prosecutor lied, but I will accept his lie as a truth and say again so that you, Judge Sloane, may not be mistaken as to my attitude, "To hell with your courts, I know what justice is."[19]

The Social Gospel

In the late nineteenth century, in spite of the power of the Gospel of Wealth, voices of dissent emerged from within the churches themselves, both Catholic and Protestant. On the Catholic side, no one pleaded the rights of workers more forcefully than James Cardinal Gibbons, archbishop of Baltimore. In particular, he argued that workers should have the right to organize in order to challenge domination and exploitation by owners and entrepreneurs.

The first national labor union, the Knights of Labor, boasted a majority of Catholic immigrant members from its inception. Uriah Stevens founded the Knights of Labor in 1869, and Terrence Powderly, Roman Catholic mayor of Scranton, Pennsylvania, began to lead that organization in 1878.

Many, however, thought labor unions inimical both to the principle of private property and to the tenets of the Christian faith. The question arose, therefore, whether Catholics should participate in labor unions at all. It was in that context that Rome, in 1884, upheld a judgment by the Canadian hierarchy that condemned the Knights of Labor. In 1887, however, James Cardinal Gibbons successfully lobbied Rome to exempt the Knights of Labor from that condemnation, clearing the way for Catholic workers to actively participate in labor organizations.

On the Protestant side, a variety of voices in the late nineteenth and early twentieth centuries challenged the Gospel of Wealth as a phenomenon fundamentally alien to the spirit of the Christian faith and launched a counter-movement that came to be known as the *Social Gospel*. While one can point to several leading figures of the Social Gospel, among them Washington Gladden of Columbus, Ohio, Walter Rauschenbusch clearly stands as the preeminent prophet of that movement.

Rauschenbusch witnessed firsthand the disastrous effects of the Gospel of Wealth on the urban poor when he pastored a small church of German immigrants in New York City in the late nineteenth century. In 1897 he began teaching at Rochester Seminary in New York and there developed a theological rationale for the Social Gospel in several books, among them *Christianity and the Social Crisis* (1907) and *A Theology for the Social Gospel* (1917).

In the first of those two books, Rauschenbusch charged that Christian advocates of the Gospel of Wealth were "religious men" who had been "cowed by the prevailing materialism and arrogant selfishness of our business world." There were alternatives, he said. "The spiritual force of Christianity should be turned against the materialism and mammonism of our industrial and social order."[20] In practical terms, his statement meant that Christian churches should reject the Gospel of Wealth and embrace instead a massive effort to minister to the poor and the dispossessed with food, clothing, and medical care.

No one articulated this vision for the white churchgoing masses more effectively than Charles Sheldon, whose best-selling novel, *In His Steps*, first appeared in 1897. In it, Sheldon tells the story of the Reverend Henry Maxwell, pastor of a fashionable church that, implicitly at least, was devoted to the principles of the Gospel of Wealth. In time, Maxwell caught the vision of the Social Gospel and challenged members of his church to deal with the social crisis of that time by responding in positive ways to the simple question, "What would Jesus do?"

> What would Jesus do in the matter of wealth? How would He spend it? What principles would regulate His use of money? Would He be likely to live in great luxury and spend ten times as much on personal adornment and entertainment as He spent to relieve the needs of suffering humanity? . . . What would Jesus do about the great army of unemployed and desperate who tramp the streets and curse the church? . . . Would Jesus care nothing for them? Would He go His way in comparative ease and comfort? Would He say it was none of His business? Would He excuse Himself from all responsibility to remove the causes of such a condition?[21]

In the novel, that simple question, "What would Jesus do?" helped transform Maxwell's church from a bastion of the Gospel of Wealth into a congregation driven by the mandates of the Social Gospel on behalf of the poor, the disenfranchised, and the dispossessed. Because of its vast popularity, Sheldon's book helped popularize the principles of the Social Gospel throughout the United States.

An African American Critique

Black Americans—whether in the ranks of labor or not—also reflected on this period and what it meant for them. Blacks, of course, were victims of intense racial discrimination in the late nineteenth century, and that discrimination bled over into the union movement. If white workers were able to unionize to demand better wages and working conditions, the trade union movement typically locked its doors against blacks, leading W. E. B. Du Bois to comment that "the greatest enemy" of the American Negro "is not the employer who robs him, but his fellow white workingman."[22]

Still, some blacks served as union organizers in spite of efforts on the part of whites to keep them out. Lucy Parsons (1853–1942), a woman of Native American, African American, and Mexican ancestry, was a labor organizer, radical socialist, and anarchist, married to Albert Parsons, one of the eight anarchists who were arrested at the Haymarket Square riots in Chicago in 1886. He was the coleader of the Central Labor Union who raised his voice on behalf of revolution if the capitalists refused to accommodate the needs of America's working people. After Albert was convicted and sentenced to death, Lucy embarked on a seven-week speaking tour with two objectives: to raise public awareness of the plight of poor and working people and to generate enough money to appeal Albert's case to the Illinois Supreme Court. In the course of that tour, she delivered more than forty speeches in seventeen states. In spite of all her efforts on her husband's behalf, he was hanged in November 1887.

Lucy was born, perhaps in slavery, in Waco, Texas, in 1853. After Albert was shot for helping register blacks to vote, the couple moved to Chicago in 1873. As Philip Foner and Robert Branham put it, she "was quite literally a revolutionary woman" and "the only woman to address the founding convention of the Industrial Workers of the World (Wobblies) in 1905."[23] On December 20, 1886, she addressed a meeting of socialists in Kansas City, Missouri:

> Do you wonder why there are anarchists in this country, in this grand land of liberty, as you love to call it? Go to New York. Go through the byways and alleys of that great city. Count the myriads starving; count the multiplied thousands who are homeless; number those who work harder than slaves and live on less and have fewer comforts than the meanest slaves. You will be dumbfounded by your discoveries, you who have paid no attention to these poor, save as objects of charity and commiseration. They are not objects of charity, they are the victims of the rank injustice that permeates the system of government, and of political economy that holds sway from the Atlantic to the Pacific. . . . But almost [their] equal is found among the miners of the West, who dwell in squalor and wear rags, that the capitalists, who control the earth, that should be free to all, may add still further to their millions. Oh, there are plenty of reasons for the existence of anarchists.[24]

Only days before the infamous events of May 1886—the nationwide strikes and the violence at Haymarket Square—T. Thomas Fortune delivered a stunning commentary on labor-capital relations before the Brooklyn Literary

Union. Like Frederick Douglass, Fortune had been born in slavery and had received virtually no formal education. He was, however, acquainted with the printer's trade and after arriving in New York in 1879, became a noted journalist. The newspaper he edited and jointly owned, the *Globe*, evolved to become the *Freeman* and later the *New York Age*.[25]

In his speech, Fortune condemned out of hand "the iniquity of privileged class and concentrated wealth [that] has become so glaring and grievous" to poor and working people. He affirmed that every man had a natural right to the necessities of life—food, air, water, and shelter. "These," he said, "are self-evident propositions," grounded in the laws of nature. Unfortunately, he said, the capitalists had abrogated these basic rights for poor and working people, and "the moment you deny to a man the unrestricted enjoyment of all the elements upon which the breath he draws is dependent, that moment you deny to him the inheritance to which he was born."

With this judgment as his premise, he maintained, "Organized society, as it obtains today . . . is an outrageous engine of torture and an odious tyranny." If it were not for the laws that support them, the capitalists "would otherwise be powerless to practice upon the masses of society the gross injustice which everywhere prevails." In fact, for many centuries past, "the aim and scope of all law have been to more securely hedge about the capitalist and the land-owner and to repress labor within a condition wherein bare subsistence was the point aimed at."

If Andrew Carnegie thought it "essential for the progress of the race, that the houses of some should be homes . . . for all the refinements of civiliza-tion," and that "we must accommodate ourselves [to] great inequality of environment [and] the concentration of business . . . in the hands of a few," Fortune flatly disagreed. "The social and material differences which obtain in the relations of mankind are the creations of man, not of God," he said. "God never made such a spook as a king or a duke; he never made such an economic monstrosity as a millionaire; he never gave John Jones the right to own a thousand or a hundred thousand acres of land, with their complement of air and water. These are the conditions of man, who has sold his birthright to the Shylocks of the world and received not even a mess of pottage for his inheritance."[26]

One might imagine that the Gospel of Wealth, born as it was of northern experience, never exerted much influence on the American South, much less on the southern Negro. That judgment is false, thanks mainly to influential white southerners who sought to coax northern entrepreneurs to invest in the South in the years after the Civil War.

Henry W. Grady, the young editor of the *Atlanta Constitution* in the late nineteenth century, was a notable case in point. In 1886 Grady spoke to the New England Society of New York and essentially announced to that august body the emergence of a "New South" with "new conditions, new adjustments and . . . new ideas and aspirations. . . . We have sowed towns and cities in the place of theories and put business above politics." Moreover, he extended a broad invitation to his northern entrepreneurial hosts. "We have smoothed the path to southward, wiped out the place where Mason and Dixon's line used to be, and hung our latch-string out to you and yours."[27]

By 1903 the intellectual who helped found the National Association for the Advancement of Colored People, W. E. B. Du Bois, worried that the "dream of material prosperity" was emerging in the South as the "touchstone of all success." That vision, he said, "is replacing the finer type of Southerner with vulgar money-getters; it is burying the sweeter beauties of Southern life beneath pretense and ostentation."[28]

In order to see the influence of the northern apostles of the Gospel of Wealth in the American South, Du Bois had to look no further than The Tuskegee Institute, founded by Booker T. Washington in Tuskegee, Alabama in 1881. In 1901, Washington published his classic text, *Up from Slavery*, where he told of his attempts to get funding for Tuskegee Institute from America's barons of industry. In that context, Washington offered a justification for the Gospel of Wealth that could easily have come from the pen of an Andrew Carnegie or a Henry Ward Beecher. "My experience in getting money for Tuskegee," he wrote, "has taught me to have no patience with those people who are always condemning the rich because they are rich, and because they do not give more money to objects of charity. In the first place, those who are guilty of such sweeping criticisms do not know how many people would be made poor, and how much suffering would result, if wealthy people were to part all at once with any large proportion of their wealth in a way to disorganize and cripple great business enterprises."

Then, echoing Russell Conwell's affirmation that "the men who get rich may be the most honest men you find in the community," Washington described his wealthy northern donors as "some of the best people in the world—to be more correct, I think I should say *the best* people in the world."[29] In *Up from Slavery*, Washington specifically mentioned several of these benefactors and friends including Andrew Carnegie, John D. Rockefeller, and the Right Reverend William Lawrence, Episcopal bishop of Massachusetts,[30] who had argued in 1901 that "it is only to the man of morality that wealth comes" and that "godliness is in league with riches."

Perhaps that context helps us better understand Washington's "Atlanta Exposition Address" of 1895, in which he told a largely white audience that if blacks wished to improve themselves, they must understand that "it is at the bottom of life we must begin, and not at the top." He assured his audience that "in all things that are purely social we [blacks and whites] can be as separate as the fingers, yet one as the hand in all things essential to mutual progress." "The wisest among my race," he said, "understand that the agitation of questions of social equality is the extremest folly." For that reason, he routinely advised blacks to "cast down your bucket where you are."[31]

W. E. B. Du Bois attacked that speech unmercifully, calling it "the Atlanta Compromise." As Du Bois saw it, the compromise was rooted in the fact that Washington had so "intuitively grasped the spirit of the age which was dominating the North" and had thoroughly learned "the speech and thought of triumphant commercialism and the ideals of material prosperity."[32]

Indeed, Du Bois satirized "triumphant commercialism" and its chief spokesperson, Andrew Carnegie, when he wrote that "all honorable men" will eventually come to see "that in the future competition of races the survival of the fittest shall mean the triumph of the good, the beautiful, and the true; that we may be able to preserve for future civilization all that is really fine and noble and strong, and not continue to put a premium on greed and impudence and cruelty."[33]

Finally, Du Bois pointed out that the Gilded Age with its Gospel of Wealth had brought nothing to the Negro except further suffering:

> Despite compromise, war, and struggle, the Negro is not free. In the backwoods of the Gulf States, for miles and miles, he may not leave the plantation of his birth; in well-nigh the whole rural South the black farmers are peons, bound by law and custom to an economic slavery, from which the only escape is death or the penitentiary. In the most cultured sections and cities of the South the Negroes are a segregated servile caste, with restricted rights and privileges. Before the courts, both in law and custom, they stand on a different and peculiar basis. Taxation without representation is the rule of their political life.[34]

Du Bois concluded that America was "a land whose freedom is to us a mockery and whose liberty a lie."[35] By 1961, when Du Bois was ninety-three years old, he was thoroughly discouraged over America's failure to implement the promise of the American Creed for African Americans. He therefore joined the American Communist Party and moved to Ghana, where he died two years later.

In 1896, in the waning years of the Gilded Age, the Supreme Court of the United States ruled in *Plessy v. Ferguson* that it was entirely legal to segregate black Americans from white Americans if the facilities were equal. Little wonder that three years later, D. P. Brown, in a speech to the New England Conference of the African Methodist Episcopal Church, dismissed the Gospel of Wealth, the elaborate projections for what capitalism might achieve in American life, and even the gains some workers had made by the century's end:

> What does the greatness or prosperity of our country amount to, to us as a race, if at the same time it shows to the civilized world either its weakness or unwillingness to protect ten millions of its most loyal citizens in the enjoyment of the simplest rights set forth in the Declaration of Independence . . . ? What is it to us if the wages of the factory employees are increased, if over the door of each of them the sign hangs out, "No Black Man Wanted Here" . . . ? Why should we shout for prosperity that means much to the white man and but little to his brother in black, when we know that it is the fixed purpose and determination to drive us from every favored avenue where we may earn our daily bread?[36]

The period of the Gospel of Wealth also coincided with a level of violence against blacks that, during the final years of the nineteenth century, was "greater than at any other period in American history," according to historian Gayraud Wilmore. Wilmore reports "unprecedented mob violence and terrorism perpetrated against Negro citizens between 1890 and 1914. Between 1885 and 1915, 3,500 Blacks were the known victims of lynch mobs, with 235 lynchings in the year 1892 alone."[37]

No one did more during that period to protest the lynching of black people than a woman we met in chapter 4—Ida B. Wells, the editor and part owner of the *Memphis Free Speech*. Wells edited that paper for three years, beginning in 1889. Then, in 1892, a mob destroyed the newspaper office in retaliation for an editorial in which Wells exposed the true motive of a white mob that had viciously murdered three black entrepreneurs. Using the capitalist system to their advantage, these three entrepreneurs had competed successfully with neighboring whites in a comparable business—an offense that led to their execution. Time and again, Wells placed before the public the murders that whites routinely inflicted on blacks in the American South during the period of the Gospel of Wealth. She took particular pains to refute the claim—typically offered by southern whites—that whites lynched blacks who had raped white women. In 1909 she pointedly asked, "Why is mob murder permitted by a Christian nation? What is the cause of this awful slaughter? This question is answered almost daily—always the same shameless falsehood that 'Negroes are lynched to protect womanhood.' . . . This is the never varying answer of lynchers and their apologists. All know that it is untrue. The cowardly lyncher revels in murder, then seeks to shield himself from public execration by claiming devotion to woman."[38]

Wells also brought to light the fact that numerous blacks were burned at the stake during this period. "Twenty-eight human beings burned at the stake, one of them a woman and two of them children, is the awful indictment against American civilization," she reported. She added, "No other nation, civilized or savage, burns its criminals; only under the stars and stripes is the human holocaust possible."[39]

"The general government," she complained, "is willingly powerless to send troops to protect the lives of its black citizens, but the state governments are free to use state troops to shoot them down like cattle, when in desperation the black men attempt to defend themselves, and then tell the world that it was necessary to put down a 'race war.'"[40]

In spite of the burnings, the lynchings, and the economic injustices wreaked on American blacks during the period of the Gospel of Wealth, the wonder is that so many blacks still kept faith in the promise of America. Wells, herself, is a case in point. She longed for the day when "mob rule shall be put down and equal and exact justice be accorded to every citizen of whatever race, who finds a home within the borders of the land of the free and the home of the brave."

In the midst of the Great Depression, when capitalism had failed the nation, Langston Hughes wrote the poem for which he is perhaps best known: "Let America Be America Again," a devastating critique of America's capitalist economy.

> I am the poor white, fooled and pushed apart,
> I am the Negro bearing slavery's scars.
> I am the red man driven from the land,
> I am the immigrant clutching the hope I seek—
> And finding only the same old stupid plan
> Of dog eat dog, of mighty crush the weak.
>
> I am the young man, full of strength and hope,
> Tangled in that ancient endless chain
> Of profit, power, gain, of grab the land!
> Of grab the gold! Of grab the ways of satisfying need!
> Of work the men! Of take the pay!
> Of owning everything for one's own greed!
> I am the farmer, bondsman to the soil.
> I am the worker sold to the machine.

I am the Negro, servant to you all.
I am the people, humble, hungry, mean—
Hungry yet today despite the dream.
Beaten yet today—O, Pioneers!
I am the man who never got ahead,
The poorest worker bartered through the years.

. . . .

O, I'm the man who sailed those early seas
In search of what I meant to be my home—
For I'm the one who left dark Ireland's shore,
And Poland's plain, and England's grassy lea,
And torn from Black Africa's strand I came
To build a "homeland of the free."

The free?

Who said the free? Not me?
Surely not me? The millions on relief today?
The millions shot down when we strike?
The millions who have nothing for our pay?
For all the dreams we've dreamed
And all the songs we've sung
And all the hopes we've held
And all the flags we've hung,
The millions who have nothing for our pay—
Except the dream that's almost dead today.

O, let America be America again—
The land that never has been yet—
And yet must be—the land where every man is free. . . .

O, yes.
I say it plain,
America never was America to me,
And yet I swear this oath—
America will be!

Out of the rack and ruin of our gangster death,
The rape and rot of graft, and stealth, and lies,
We, the people, must redeem
The land, the mines, the plants, the rivers.
The mountains and the endless plain—
All, all the stretch of these great green states—
And make America again!

Capitalism and Systemic Racism

Having now explored how some blacks assessed American capitalism and the myths that sustained it during the Gilded Age, it is time to explore other ways in which the mythic dimensions of American capitalism have played themselves out in American life.

In 2016, Kathy Miller, a former campaign chair for Donald Trump in Mahoning County, Ohio, gave voice to a belief pervasive among whites about economic opportunities for blacks in America's capitalist system. "If you're black and you haven't been successful in the last 50 years," Miller said, "it's your own fault. You've had every opportunity, it was given to you. You've had the same schools everybody else went to. You had benefits to go to college that white kids didn't have. You had all the advantages and didn't take advantage of it."

Malcolm X tells a story that stands as a rebuke to Miller—a story that aptly captures the experience of millions of America's blacks both before Malcolm's time and after. "One day . . . something happened which was to become the first major turning point in my life," Malcolm recalled:

> I happened to be alone in the classroom with Mr. Ostrowski, my English teacher [at Mason Junior High School, Mason, Michigan]. . . . He told me, "Malcolm, you ought to be thinking about a career. Have you been giving it thought?" The truth is, I hadn't. I never figured out why I told him, "Well, yes sir. I've been thinking I'd like to be a lawyer." . . . Mr. Ostrowski looked surprised, I remember, and leaned back in his chair and clasped his hands behind his head. He kind of half-smiled and said, "Malcolm, one of life's first needs is for us to be realistic. Don't misunderstand me, now. We all here like you, you know that. But you've got to be realistic about being a nigger. A lawyer—that's no realistic goal for a nigger. You need to think about something you can be. You're good with your hands—making things. . . . Why don't you plan on carpentry?

Never mind that Malcolm was one of three students who vied for top scholastic honors in that class.[41]

Malcolm's story helps us grasp why capitalism has so often failed to work for American blacks. If the power structure takes pains to exclude you from the system, then clearly the system will fail you. In the United States, privileged whites have often gone out of their way to exclude blacks from the potential benefits of a capitalist economy.

Virtually all American blacks have had experiences comparable to Malcolm's. Michael Eric Dyson, for example, recalls that after Princeton University had accepted him for graduate studies, the president of his undergraduate institution, Carson-Newman College, discouraged him from enrolling:

> The president wasted no time in summoning me to his office. . . . He demanded that I produce proof on the spot that I'd gotten into Princeton. . . . I whipped out my offer letter. . . . He wasn't pleased, but neither was he deterred. I was especially nervous because I owed the school seven thousand dollars in unpaid tuition. Sneering, the president looked me straight in the eyes and told me that I should get a job and pay my bill instead of going to Princeton.[42]

These two stories bear out Carol Anderson's contention, cited in chapter 1, that what triggers "white rage" against blacks is always "black advancement. It is not the mere presence of black people that is the problem; rather, it is blackness with ambition, with drive, with purpose, with aspirations, and with demands for full and equal citizenship."

The story Anderson tells differs from the stories of Malcolm X and Eric Dyson in one fundamental sense. In the cases of Malcolm X and Dyson, individual actors sought to thwart their success. But as Anderson notes, there is something far larger and far more powerful at work in American life than the bigotry of a single teacher or a single college president. Anderson tells us that what typically erects the roadblocks to black advancement are the great organizational systems in the United States—"the courts, the legislatures, and a range of government bureaucracies,"[43] not to mention economic structures, educational structures, and even religious structures that often bless those roadblocks with divine sanction, as noted in chapter 4.

There is a phrase that describes this reality—*systemic racism*. This phrase refers to the vast inequalities that are embedded into the economic systems and social structures in which virtually all Americans participate. Systemic racism tends to insure that whites benefit from a capitalist economy while blacks do not, that privileged whites grow richer while underprivileged blacks grow poorer, and that the doors of opportunity remain, for the most part, closed to those on the bottom rungs of the ladder.

Because American capitalism is so shrouded in myth, however—because its beneficiaries have so often believed it God-ordained and an accurate reflection of the natural order of things—whites who benefit from America's capitalist system have seldom been able to discern the extent to which systemic racism restricts for people of color the possibility of genuine economic equality.

Some whites, seeking to rebut the truth that systemic racism is a fact of American life and has been for a very long time, point to blacks who have succeeded financially in extraordinary ways. But those are exceptions, not the rule, as Jeremiah Wright, former senior pastor of Trinity United Church of Christ in Chicago, pointed out in a sermon he preached on April 13, 2003: "For every one Oprah, a billionaire," Wright said, "you got five million blacks who are out of work. For every one Colin Powell, a millionaire, you got ten million blacks who cannot read. For every one 'Condeskeeza' Rice, you got one million in prison. . . . For every one Tiger Woods, we got ten thousand black kids who will never see a golf course."[44]

One additional myth rounds out the mythic mix in which American capitalism is embedded—the notion of rugged individualism. More than any other factor, this one myth underpins the resistance of many whites to the very idea of "white privilege." "Nobody gave me a thing," they often say. "I worked hard for my money and I made it on my own."

There is, however, not one American—not one—who can plausibly claim to have "made it on my own." Those who experience economic success in the United States may well work hard, but they often benefit from systems and structures that have tilted the scales in their favor. Some of those systems were put in place decades, even centuries ago, but because—as noted often in this book—the American people typically live in the eternal present with little or no sense of history, they have long since forgotten about laws that were made, doors that were opened, and economic structures that were put in place that allow some to thrive while others do not. When those laws and doors and structures favor whites at the expense of blacks, we can legitimately speak of two realities: *systemic racism*—a form of racism that is embedded into the American economic system; and *white privilege*—advantages that accrue to whites precisely because of racist structures that have been built into the American economic system for many years.

If we want examples of laws and doors and structures that were put in place years ago and have tilted the scales in favor of whites at the expense of blacks, we must begin with slavery—a vast economic system of human bondage and death that was rooted in notions of white supremacy and black degradation.

Following Reconstruction, those laws and doors and structures persisted in other forms. One of those forms was the practice, common in the South until World War II, of arresting blacks on charges as flimsy as "vagrancy"—in effect, unemployment—and leasing these convicts to privately run farms, factories, and mines, a practice that often resulted in the convict's death. Douglas A. Blackmon described that practice as "slavery by another name."[45]

Sharecropping was also "slavery by another name"—an economic system that kept southern blacks in virtual bondage during the Gilded Age when the barons of industry in northern states were amassing stupendous fortunes.

Frederick Douglas explained what the system of sharecropping meant for blacks:

> The same class that once extorted his labor under the lash now gets his labor by a mean, sneaking, and fraudulent device. That device is a trucking system which never permits him [the black tenant farmer] to see or to save a dollar of his hard earnings.... The highest wages paid him is eight dollars a month, and this he receives only in orders on the store, which, in many cases, is owned by his employer. The script has purchasing power on that one store, and that one only.... The laborer is by this arrangement ... completely in the power of his employer. He can charge the poor fellow what he pleases and give what kind of goods he pleases, and he does both. His victim cannot go to another store and buy, and this the storekeeper knows.

In a line that clearly echoed the "Opinion of the Court" written by Supreme Court Justice Roger B. Taney in the Dred Scott decision, Douglass affirmed that "The only security the wretched Negro has under this arrangement is the conscience of the storekeeper—a conscience educated in the school of slavery, where the idea prevailed in theory and practice that the Negro had no rights which men were bound to respect."[46]

If one wants other examples of laws and doors and structures that tilted the scales in favor of whites at the expense of blacks, they are not hard to find. In 1785, the federal government passed the Land Ordinance Act that permitted American citizens to purchase 640 acres of land at one dollar per acre. Since blacks were not citizens, however, they were denied participation in what amounted to a great entitlement for whites.

Seventy-seven years later, in 1862, Congress passed the Homestead Act, signed into law by President Lincoln. That law provided that any American citizen could claim 160 acres of western land, provided he or she would improve the land, live there for five years, and build a dwelling. But once again, since blacks were enslaved and therefore not American citizens, they could not take advantage of this second entitlement initiative until the Fourteenth Amendment granted them citizenship in 1868. As a result, relatively few blacks benefited from this program.

It goes without saying that land acquired by white Americans by virtue of the Land Ordinance Act and the Homestead Act has been passed down through the years to the heirs of those original settlers. Millions of white Americans still benefit from those congressional actions that date to 1785 and 1862. In fact, historians estimate that some 93 million white Americans alive today still benefit from the Homestead Act alone.[47] At the very same time, by refusing them citizenship, Congress effectively barred most black

Americans from these significant entry points into the engine of American capitalism.

Another example can be found in the Social Security Act, which Congress passed and President Franklin Roosevelt signed into law in 1935 as part of the New Deal. That Act specifically excluded from its benefits "agricultural labor," "domestic service in a private home," and "casual labor not in the course of the employer's trade or business."[48] Obviously, these provisions excluded many blacks who worked in precisely those pursuits.

We discover other examples in the housing and real estate industries. The National Housing Act of 1934, another New Deal effort, aimed to make housing more affordable and to cut the rate of housing foreclosures that had accelerated during the Great Depression. As part of that initiative, the Federal Housing Administration created "residential security maps" to help lenders determine whether a given property was a wise investment. Those maps divided cities into four districts: green areas were good investments, blue areas were less so, yellow indicated areas that were in decline, and red marked out areas that had already declined, areas where low-income families—often black families—typically lived. Needless to say, realtors habitually steered white clients away from those redlined parts of the city.

Cornell Belcher described the result: "Of the over 120 billion dollars in federal home-owner subsidies that were disbursed between 1934 and 1962, only 2% went to families of color. . . . A majority of us can expect to inherit from our parents the proceeds from what is for most middle-class people their greatest asset, their home, when they pass on. Because of redlining, generations of people of color have had no homes, or have had homes of lesser value, to pass on and assist the next generation in accumulating wealth."[49] Rich Benjamin adds, "Some scholars now call the government's handiwork a '$120 billion head start' on white home ownership, on white equity, and on white's ability to pass along wealth from one generation to the next."[50] No wonder that by 2011 the median white household had $111,146 in wealth while the median black family was worth $7,111.[51] That reality—and the forces that helped produce it—is the essence of systemic racism.

Every law and statute described thus far has contributed mightily—and still contributes—to the reality of white privilege in the United States. But there is still more, for white privilege also means that white people never have to fear that the police might pull them over simply because of the color of their skin. Likewise, whites never worry that grocery store personnel might follow them from aisle to aisle because they associate dark skin with robbery.

Further, every law and statute described thus far was part and parcel of the overarching system of Jim Crow segregation that defined the lives of African

American citizens from the end of Reconstruction in 1877 until the Supreme Court ruled against segregated schools in *Brown v. Board of Education* (1954) and the Civil Rights Movement launched a massive challenge to the system of racial segregation in 1955.

Fred Gray—attorney for Martin Luther King Jr., Rosa Parks, the Montgomery Bus Boycott, the 1965 Selma March, and many other leaders and initiatives that defined the Freedom Movement—described in his autobiography the scope of Jim Crow segregation. "By my junior year at Alabama State, I understood more fully that everything was completely segregated not only in Montgomery, but throughout the South and in many places across the nation. In Alabama's capital city—the 'Birthplace of the Confederacy'—churches, schools, hospitals, and places of public accommodation were all segregated. Whites and blacks were segregated from the time they were born until the time they were buried in segregated cemeteries. If a person of color had a claim against a white person there was very little likelihood he would obtain justice." Gray therefore decided to go to law school and "return to Montgomery and use the law to destroy everything segregated I could find."[52]

The work of Fred Gray, Martin Luther King, and the entire Civil Rights Movement was remarkably successful. It was so successful that it triggered a massive reaction designed to reverse those gains, a reaction in sync with Carol Anderson's claim, noted in chapter 1, that "for every action of African American advancement, there's a reaction, a backlash," often orchestrated by "the courts, the legislatures, and a range of government bureaucracies."[53]

Another lawyer, Michelle Alexander, has described the backlash against the Freedom Movement of the 1960s as "the new Jim Crow"—an effort to incarcerate black people through a massive "war on drugs," launched by President Ronald Reagan's administration in 1982. "I came to see," Alexander wrote, "that mass incarceration in the United States had, in fact, emerged as a stunningly comprehensive and well-disguised system of racialized social control that functions in a manner strikingly similar to Jim Crow."[54]

Consider the following facts: (1) The government declared its War on Drugs when illegal drug use was actually declining. (2) The CIA, by its own admission, supported guerrilla armies in Nicaragua that were smuggling illegal drugs into America's inner cities and blocked efforts by law enforcement to investigate the networks that supplied those drugs. (3) Thanks to the War on Drugs, the United States has the highest incarceration rate in the world, six to ten times greater than any other industrialized nation in the world. (4) The War on Drugs resulted in an explosion of incarceration of black and brown people, so much so that "the United States," Alexander reported, "now has the highest rate of incarceration in the world, dwarfing the rates of nearly every developed country, even surpassing those in highly repressive regimes like Russia, China, and Iran." In fact, she wrote, "the United States imprisons a larger percentage of its black population than South Africa did at the height of apartheid."[55] (5) Finally, a report to the United Nations Human Rights Committee concluded that "if current trends continue, one of every three black American males born today can expect to go to prison in his lifetime."[56] In Washington D.C., those numbers are far worse. Alexander reported that "in . . . our nation's capital, it is estimated that three out of four young black men (and nearly all those in the poorest neighborhoods) can expect to serve time in prison."[57]

As Alexander notes, incarceration is only the beginning of this "new Jim Crow." "Once . . . released," she notes, "[ex-prisoners] are often denied the right to vote, excluded from juries, and relegated to a racially segregated and subordinated existence. Through a web of laws, regulations, and informal rules, all of which are powerfully reinforced by social stigma, they are confined to the margins of mainstream society and denied access to the mainstream economy. They are legally denied the ability to obtain employment, housing, and public benefits—much as African Americans were once forced into a segregated, second-class citizenship in the Jim Crow era."[58]

Conclusions

For purposes of this chapter, the most important phrase in Alexander's last question is this: "denied access to the mainstream economy." The new Jim Crow, coupled with the vast and privatized prison-industrial complex, has served—and continues to serve—to lock young blacks out of America's capitalist system just as surely as Mr. Ostrowski sought to block young Malcolm from entering into that system in the late 1930s.

At the very same time, as late as 2017, many whites—especially white evangelical Christians—seemed oblivious to this reality and continued to buy into the assumptions that undergirded the Gospel of Wealth a hundred years before. A poll conducted by the *Washington Post* and the Kaiser Family Foundation in 2017 found that "46 percent of all Christians [and 53 percent of white evangelical Protestants] said that a lack of effort is generally to blame for a person's poverty, compared with 29 percent of all non-Christians."[59] This twenty-first-century version of the Gospel of Wealth served as one more ideological support for the Myth of White Supremacy.

Michelle Alexander confessed that she came quite reluctantly to the conclusions she presented in her book, *The New Jim Crow*. "Ten years ago," she writes, "I would have argued strenuously against the central claim made here –

namely, that something akin to a racial caste system currently exists in the United States." And she frankly admits that her readers will have "difficulty . . . seeing what most everyone insists does not exist."[60] Indeed, the people who resist the thesis of Alexander's book likely do so for the same reason that I had difficulty for such a long time accepting the central premise that I have developed in *this* book—that the Myth of White Supremacy plays a crucial role in defining the meaning of the American nation. Many of us find it difficult to process these realities because of the persistent power of a fifth American myth—the Myth of the Innocent Nation, which we shall explore in chapter 7.

Notes

1. Walter Johnson, "Slavery, Racial Capitalism, and Justice," in Walter Johnson with Robin D. G. Kelley, eds., *Boston Review: Forum I: Race, Capitalism, Justice* (Cambridge: Boston Critic, Inc., 2017), 25–27. See also Johnson, *River of Dark Dreams: Slavery and Empire in the Cotton Kingdom* (Cambridge: Belknap Press, 2013), which explores slavery's contribution to global capitalism.

2. Daniel Seely Gregory, *Christian Ethics*, 1875, cited in Ralph Henry Gabriel, *The Course of American Democratic Thought*, 2d ed. (New York: Ronald Press, 1956), 157; William Lawrence, "The Relation of Wealth to Morals," 1901, in Conrad Cherry, ed., *God's New Israel: Religious Interpretations of American Destiny*, rev. ed. (Chapel Hill: University of North Carolina Press, 1998), 252; and Charles Arthur Conant, *The United States in the Orient: The Nature of the Economic Problem* (Boston: Houghton Mifflin, 1900), 2.

3. William Lawrence, "The Relation of Wealth to Morals," 1901, in Cherry, ed., *God's New Israel*, 250–252.

4. Russell Conwell, *Acres of Diamonds* (New York: Harper and Row, 1905 [1890]), 18.

5. Sidney E. Mead, *The Lively Experiment: The Shaping of Christianity in America* (New York: Harper and Row, 1963), 143.

6. Henry Ward Beecher, "The Tendencies of American Progress," 1870, in Cherry, ed., *God's New Israel*, 237, 242, and 245.

7. Quoted in Henry F. May, *Protestant Churches and Industrial America* (New York: Harper and Row, 1967), 69.

8. Sydney Ahlstrom, *A Religious History of the American People* (New Haven: Yale University Press, 1972), 767.

9. Andrew Carnegie, "Wealth," 1889, in Robert A. Mathisen, ed., *The Role of Religion in American Life: An Interpretive Historical Anthology* (Dubuque, Iowa: Kendall/Hunt Publishing, 1994), 168 and 173.

10. Josiah Strong, "Our Country," 1885, in Winthrop Hudson, ed., *Nationalism and Religion in America: Concepts of American Identity and Mission* (New York: Harper and Row, 1970), 115–116.

11. James Henderson Berry, *Congressional Record*, 55th Congress, 3d sess., vol. 32, pt. 2 (Washington, D.C.: Government Printing Office, 1899), 1299.

12. Beveridge cited in James Oliver Robertson, *American Myth, American* Reality (New York: Hill and Wang, 1980), 272; Kitchell cited in Emily Rosenberg, *Spreading the American Dream: American Economic and Cultural Expansion, 1890–1945* (New York: Hill and Wang, 1982), 22.

13. For an elaboration of this point, see Rosenberg, *Spreading the American Dream*, 38, 48–49, and 230–231.

14. Conant cited in Rosenberg, *Spreading the American Dream*, 50.

15. Rosenberg, *Spreading the American Dream*, 25.

16. Arthur M. Schlesinger Jr., *Orestes A. Brownson: A Pilgrim's Progress* (Boston: Little, Brown and Co., 1939), 90.

17. Howard Zinn narrates these events in *A People's History of the United States* (New York: Harper and Row, 1980), 263–265.

18. John R. Commons, *History of the Labor Movement in the United States* (New York: Macmillan, 1936), 2:373–374.

19. Speech of Jack White cited in Zinn, *A People's History*, 325–326.

20. Walter Rauschenbusch, *Christianity and the Social Crisis* (New York: MacMillan, 1913 [1907]), 369–372.

21. Charles Sheldon, *In His Steps* (Chicago: John C. Winston Co., 1957 [1897]), 254–259.

22. Cited in Zinn, *A People's History*, 328–329.

23. Philip S. Foner and Robert James Branham, eds., *Lift Every Voice: African American Oratory, 1787–1900* (Tuscaloosa: University of Alabama Press, 1998), 655–656.

24. Lucy Parsons, "I Am an Anarchist," 1886, in Foner and Branham, eds., *Lift Every Voice*, 657.

25. See description of Fortune in Foner and Branham, eds., *Lift Every Voice*, 642.

26. T. Thomas Fortune, "The Present Relations of Labor and Capital," 1886, in Foner and Branham, eds., *Lift Every Voice*, 642–644.

27. Paul M. Gaston, *The New South Creed: A Study in Southern Mythmaking* (New York: Knopf, 1970), 17, 87–88. For the full text of Grady's speech, see Joel Chandler Harris, ed., *Life of Henry W. Grady, Including His Writings and Speeches* (New York, 1890).

28. W. E. B. Du Bois, *The Souls of Black Folk*, 1903, in *Three Negro Classics* (New York: Avon Books, 1965), 264.

29. Booker T. Washington, *Up From Slavery*, 1901, in *Three Negro Classics*, 126–127.

30. Ibid., 131–132, 176, and 190–191.

31. Ibid., 146–150.

32. Du Bois, *The Souls of Black Folk*, 241.

33. Ibid., 321.

34. Ibid., 239.

35. Ibid., 350.

36. D. P. Brown, "The State of the Country from a Black Man's Point of View," 1899, in Foner and Branham, eds., *Lift Every Voice*, 893–894.

37. Gayraud Wilmore, *Black Religion and Black Radicalism: An Examination of the Black Experience in Religion* (New York: Doubleday, 1973), 190 and 192.

38. Ida B. Wells, "Lynching, Our National Crime," 1909, in Marcia Y. Riggs, ed., *Can I Get a Witness? Prophetic Religious Voices of African American Woman: An Anthology* (Maryknoll, N.Y.: Orbis, 1997), 147–148.

39. Ibid., 147.

40. Wells, "Lynch Law in All its Phases," in *Can I Get a Witness?* 94.

41. Alex Haley, *The Autobiography of Malcolm X* (New York: Ballantine Books, 1964), 37–38.

42. Michael Eric Dyson, *Tears We Cannot Stop: A Sermon to White America* (New York: St. Martin's Press, 2017), 46–47.

43. Carol Anderson, *White Rage: The Unspoken Truth of our Racial Divide* (New York: Bloomsbury, 2016), 3.

44. Jeremiah Wright, "Confusing God and Government," sermon preached at Trinity United Church of Christ, Chicago, April 13, 2003, www.blackpast.org/2008-rev-jeremiah-wright-confusing-god-and-goverment, accessed February 3, 2018.

45. Douglas A. Blackmon, *Slavery by Another Name: The Re-Enslavement of Black Americans from the Civil War to World War II* (New York: Anchor Books, 2008).

46. Frederick Douglass, "I Denounce the So-Called Emancipation as a Stupendous Fraud," 1888, in Foner and Branham, eds., *Lift Every Voice*, 706, 698, and 703.

47. "Effects of the Homestead Act of 1862," http://www.grit.com/farm-and-garden/homestead-act-of-1862, accessed April 28, 2017.

48. "The Social Security Act of 1935," https://www.ssa.gov/history/35act.html, accessed April 28, 2017.

49. Cornell Belcher, *A Black Man in the White House: Barack Obama and the Triggering of America's Racial-Aversion Crisis* (Healdsburg, Calif.: Water Street Press, 2016), 91–93.

50. Rich Benjamin, *Searching for Whitopia: An Improbable Journey to the Heart of White America* (New York: Hachette Books, 2009), 187.

51. Laura Sullivan, Tatjana Meschede, Lars Dietrich, Thomas Shapiro, Amy Traub, Catherine Ruetschlin, and Tamara Draut, *The Racial Wealth Gap: Why Policy Matters*, a study sponsored by Demos and the Institute for Assets and Social Policy, Brandeis University, 1, http://www.demos.org/sites/default/files/publications/RacialWealth-Gap_1.pdf, accessed August 9, 2017; and Brad Plumer, "These Ten Charts Show the Black-White Economic Gap Hasn't Budged in 50 Years," *The Washington Post*, August 28, 2013, https://www.washingtonpost.com/news/wonk/wp/2013/08/28/these-seven-charts-show-the-black-white-economic-gap-hasnt-budged-in-50-years/?utm_term=.8641ffa9aab0, accessed August 9, 2017.

52. Fred D. Gray, *Bus Ride to Justice: The Life and Works of Fred D. Gray* (rev. ed., Montgomery: NewSouth Books, 1995), 13.

53. Carol Anderson, "Ferguson Isn't about Black Rage against Cops. It's White Rage against Progress," *Washington Post*, August 29, 2014, https://www.washingtonpost.com/opinions/ferguson-wasnt-black-rage-against-copsit-was-white-rage-against-progress/2014/08/29/3055e3f4–2d75–11e4-bb9b-997ae96fad33_story.html?utm_term=.4d1a9a3e855o, accessed September 10, 2014; and Anderson, *White Rage*, 3.

54. Michelle Alexander, *The New Jim Crow: Mass Incarceration in the Age of Colorblindness* (New York: The New Press, 2010), 4.

55. Ibid., 5–6.

56. "Report of the Sentencing Project to the United Nations Human Rights Committee Regarding Racial Disparities in the United States Criminal Justice System," August 2013, 1.

57. Alexander, *The New Jim Crow*, 6–7.

58. Ibid., 4.

59. Julie Zauzmer, "Christians Are More than Twice as Likely to Blame a Person's Poverty on Lack of Effort," *Washington Post*, August 3, 2017, https://www.washingtonpost.com/news/acts-of-faith/wp/2017/08/03/christians-are-more-than-twice-as-likely-to-blame-a-persons-poverty-on-lack-of-effort/?utm_term=.02f445c39afo, accessed August 9, 2017.

60. Alexander, *The New Jim Crow*, 2, 12.

CHAPTER SEVEN

The Myth of the Innocent Nation

The Twentieth and Twenty-First Centuries

In his splendid memoir that describes what it meant to grow up in the 1960s and 1970s, Lawrence Wright reflects on the innocence that characterized America during the period of World War II. "When my father went off to war," Wright recalls, "I understood that he was going to make the world safe for democracy and that that was what the world wanted. . . . [He had] matured in a magic age, the 1940s, when great evil and great good faced each other. In that splendid moment he knew which side he was on. He was an American farm boy doing what God and his country had designed for him. . . . Here he was, saving the world. I grew up expecting to inherit his certainty."[1]

The fact is, a profound sense of innocence characterized the American experience for much of the twentieth century and especially between World War I and the 1960s. Some periods were exceptions to that generalization, of course. The Great Depression, for example, generated enormous doubt and despair among both blacks and whites. Still, in the mainstream of American life, most had no doubt about the ultimate meaning of their nation: America stood for good against evil, right against wrong, democracy against tyranny, and virtue against vice. What can account for this extraordinary sense of innocence that many in later years would view as profoundly naive?

The Ahistorical Dimensions of American Innocence

By the twentieth century, America was heir to all the myths we have considered in this book, and all these myths sustained the nation's sense of innocence. The myth of America as a Christian Nation is a case in point.

By the early twentieth century fundamentalists worried that America had deserted its Christian moorings, although most Americans who claimed the Christian faith remained confident that America was a Christian civilization. That perception alone was enough to sustain a powerful sense of innocence.

In addition, the Myth of the Chosen Nation was still a vibrant, dynamic theme in American life and culture. As Lawrence Wright noted in his memoir, "America had a mission—we thought it was a divine mission—to spread freedom, and freedom meant democracy, and democracy meant capitalism, and all that meant the American way of life."[2] Would God choose America for such a mission if America lacked the qualities of goodness, virtue, and innocence?

In my judgment, however, the two most important myths sustaining America's sense of innocence in the early twentieth century were the myths of Nature's Nation and the Millennial Nation. Important in this context is the way those myths converged to preclude any meaningful sense of history in the United States.

The notion of Nature's Nation pointed Americans to a mythic time when the world first began and all was good and right and true—the time of Eden before the fall. It was easy to imagine that the United States was a virtual re-creation of this golden age, an age that stood on the front end—and therefore outside the boundaries—of human history.

At the same time, the notion of the Millennial Nation pointed Americans to another golden age that would conclude the human saga. Because the millennium was also characterized by perfection, it, too, stood outside the boundaries of human history, this time on the back end. By restoring the virtues of the first perfect age, Americans imagined they would usher in the second perfect age and thereby bless the world.

By identifying itself so completely with these mythic periods of perfection, America lifted itself above the plane of ordinary human history where evil, suffering, and death dominated the drama of human existence. America became, as the Great Seal of the United States so clearly states, a *novus ordo seclorum*, a new order of the ages. Other nations were mired in the bog of human history, but not the United States. Other nations had inherited the taint of human history, but not the United States. Other nations had been compromised by human history, but not the United States. In effect, then, America had removed itself from the power of human history with all the ambiguity that history inevitably bears. In this way, America emerged as an innocent child among the nations of the world, without spot or wrinkle, unmarred and unblemished by the finite dimensions of human history.

President Ronald Reagan perhaps put it best when he said in his State of the Union address of 1987, "The calendar can't measure America because we were meant to be an endless experiment in freedom, with no limit to our reaches, no boundaries to what we can do, no end point to our hopes."[3]

Having rejected the bounds of finite human history, it is little wonder that when America launched a war against Islamic terrorists in retaliation for the September 11, 2001, attacks, U.S. military strategists initially called the war "Operation Infinite Justice." They finally scuttled that phrase when people of religious faith—Muslims, Christians, and Jews—pointed out that only God can dispense "infinite justice."

Indeed, the starting point for the American illusion of innocence lies in the way Americans typically deal with history and its contents. Henry Ford perhaps put it best when he said flatly "History is bunk." If Americans wish to say that someone is irrelevant to a particular situation, we often say to that person, "You're history." American students typically avoid history, believing that history itself is irrelevant. We bulldoze buildings of any age at all in order to create something that is bright, shining, and new. These are just some of the ways that Americans routinely reject the reality of history. The truth is that many Americans live their lives in the eternal present, a present informed and shaped not by history but by those two golden epochs that bracket human time.

Because many Americans so often reject history, they also reject the most fundamental contents of history, especially finitude, suffering, and death. In 1963 Jessica Mitford published an important book called *The American Way of Death*. While many cultures cope with death by embracing it—by handling the corpse, for example—Americans, Mitford noted, have adopted funeral practices that effectively mask the reality of death so that it never intrudes on the perfect world they seek to create.[4]

Americans often deal with suffering in the very same way, as the patterns of our neighborhoods abundantly attest. Indeed, one could argue that racial segregation has always had more to do with poverty, suffering, and death than with color. In this scenario, whites despised blacks because black skin became in the United States a powerful symbol of the suffering and death that no one wanted and with which no one wished to come into contact. And so for many years white America has segregated blacks into neighborhoods far removed from the manicured lawns and the beautiful homes of the privileged. This is the truth to which James Baldwin pointed when he wrote, "White Americans do not believe in death, and this is why the darkness of my skin so intimidates them."[5]

Our prison system performs much the same function, effectively removing from the daily lives of privileged Americans the black, the brown, and the poor. Society's concern to remove them from the perfect world we seek to create is particularly evident in its resistance to prevention and its commitment to punishment. By and large, Americans would far prefer to lock people up than to provide the kinds of programs that might prevent crime in the first place or that might rehabilitate offenders. When one couples that reality with a privatized prison system that encourages incarceration, we find we cannot build prisons quickly enough to cope with the vast population that we seek to place behind bars.

The point I seek to make through all these examples should be clear: privileged Americans are committed to creating for themselves a perfect world in a golden age that has little to do with the tragic contents of human history with which so many people, both in the United States and in so many other parts of the world, must deal every day. In this context, historian Edward T. Linenthal, describing the April 19, 1995, bombing of the Alfred P. Murrah Federal Building in Oklahoma City, wrote, "There was, seemingly, nowhere in the storehouse of American meaning to place the bombing, to make sense of it. It was, quite literally, 'out of place.'" It was out of place, Linenthal wrote, because it "activated enduring convictions that Americans were peaceable citizens of an innocent and vulnerable nation in a largely wicked world. Thus, the evocative power of headlines: 'Myth of Midwest safety shattered' . . . [and] 'American innocence buried in Oklahoma.'"[6]

Similarly, Mark Slouka suggested that Americans found the September 11, 2001, attack on the Pentagon and the World Trade Center particularly traumatic because

it simultaneously exposed and challenged the myth of our own uniqueness. A myth most visible, perhaps, in our age-old denial of death.

Consider it. Here in the New Canaan, in the land of perpetual beginnings and second chances, where identity could be sloughed and sloughed again and history was someone else's problem, death had never been welcome. Death was a foreigner—radical, disturbing, smelling of musty books and brimstone. We wanted no part of him.

And now death had come calling. That troubled brother, so long forgotten, so successfully erased, was standing on our porch in his steel-toed boots, grinning. He'd made it across the ocean, passed like a ghost through the gates of our chosen community. We had denied him his due. . . . Yet here he was.

Slouka concluded, "This was not just a terrorist attack. This was an act of metaphysical trespass."[7]

Since September 1, 2011, the United States has grown far more familiar with wholesale death from terror attacks. Still and all, the American predisposition to cling to an image of the nation as fundamentally innocent remains firmly embedded in the American psyche and has its deepest roots in the two great myths that gripped the imagination of the American people when the nation was young—the Myth of Nature's Nation and the Myth of the Millennial Nation.[8]

The Paradox of the Myth of Innocence

Any exploration of the history of the myth of innocence almost invariably reveals that it finally transforms itself into its opposite. Indeed, it typically encourages those who march under its banner to repress those they regard as corrupted or defiled. Paradoxically, then, the innocent become guilty along with the rest of the human race, though the myths they have embraced prevent them from discerning their guilt.

The dynamics of this paradox are illumined by two Christian traditions that first emerged on the nineteenth-century American frontier and that I presented in chapter 4—the Latter-day Saints (Mormons) and the Disciples/Churches of Christ. These two traditions take us to the heart of America's mythic self-understanding, for both embraced the recovery of pure beginnings (primitive church) as the means to usher in the golden age at the end of time (millennium). Like the larger nation, therefore, they stood with one foot in the dawn of time—or at least the only time that mattered for them—and the other in the world's evening shadows, and both, like the larger nation, regarded the intervening history as essentially irrelevant. And because they had leapfrogged over human history, both traditions imagined that they had achieved a level of purity and innocence denied to those earthlings still rooted in the messy ambiguities of ordinary time and space.[9]

Though defending their innocence all the while, it was therefore not uncommon for early adherents to these two traditions to threaten other Christians with divine retribution, rooted in the innocence both presumed about themselves. A single example from each tradition will suffice.

With respect to the Disciples/Churches of Christ, one of their preachers, John R. Howard, warned in 1843 that "the coming of the Lord, in vengeance to destroy his enemies, cannot . . . be very far off. . . . And should *you* not be found among his true people—his genuine disciples—but arrayed in opposition against them, he will 'destroy' you 'with the *breath* of his *mouth*, and with the *brightness* of his *coming*.'"[10]

On the Mormon side of the ledger, Parley Pratt, an early Mormon missionary, published in 1837 *A Voice of Warning*, a book that Mormon scholars have regarded as "the most important of all non-canonical Mormon books" and "the most important missionary pamphlet in the early history of the church."[11] In that book, Pratt argued that the Mormon faith "is the gospel which **God** has commanded us to preach. . . . And no other system of religion . . . is of any use; every thing different from this, is a perverted gospel, bringing a curse upon them that preach it, and upon them that hear it." In fact, all who resisted the Mormon message "shall alike feel the hand of the almighty, by pestilence, famine, earthquake, and the sword: yea, ye shall be drunken with your own blood . . . until your cities are desolate . . . until all lyings, priestcrafts, and all manner of abomination, shall be done away."[12]

Both these traditions asserted their innocence on the grounds that they had fully replicated the perfections of the first age. As it turned out, however, they fell into the guilt of history in spite of themselves. The innocence they presumed prompted an arrogance they could not admit, for the myth of innocence shielded them from their sins. So they persisted in their claims to perfection, even as they broke community and ruptured relations with their brothers and sisters in other communities of the Christian faith.

These two traditions provide a microcosmic window onto the myth of innocence that played itself out in the early years of the larger Republic, for both emerged and grew up when the nation was young and borrowed from the larger culture the mythic themes that defined them. For this reason, when we explore the mythic dimensions of these two traditions, we can learn much about the mythic dimensions of the nation at large.

Like the Mormons and Disciples/Churches of Christ, the larger nation grounded its sense of innocence in the way it identified with the golden age of the past (the time of creation) and the golden age of the future (the millennium). Since America refused to admit its debt to human history and imagined itself a "new order of the ages," it also imagined it could lead the world into a golden age of "liberty and justice for all."

The problems emerged when other nations resisted the American version of "liberty and justice for all"; or when America failed—as it often did—to separate its vision of "liberty and justice for all" from its own political, economic, and military interests; or when, on the domestic front, it confused "liberty and justice for all" with liberty and justice for whites. In this way, while proclaiming its innocence and the purity of its motives, America—like the other nations of the world—also fell into the guilt of history. This is the point, however, that white Americans often failed to see, since the Myth of the Innocent Nation shielded them from the realities that were so apparent to minorities at home and to so many others around the world.

America: The Innocent Nation

While the myth of innocence was implicit in American culture at the time of the founding, it became especially prominent in American life from World War I to the Vietnam War.

World War I

The way America defined its role in World War I established the essential pattern to which the myth of innocence would conform itself for the rest of the twentieth century. No one did more to define that pattern than President Woodrow Wilson who viewed the enemy as implacably evil. In a message to the Congress on April 2, 1917, Wilson described the Imperial German government as one "which has thrown aside all considerations of humanity and of right and is running amuck."[13] When the war was over and Wilson presented the treaty for ratification, he reflected once again on what he regarded as the demonic character of the Imperial German government. America entered this war, he said, "because we saw the supremacy, and even the validity, of right everywhere put in jeopardy and free government likely to be everywhere imperiled by the intolerable aggression of a power which respected neither right nor obligation and whose every system of government flouted the rights of the citizen as against the autocratic authority of his governors."[14]

At the same time, Wilson presented the American cause as righteous, innocent, and free of self-interest. Shortly after America entered the war in 1917, Wilson explained to the American people that "there is not a single selfish element so far as I can see, in the cause we are fighting for. We are fighting for what we believe and wish to be the rights of mankind and for the future peace and security of the world."[15]

Two weeks earlier, he presented a similar case to the U.S. Congress: "We have no selfish ends to serve. We desire no conquest, no dominion. We seek no indemnities for ourselves, no material compensation for the sacrifices we shall freely make. We are but one of the champions of the rights of mankind."[16]

When the war was over, he confirmed that judgment. "The United States entered the war upon a different footing from every other nation except our associates on this side of the sea," he said. "We entered it, not because our material interests were directly threatened or because any special treaty obligations to which we were parties had been violated." Rather, America entered the war "only as the champion of rights which she was glad to share with free men and lovers of justice everywhere. . . . We were welcomed as disinterested friends. . . . We were generously accepted as the unaffected champions of what was right." [17]

Wilson could make these claims because he so completely grounded the American mission in what he imagined were the principles built into the natural order from the time of creation. Accordingly, in a speech to the Senate on January 22, 1917, he stated flatly, "American principles [and] American policies . . . are the principles of mankind, and must prevail." [18]

Wilson also believed that American principles and policies would usher in a final golden age for all humanity. American soldiers fought, he said, not for a penultimate or short-term peace, but "for the ultimate peace of the world." He hoped, like the British politician David Lloyd George, that this conflict would be the war to end all war. Further, through the implementation of American principles and policies, he hoped to make the world "safe for democracy." [19] Clearly, Wilson aimed for nothing less than a golden age of liberty, democracy, and justice for all humankind, a goal that allowed him to imagine that American involvement in the war was innocent of self-serving motivations.

One fact belied that conviction, however—the widely held ambition so baldly stated by Senator Albert Beveridge only twenty years before that "we are enlisted in the cause of American supremacy, which will never end until American commerce has made the conquest of the world." When one combines that objective with the fact that American commercial investments abroad quadrupled between 1897 and 1914, it becomes apparent that American entry into World War I was hardly free of self-serving motivations. Wilson described how German attacks on American vessels had produced a "very serious congestion of our commerce . . . which is growing rapidly more and more serious every day." Indeed, he noted, American commerce suffered not only from direct attack, but from the many commercial vessels that sat idly in port "because of the unwillingness of our ship-owners to risk their vessels at sea without insurance or adequate protection." [20]

When the war was over, Edward N. Hurley, head of the U.S. Shipping Board, confirmed the way Americans at that time often confused the dream of universal peace and justice with the dream of the economic conquest of the world. In a memo to Bernard Baruch, head of the War Industries Board, Hurley wrote, "If America would invest substantially in the essential raw materials of all foreign countries . . . America would then be in a position to say to the rest of the world, that these commodities would be sold at a fair price. . . . In what better way could we be of real service than by the use of our financial strength to control the raw materials for the benefit of humanity?" [21]

Nonetheless, Wilson obscured the commercial motivation for American involvement in the war when he told the Congress, "I have spoken of our commerce and of the legitimate errands of our people on the seas, but you will not be misled as to my main thought. . . . I am thinking not only of the rights of Americans to go and come about their proper business by way of the sea, but also of something much deeper, much more fundamental than that. I am thinking of those rights of humanity without which there is no civilization."[22]

There is no reason to doubt Wilson's sincerity when he claimed that his foremost consideration was the "rights of humanity without which there is no civilization," but why did he obscure the commercial motivation for American involvement in the war? It is safe to say that Wilson—along with many other Americans—might not have discerned the dimensions of self-interest inherent in American commerce. After all, they had for many years believed that capitalism and commercial activity simply reflected the universal "principles of mankind."

One other event belied American claims during World War I that it was an innocent participant, altogether free of self-interested motivation. When the government took extraordinary steps to punish dissenters and to convince the American people to support the war, one can only conclude that the official rationale—to secure the rights of all mankind—was not all that self-evident, and that many Americans detected a dimension of self-interest that the government refused to admit.

Indeed, the Committee on Public Information (CPI), directed by Denver newsman George Creel, aimed a vigorous propaganda campaign directly at the American people. Employing artists, musicians, journalists, historians, and a host of other creative professionals, the CPI produced patriotic posters, books like *German War Practices*, and films like *The Beast of Berlin*, all designed to demonize the enemy and portray the American cause as both innocent and righteous. Strikingly, Creel never admitted that CPI productions were propagandistic in any sense at all. Rather, they simply presented "value-free" facts that were self-evident to any reasonable observer—a conclusion completely in harmony with the notion that America was an "innocent nation," standing for "the principles of mankind."[23]

By and large, the American public responded positively to the campaign, demonizing all things German and equating German people, German language, and German culture with disloyalty to American principles and the American mission. Schools throughout the country, for example, dropped the study of the German language, and while Americans continued to eat "sauerkraut," they renamed it "liberty cabbage."

Still, there were dissenters. Consequently, the CPI censored materials that disagreed with its own propaganda and sought to squelch those who dared to question the dominant ideology. The Espionage and Sedition Acts, in fact, essentially made criticism of the government and its war policies illegal. Passed on June 15, 1917, the Espionage Act made it possible to fine dissenters up to $10,000 and imprison them for up to twenty years. Possible offenses included disloyalty, statements that might interfere with the war effort, giving aid to the enemy, refusing duty in the armed services, or inciting insubordination in the armed services. Passed almost a year later, on May 16, 1918, the Sedition Act extended these penalties to anyone who spoke, wrote, or printed anything that might be considered "disloyal, profane, scurrilous, or abusive" about the government, the Constitution, or the armed services.

The irony, of course, lies in the fact that while America sought, through participating in World War I, to secure the rights of all mankind and to make "the world safe for democracy," it abridged the rights of American citizens and undermined the democratic process in the homeland. In this way, the myth of innocence turned in upon itself. When all was said and done, America participated in the guilt that inevitably belongs to participants in human history in spite of every effort to avoid it. Most Americans, however, could scarcely discern that guilt, so strong was the myth of America as the Innocent Nation.

The notion of national innocence not only blinded President Wilson to the nation's self-serving motivations in World War I— its drive toward "American supremacy" and the economic "conquest of the world." As I noted in chapter 1, it also blinded him to the degree of white supremacy that flourished within the borders of the United States.

Wilson served as president of Princeton University between 1902 and 1910—a time when Paul Robeson, an African American destined to achieve great fame as an athlete, an actor, and a singer, was growing up in the shadow of that institution. The Witherspoon Street Presbyterian Church called his father, the Reverend W. D. Robeson, to pastor that congregation in 1898, the same year Paul was born.

Robeson later recalled that "the Princeton of my boyhood . . . was for all the world like any small town in the deep South," a town that routinely practiced "the most rigid social and economic patterns of White Supremacy. . . . Rich Princeton was white. . . . The people of our small Negro community were, for the most part, a servant class—domestics in the homes of the wealthy, serving as cooks, waiters and caretakers at the university, coachmen for the town and laborers at the nearby farms and brickyards. . . . The grade school that I attended was segregated and Negroes were not permitted in any high school." Princeton, Robeson flatly affirmed, "was Jim Crow."

In that context, his father became a "bridge between the Have-nots and the Haves," and working in that capacity, was well known and respected throughout the Princeton community, even by the president of the university:

> But though the door of the university president might be open to him, Reverend Robeson could not push open the doors of that school for his son, when Bill was ready for college. The pious president, a fellow Presbyterian, said: No, it is quite impossible. That was Woodrow Wilson . . ., advocate of democracy for the world and Jim Crow for America![24]

World War II

The American experience in World War I prepared the country to imagine itself an innocent, disinterested participant in the conflicts of the world. Grounded in the laws of "Nature and Nature's God" and defined by Christian virtues, America stood poised to lead the world into a golden age of liberty and justice for all. American involvement in World War II only confirmed the validity of these myths in the minds of the American people. In part, this was because in that particular war, the face of evil seemed so thoroughly apparent.

President Franklin D. Roosevelt framed the issues in his message to the Congress on January 6, 1942, only a month after the Japanese attacked Pearl Harbor. Above all else, Roosevelt sought to portray the Axis forces as fundamentally demonic and America as fundamentally good:

> Our enemies are guided by brutal cynicism, by unholy contempt for the human race. We are inspired by a faith which goes back through all the years to the first chapter of the Book of Genesis: "God created man in His own image." We on our side are striving to be true to that divine heritage. We are fighting, as our fathers have fought, to uphold the doctrine that all men are equal in the sight of God. Those on the other side are striving to destroy this deep belief and to create a world in their own image—a world of tyranny and cruelty and serfdom. . . . There never has been—there never can be—successful compromise between good and evil. Only total victory can reward the champions of tolerance and decency, and freedom, and faith.[25]

In this way, Roosevelt kept alive the theme of American innocence that had been articulated so well by Woodrow Wilson a quarter of a century earlier.

In addition, Roosevelt grounded the theme of American innocence in the very same myths to which Wilson had appealed. He invoked the Myth of Nature's Nation when he declared the American cause a universal cause. Americans were fighting, he said, "not only for ourselves, but for all men, not only for one generation, but for all generations."[26] And he invoked the venerable Myth of the Millennial Nation when he declared the American intention "to cleanse the world of ancient evils, ancient ills" and "to make very certain that the world will never suffer again."[27] Here is the old, familiar pattern: The anticipated golden age of liberty and justice for all is grounded in the golden age of creation. By identifying with these mythic times that bracketed the history of humankind, America emerged as God's agent for good in a sinful world. Perhaps most striking, one of the myths to which Roosevelt appealed was the Myth of the Christian Nation. "The world is too small to provide adequate 'living room' for both Hitler and God. In proof of that[, the] Nazis have now announced their plan for enforcing their new German, pagan religion throughout the world—the plan by which the Holy Bible and the Cross of Mercy would be displaced by 'Mein Kampf' and the swastika and the naked sword."[28]

Significantly, it was the way this "innocent nation" treated blacks during and following World War II that became, for James Baldwin, "a turning point in the Negro's relation to America. To put it briefly, and somewhat too simply, a certain hope died, a certain respect for white Americans faded." Then Baldwin explained:

> You must put yourself in the skin of a man who is wearing the uniform of his country, is a candidate for death in its defense, and who is called a "nigger" by his comrades-in-arms and his officers; who is almost always given the hardest, ugliest, most menial work to do; who knows that the white G.I. has informed the Europeans that he is subhuman . . . ; who does not dance at the U.S.O. the night white soldiers dance there, and does not drink in the same bars white soldiers drink in; and who watches German prisoners of war being treated by Americans with more human dignity than he has ever received at their hands. And who, at the same time, as a human being, is far freer in a strange land than he has ever been at home. *Home!* The very word begins to have a despairing diabolical ring. You must consider what happens to this citizen, after all he has endured, when he returns home: search, in his shoes, for a job, for a place to live; ride, in his skin, on segregated buses; see, with his eyes, the signs saying "White" and "Colored," and especially the signs that say "White Ladies" and "Colored *Women*"; look into the eyes of his wife; look into the eyes of his son; listen, with his ears, to political speeches, North and South; imagine yourself being told to "wait." And all this is happening in the richest and freest country in the world, and in the middle of the twentieth century.[29]

That is the context for the story Toni Morrison relates of Isaac Woodard, a black veteran of World War II who, in 1946, returned from Europe to his home in North Carolina. "He had spent four years in the army," Morrison writes, "—in the Pacific Theater (where he was promoted to sergeant) and in the Asiatic Pacific (where he earned a campaign medal, a World War II Victory Medal, and the Good Conduct Medal)." Woodard was on a Greyhound bus on the final leg of his journey:

> When the bus reached a rest stop, he asked the bus driver if there was time to use the restroom. They argued, but he was allowed to use the facilities. Later, when the bus stopped in Batesburg, South Carolina, the driver called the police to remove Sergeant Woodard (apparently for going to the bathroom). The chief, Linwood Shull, took Woodard to a nearby alleyway where he and a number of other policemen beat him with their nightsticks. Then they took him to jail and arrested him for disorderly conduct. During his night in jail, the chief of police beat Woodard with a billy club and gouged out his eyes. The next morning Woodard was sent before a local judge, who found him guilty and fined him fifty dollars. Woodard asked for medical care and two days later it arrived. Meantime, not knowing where he was and suffering from mild amnesia, he was taken to a hospital in Aiken, South Carolina. Three weeks after he was reported missing by his family, he was located and rushed to an army hospital in Spartanburg. Both eyes remained damaged beyond repair. He lived, though blind, until 1992, when he died at age seventy-three. After thirty minutes of deliberation, Chief Shull was acquitted of all charges, to the wild applause of an all-white jury.[30]

The Communist Threat

I have observed several times that it is far easier to think of one's self as righteous and pure if one confronts an enemy that can be characterized as utterly evil. Germany became that enemy during World War I, and Germany, Japan, and Italy all presented Americans with the face of evil during World War II. By the 1950s, those wars were over and the enemy had disappeared. But communism—symbolized best by the Soviet Union—emerged to fill the void. In that context, one American summoned the nation to "faith in Jesus Christ" as the best and surest defense against "godless" Communism. That American was Billy Graham.

Graham came to national prominence in 1949 when he held a revival in Los Angeles and told the crowd, "Do you know that the Fifth Columnists, called Communists, are more rampant in Los Angeles than any other city in America?" Graham saw a solution, a solution rooted deeply in William Tyndale's notion of the national covenant (see chapter 2). "If we repent, if we believe, if we turn to Christ in faith and hope, the judgment of God can be stopped."[31]

Graham's appeal to the nation to turn to Christ as the way to fulfill the requirements of the national covenant and thereby defeat godless communism became a feature of Graham's preaching for many years. In sermon after sermon, he appealed to the covenant theme. On one occasion, he counseled his audience, "Until this nation humbles itself and prays and . . . receives Christ as Savior, there is no hope for preserving the American way of life." On another occasion, he flatly stated, "Only as millions of Americans turn to Jesus Christ at this hour and accept him as their Savior, can this nation possibly be spared the onslaught of a demon-possessed communism."[32] William G. McLoughlin Jr., a historian of American religion at Brown University, observed in 1960 that "scarcely one of his Sunday afternoon sermons over a nine-year period has failed to touch on communism."[33]

Graham perhaps did as much as any other American in the 1950s to divide the world into good versus evil. "Christian America" embodied good while communism and the Soviet Union embodied evil. "America," he said in 1952, "is the last bulwark of Christian civilization." On the other hand, "Communism is . . . master-minded by Satan," and the two were engaged in a life and death struggle. In this way, Graham reaffirmed the myth of American innocence.

Little wonder that Graham rejoiced when Dwight Eisenhower was elected president in 1952. After Eisenhower prayed at his own inauguration, Graham exulted, "The overwhelming majority of the American people felt a little more secure realizing that we have a man who believes in prayer at the helm of our government at this critical hour." After he attended a prayer meeting with Eisenhower in 1953, Graham affirmed that "God is giving us a respite, a new chance. . . . We are no longer going to be pushed around" by the Communists.[34]

By 1955 the innocence that Americans believed was their birthright seemed to have been realized. As William Lee Miller put it, "Ike was in his White House and all was right with the world."[35] By then Americans had inherited the entire mythic history of the Republic. They understood themselves as an Innocent Nation, standing with one foot in the golden age of the past (Nature's Nation) and the other in the golden age of the future (the Millennial Nation). They had been chosen by Almighty God to enlighten the world with liberty and justice for all. And if America was not altogether a Christian nation, at least it was infused with the virtues taught by the Christian faith.

An African American Critique of the Myth of American Innocence

Suddenly, almost without warning, a bombshell dropped into the idyllic American garden of the 1950s. We call that bombshell the 1960s. When we use the phrase *the 1960s*, we don't mean a decade that ran from 1960 to 1969.

Rather, we mean a period of American history defined by intense social unrest that focused especially on racial discrimination and civil rights, on the one hand, and the Vietnam War, on the other. In a very real sense, that period began in Montgomery, Alabama, in 1955, when Rosa Parks refused to give up her seat on a city bus to a white man. It is difficult to determine precisely when that period ended, but one convenient date is March 29, 1973, when the last American combat troops left Vietnam.

By any measure, the 1960s was a watershed in American history. It shattered the sense of innocence that prevailed in the 1950s and exposed layers of guilt that, in turn, deeply divided the nation. In the beginning of this chapter, we noted how Lawrence Wright envied his father. "He matured in a magic age, the 1940s," Wright recalled, "when great evil and great good faced each other." And Wright "grew up expecting to inherit his [father's] certainty."

Yet, as a child of the 1960s, he found himself part of a disillusioned generation, entertaining the deepest doubts regarding the meaning of the United States. "It is easy to understand my anger, and the anger of my generation when we realized that our country had taken a wrong turn," Wright wrote. "Eisenhower was right: we had forfeited our moral position. We had surrendered our anticolonial past. Now that we were compromised, the world did not divide so neatly between good and evil."[36]

The Black Revolution

Black Americans emerged in the 1960s as some of the nation's most insightful social critics, offering important critiques of the myth of American innocence. In this limited space, I will consider five: Martin Luther King Jr., Angela Davis, James Baldwin, Eldridge Cleaver, and Malcolm X. We will hear their critiques in the context of the two most important events in this period: the civil rights movement and the war in Vietnam.

Martin Luther King Jr.

On December 1, 1955, Rosa Parks refused to abandon her seat on a Montgomery, Alabama, city bus for a white man. For this infraction of the southern code, she was arrested. The black community in Montgomery, under the leadership of Martin Luther King Jr., a young minister for the Dexter Avenue Baptist Church, responded with a massive nonviolent bus boycott that crippled downtown businesses and eventually won bus desegregation. Similar protests, organized and executed by blacks, soon erupted in other parts of the South.

Inspired by King's nonviolent philosophy, blacks protested the segregation of southern restaurants in a series of lunch-counter sit-ins, staged in numerous southern cities, beginning in 1960. The following year, they protested the segregation of interstate buses in the South that continued despite a 1946 Supreme Court ruling (*Morgan v. Virginia*) and an Interstate Commerce Commission order in 1955, both of which had made segregation on interstate travel facilities illegal. The Congress of Racial Equality (CORE), led by James Farmer, commissioned "freedom rides," buses that carried blacks and whites together through many sections of the American South, testing whether the federal government would enforce its own laws. Though nonviolent themselves, protesters in almost all these efforts met with violence, instigated by whites.

Because the Montgomery Bus Boycott catapulted Martin Luther King into national leadership of the Civil Rights Movement, it is important to come to terms with his character and his commitments. First, it is impossible to understand King apart from his allegiance both to the American nation and to the American Creed. At the same time, he was convinced that, through years of segregation and racial discrimination, the nation had sold its soul and abandoned its founding aspirations. In his view, most white Americans had no clear sense of the nation's meaning or, if they did, they paid it no serious heed. He therefore determined to call the nation back to its own noblest ideals.

Perhaps nowhere did King make that case more effectively than in his "I Have a Dream" speech, delivered to the throngs of people who had assembled for a massive March on Washington in 1963—a march that A. Philip Randolph and others had proposed as early as 1941. At one point in that speech he told the crowd, "When the architects of our republic wrote the magnificent words of the Constitution and the Declaration of Independence, they were signing a promissory note to which every American was to fall heir." That note, King believed, promised "that all men, yes, black men as well as white men, would be guaranteed the unalienable rights of life, liberty, and the pursuit of happiness." Nevertheless, he noted,

> It is obvious today that America has defaulted on this promissory note in so far as her citizens of color are concerned. Instead of honoring this sacred obligation, America has given the Negro people a bad check; a check which has come back marked "insufficient funds." We refuse to believe that there are insufficient funds in the great vaults of opportunity of this nation. And so we've come to cash this check, a check that will give us upon demand the riches of freedom and the security of justice.

King explained that this dream was "a dream deeply rooted in the American dream that one day this nation will rise up and live out the true meaning of its creed—we hold these truths to be self-evident, that all men are created equal."[37] For King, the true meaning of the American Creed demanded racial integration at every significant level of American life.

Nor can one understand King apart from his Christian heritage. A Baptist minister himself, and the son and the grandson of Baptist ministers, King understood the message of Jesus on the value of every human being. In addition, the works of Reinhold Niebuhr—especially his book *Moral Man and Immoral Society*—had convinced King that dispossessed people must challenge their oppressors through "direct action"—behavior that would inconvenience the oppressor in some significant way. Finally, inspired both by Jesus and by India's Mahatma Gandhi, King preached a message of nonviolent resistance against the policies of segregation and discrimination. King argued that only a nonviolent approach to these issues would preserve the integrity of the protesters while revealing the racist dimensions of American life for all to see.

That strategy paid especially rich dividends in 1963 when King led a protest march through the streets of Birmingham, Alabama. Television cameras were rolling when Sheriff Eugene "Bull" Connor's men turned police dogs and high-powered fire hoses on the nonviolent demonstrators, most of them children. The next day, pictures of police hosing demonstrators and clubbing young black girls appeared in newspapers and magazines throughout the United States and the world. These events captured the imaginations of many young whites throughout the nation. The issues for them were clear: Blacks were only demanding what the American Creed had promised them, but their parents' generation had refused to make that promise good.

Lawrence Wright was a case in point. "In Dallas," he recalled,

> we didn't know what to make of the Freedom Riders. When the first busload . . . approached Anniston, Alabama, in 1961, a mob punctured the bus's tires and set it on fire. The next bus made it to Birmingham, where the police stood aside and let the white mob beat the riders nearly to death. . . . I didn't clearly understand that the Freedom Riders were not fighting back. Nonviolence was such a foreign idea to me that I assumed the blacks and several whites on the buses had provoked the mob and got what was coming to them. I didn't grasp the philosophy of nonresistance—but then nothing in my years of churchgoing had prepared me to understand the power of suffering, or redemptive love.

Wright found it "unsettling to hear Martin Luther King . . . talking about Jesus." He recalled King's words at the 1960 lunch-counter sit-ins in Durham, North Carolina: "I am still convinced that Jesus was right. . . . I can hear Him saying, 'He who lives by the sword will perish by the sword.' I can hear him crying out, 'Love thy enemies.'"

King's rhetoric, coupled with black-led struggles for equal opportunity, caused Larry Wright—as it caused a whole generation of white youth—to raise serious questions about the meaning of the American experiment. King's injunctions to "love thy enemies" were themes, Wright recalled, that "I also heard nearly every Sunday, but didn't we, as a nation, live by the sword? . . . Our doctrine was brotherly love. And yet no one ever proposed that Jesus might return as a Negro."[38]

If Martin Luther King Jr. and the nonviolent, southern phase of the civil rights movement called on America to "live out the true meaning of its creed," other blacks wondered whether the American Creed had been so badly betrayed that there was little left to retrieve. As a result, many of these blacks turned their backs on nonviolence as a workable strategy for change and embraced black power instead. Some in this group advocated socialism and the overthrow of capitalism. James Forman, for example, wrote, "Our fight is against racism, capitalism and imperialism, and we are dedicated to building a socialist society inside the United States."[39]

Who were these radicals, many of whom had lost faith both in America and the American Creed?

Angela Davis

One was a woman named Angela Davis. Born in 1944, Davis grew up in Birmingham, Alabama, where whites rigidly maintained segregation by custom and by law, enforced by intimidation, violence, and the threat of violence. She recalled in her autobiography what life was like for her as a child:

> Near my father's service station downtown was a movie house called The Alabama. . . . A luxurious red carpet extended all the way to the sidewalk. On Saturdays and Sundays, the marquee always bore the titles of the latest children's movies. . . . We weren't allowed in The Alabama—our theaters were the Carver and the Eighth Avenue, and the best we could expect in their roach-infested auditoriums was reruns of Tarzan. . . . Downtown . . ., if we were hungry, we had to wait until we retreated back into a Black neighborhood, because the restaurants and food stands were reserved for whites only. . . . If we needed to go to the toilet or wanted a drink of water, we had to seek out a sign bearing the inscription "Colored." Most Southern Black children of my generation learned how to read the words "Colored" and "White" long before they learned "Look, Dick, look."[40]

She learned as a child "the prevailing myth . . . that poverty is a punishment for idleness and indolence. If you had nothing to show for yourself, it meant that you hadn't worked hard enough." Further, at Carrie A. Tuggle Elementary School, many of her teachers "tended to inculcate in us the official, racist explanation for our misery" and explained to the children that if they would only work hard, "[we could] lift ourselves singly and separately out of the muck and slime of poverty by 'our own bootstraps.'"

These explanations made less and less sense to Davis. She knew how hard her parents had worked, and "it didn't make sense to me that all those who had not 'made it' were suffering for their lack of desire and the defectiveness of their will to achieve a better life for themselves. If this were true, then, great numbers of our people—perhaps the majority—had really been lazy and shiftless, as white people were always saying."[41]

At the age of fourteen, Davis left Birmingham to participate in a program in New York City that brought black students from the South to integrated schools in the North. There she first read the *Communist Manifesto* and there she first encountered a circle of blacks devoted to Marxist ideals. She later recalled that "the *Communist Manifesto* hit me like a bolt of lightning."[42]

In 1963 Angela Davis was studying in France when she read in an English-language newspaper a story about some murders in her own hometown of Birmingham: "I saw a headline about four girls and a church bombing. At first I was only vaguely aware of the words. Then it hit me! It came crashing down all around me. Birmingham. 16th Street Baptist Church. The names. I closed my eyes, squeezing my lids into wrinkles as if I could squeeze what I had just read out of my head. . . . I kept staring at the names. Carole Robertson. Cynthia Wesley. Addie Mae Collins. Denise McNair."

Davis had known each of these girls and known them well. "When the lives of these four girls were so ruthlessly wiped out," she wrote, "my pain was deeply personal." In time she began to think clearly about the meaning of these murders. "This act was not an aberration," she wrote. "On the contrary, it was logical, inevitable. The people who planted the bomb in the girls' restroom in the basement of 16th Street Baptist Church were not pathological but rather the normal products of their surroundings." Whoever committed this act, she believed, "wanted to terrorize Birmingham's Black population," regardless of who might be killed. "The broken bodies of Cynthia, Carole, Addie Mae and Denise were incidental to the main thing—which was precisely why the murders were even more abominable than if they had been deliberately planned."[43]

In 1968 Angela Davis joined the Communist Party.[44] In 1970 Governor Ronald Reagan fired her from her position as professor of philosophy at

UCLA on the grounds that ""the board will not tolerate any Communist activities at any state institution." In that same year, she found herself on the FBI's "Ten Most Wanted" list. The bureau charged her with planning the rescue of three San Quentin prisoners and supplying the gun that killed four people during the rescue attempt. In 1972, thanks to a massive international campaign, she was acquitted.

The year before her acquittal, Davis wrote from her cell in the Marin County, California, jail of the system she had come to reject. She wrote of "unjust laws, bolstering the oppression of Black people." She wrote of the "racist oppression [that] invades the lives of Black people on an infinite variety of levels." And she wrote of the police who, she said, were "the oppressor's emissaries, charged with the task of containing us within the boundaries of our oppression."[45] Quite clearly, for Angela Davis, the notion that America was an Innocent Nation was a myth completely lacking in legitimacy or justification.

The story of Angela Davis helps us understand in considerable depth how and why the meaning of America was unraveling in the 1960s and early 1970s, at least within the black community. Indeed, Davis viewed her story as the story of a much larger cause. "The forces that have made my life what it is are the very same forces that have shaped and misshaped the lives of millions of my people," she wrote.[46] This is why her story demands thoughtful consideration.

James Baldwin

By any measure, James Baldwin provided the literary voice for the Civil Rights Movement. Born in 1924, some thirty years before the rise of that movement, he experienced the brunt of racism and segregation as a youth growing up in Harlem. At only 24 years old, he fled the United States and settled in France where he spent much of his life.

It is safe to say that no one during the 1960s mounted a more devastating critique of white supremacy and the myth of innocence that gave it protection than James Baldwin. For example, in his "Letter to My Nephew," one of the essays of his 1963 classic, *The Fire Next Time*, Baldwin spoke forcefully of the myth of American innocence and the terror for which it provided cover. "My country and my countrymen," he said, "have destroyed and are destroying hundreds of thousands of lives and do not know it and do not want to know it." Indeed, most of all "it is the innocence which constitutes the crime."

Baldwin then explained to his nephew what his nephew already knew from experience—the nature of the terror for which the myth of innocence provided cover:

This innocent country set you down in a ghetto in which, in fact, it intended that you should perish. Let me spell out precisely what I mean by that, for the heart of the matter is here, and the root of my dispute with my country. You were born where you were born and faced the future that you faced because you were black and *for no other reason*. The limits of your ambition were, thus, expected to be set forever. You were born into a society which spelled out with brutal clarity, and in as many ways as possible, that you were a worthless human being. You were not expected to aspire to excellence: you were expected to make peace with mediocrity. Wherever you have turned, James, in your short time on this earth, you have been told where you could go and what you could do (and *how* you could do it) and where you could live and whom you could marry.

And then, fully anticipating the objections from whites whose sense of innocence would prompt both denial and disbelief, Baldwin continued, "I know your countrymen do not agree with me about this, and I hear them saying, 'You exaggerate.' [But] they do not know Harlem, and I do. So do you."[47]

Significantly, Baldwin grounded the myth of American innocence in America's failure—perhaps its refusal—to grasp its own history and the guilt its history bears. "These innocent people . . . [are] still trapped in a history which they do not understand; and until they understand it, they cannot be released from it," Baldwin wrote. Typically, however, they could not afford to grapple with their history, and what prevented that grappling was "the danger" which, "in the minds of most white Americans," was "the loss of their identity," which was rooted in black subservience. Indeed, Baldwin wrote, "the black man has functioned in the white man's world as a fixed star, as an immovable pillar: and as he moves out of his place, heaven and earth are shaken to their foundations."[48]

On November of 1970, shortly after the FBI placed Angela Davis's name on its Ten Most Wanted Fugitive List and following her capture, *Newsweek* placed a photo of a handcuffed Davis on its cover with the headline, "Angela Davis: Black Revolutionary."[49] In response, Baldwin penned "An Open Letter to My Sister, Miss Angela Davis." In that letter he returned to the myth of innocence and how it was rooted in white America's refusal to come to terms with the terrors of its history. America was "on the edge of absolute chaos," he wrote. The period of the black revolution "was a day which Americans never expected or desired to see, however piously they may declare their belief in 'progress and democracy.'" They were not prepared because white Americans "never expected to be confronted with the algebra of their history."

Blacks, on the other hand, understood all too well "the algebra of [American] history" and the impact of that history on black consciousness and black self-esteem:

The American triumph—in which the American tragedy has always been implicit—was to make black people despise themselves. When I was little I despised myself, I did not know better. And this meant, albeit unconsciously, or against my will, or in great pain, that I also despised my father. *And* my mother. *And* my brothers. *And* my sisters. Black people were killing each other every Saturday night out on Lenox Avenue, when I was growing up; and no one explained to them, or to me, that it was *intended* that they should; that they were penned where they were, like animals, in order that they should consider themselves no better than animals. Everything supported this sense of reality, nothing denied it: and so one was ready, when it came time to go to work, to be treated as a slave.

While the question of the American future was far from clear in 1970, of one thing Baldwin was certain—that blacks, unlike whites, had come to terms with their history and, through that action, had taken decisive steps toward freedom. Baldwin therefore encouraged Davis with this assessment: "What has happened, it seems to me, and to put it far too simply, is that a whole generation of people have assessed and absorbed their history, and, in that tremendous action, have freed themselves of it and will never be victims again." Indeed, Baldwin wrote, "we must fight for your life as though it were our own—which it is—and render impassable with our bodies the corridor to the gas chamber. For, if they take you in the morning, they will be coming for us that night."[50]

Eldridge Cleaver

Eldridge Cleaver, minister of information of the Black Panther party, offered a striking critique of several American myths in *Soul on Ice*, a book that he wrote from his cell at Folsom Prison. He began his critique with the myth of American innocence and the way that myth was rooted in white America's denial of its history. The white youth of America, he wrote,

> must face and admit the moral truth concerning the works of their fathers. That such venerated figures as George Washington and Thomas Jefferson owned hundreds of black slaves, that all of the Presidents up to Lincoln presided over a slave state, and that every President since Lincoln connived politically and cynically with the issues affecting the human rights and general welfare of the broad masses of the American people,

Cleaver rejoiced that at last, in the midst of the revolution of the 1960s, "these facts weigh heavily upon the hearts of these young people."[51]

For Cleaver, however, the problem was not just America. It was the entire white race "whose heroes have been revealed as villains and its greatest heroes as the arch-villains; . . . heroes whose careers rested on a system of foreign and domestic exploitation, rooted in the Myth of White Supremacy and the manifest destiny of the white race."[52] For many years, white Americans could not discern these realities, protected as they were by the myths presented in this book. As Cleaver noted, "Even when confronted with overwhelming evidence to the contrary, most white Americans have found it possible, after steadying their rattled nerves, to settle comfortably back into their vaunted belief that America is dedicated to the proposition that all men are created equal and endowed by their Creator with certain inalienable rights—life, liberty and the pursuit of happiness." Indeed, Cleaver observed, "It is remarkable how the system worked for so many years, how the majority of whites remained effectively unaware of any contradiction between their view of the world and that world itself."[53]

However one might regard Eldridge Cleaver, his words can help us understand the dynamics that accompanied the erosion of America's myths in the 1960s and 1970s, especially the myth of America as an Innocent Nation.

Malcom X

Typically, blacks who argued as Cleaver did were northern and urban, or perhaps western and urban like Cleaver himself, but generally not southern or rural. In their view, King's nonviolent strategies might work well in the South but were unsuited to major urban centers outside the South like New York, Boston, Los Angeles, and Chicago. They also differed with King's support for racial *integration*. Often more militant than King, these blacks rejected the ideal of integration, insisting on racial *separation* instead. They increasingly abandoned the banner of civil rights, defined by Martin Luther King, and embraced instead the banner of black power.

No one typified this more militant tradition better than Malcolm X. Malcolm spent his early years in Michigan, though he experienced there the same intense level of discrimination that so many Americans today associate only with the historic American South. I noted, for example, in the chapter on American capitalism how, when Malcolm told his eighth grade teacher in Mason, Michigan, that he wanted to become a lawyer, his teacher told him, "That's no realistic goal for a nigger." His teacher's statement, Malcolm later recalled, was a turning point in his life.[54]

Later, in Boston's Roxbury district, Malcolm found that jobs of all kinds were closed to blacks. After a short career of thieving, hustling, and pimping, he landed in prison where he encountered a new religion, the Nation of Islam, popularly styled the Black Muslim tradition. He embraced that faith and soon became its most prominent spokesperson. His new faith taught him that "the only way the black people caught up in this society can be saved is not to *integrate* into this corrupt society, but to *separate* from it, to a land of our *own*, where we can reform ourselves, lift up our moral standards, and try to be godly."

Malcolm carefully distinguished between *separation* and *segregation*. "We reject *segregation* even more militantly than you say you do," Malcolm told more moderate black leaders. "Segregation is that which is forced upon inferiors by superiors. But *separation* is that which is done voluntarily, by two equals—for the good of both!" Separation, he said, was important, since "as long as our people here in America are dependent upon the white man, we will always be begging him for jobs, food, clothing, and housing. And he will always control our lives, regulate our lives, and have the power to segregate us."[55]

Especially in his early years, Malcolm strongly criticized Martin Luther King on this issue. "I knew," he wrote, "that the great lack of most of the big-name 'Negro leaders' was their lack of any true rapport with the ghetto Negroes. How could they have rapport when they spent most of their time 'integrating' with white people?"[56] Malcolm therefore argued for a strategy he called "black nationalism."[57] He meant by this term that blacks should strive for total independence from whites. He meant that blacks should run their own farms, their own businesses, and their own banks. He meant that blacks should cultivate their own traditions and value their own heritage and culture.

His embrace of the Nation of Islam symbolized his deepest misgivings both about America and about the Christian faith. In his judgment, western society in general and America in particular had "become overrun with immorality, and God is going to judge it, and destroy it."[58] For these reasons and more, Malcolm rejected his Anglo and Christian surname, "Little" and adopted instead the name, "X." The X, he said, symbolized his African name, long since sacrificed to the racism that dominated Anglo-American culture.

Malcolm differed profoundly from Martin Luther King on the issue of violence. "I'm not for wanton violence," he said. "I'm for justice." This meant for Malcolm, however, that violence might sometimes be appropriate: "I believe it's a crime for anyone who is being brutalized to continue to accept that brutality without doing something to defend himself. If that's how 'Christian' philosophy is interpreted, if that's what Gandhian philosophy teaches, well, then, I will call them criminal philosophies."[59] In 1964 Malcolm made his position unmistakably clear: "We should be peaceful, law-abiding—but the time has come for the American Negro to fight back in self-defense whenever and wherever he is being unjustly and unlawfully attacked."[60]

Malcolm and his message grew immensely popular with American blacks, especially the younger generation of blacks who lived in northern cities. Typified by second-wave leaders of the civil rights movement like H. Rap Brown and Stokely Carmichael, those blacks modeled their protest on Malcolm's strategies and essentially rejected King's nonviolent tactics along with his dream of racial integration.

By the 1990s, Malcolm's vision remained the model for thousands of blacks throughout America. In 1991, for example, Sam Fulwood explained how "my generation . . . is so disillusioned by the persistent racism that continues to define and limit us that we are abandoning efforts to assimilate into the mainstream of society." Although they were the "sons and daughters of those who faced the dogs, water hoses and brutal cops" for the sake of integration, thousands of black professionals, Fulwood reported, were "turning away from our parents' great expectations of an integrated America." He told how "many middle-class black executives are moving out of their corporate roles to create fulfilling jobs that serve black customers. Black colleges are experiencing a renaissance. Black organizations—churches, fraternities, sororities, and professional groups—are attracting legions of new members. And, most surprising to me, upscale blacks are moving to neighborhoods that insulate them from the slings and arrows of the larger society." And why? "Trying to explain my life to white people, who just don't care to understand," Fulwood explained, "is taxing and, ultimately, not worth the trouble. Sort of like singing 'Swing Low, Sweet Chariot' *en francais*. Why bother? Once translated, it's just not the same song."[61]

What, then, should we make of the Black Revolution and these five leaders? Simply put, each articulated what every African American had always known, that powerful American myths had long defined the American Creed, subverted its true meaning, and crippled its ability to fulfill its promise for all human beings. As a result, blacks formed the vanguard of the counterculture of the 1960s. Some, like Martin Luther King, called on Americans "to live out the true meaning of the American creed." Others, like Malcolm X, argued that if blacks were to find any meaning in the American experience, they would have to find that meaning in themselves.[62]

The Vietnam War

American involvement in Vietnam grew from small beginnings. In the aftermath of World War II, numerous Asian and African nations, colonized by European powers, declared their independence from European colonial domination. Among these was the Democratic Republic of Vietnam, led by

Ho Chi Minh, who in 1945 declared his country's independence in words borrowed from Thomas Jefferson: "We hold these truths to be self-evident, That all men are created equal."

When the French, dominant in that region since the nineteenth century, refused to abandon Vietnam and sought to establish a new colonial outpost in the southern provinces, the First Indochina War erupted in 1946. Ho Chi Minh increasingly turned to Red China for support, while the French turned to America and Great Britain.

The government of the United States sympathized with Ho Chi Minh and his declarations of independence for his nation. At the same time, America feared the expansion of communism in Southeast Asia and increasingly provided support for French control of that region. That support began under the Harry Truman administration but accelerated under President Dwight Eisenhower. In 1953 the United States paid $1 billion to achieve its objective—two-thirds of the cost of the French occupation. In 1954 President Eisenhower articulated the infamous "domino theory": "You have a row of dominoes set up, you knock over the first one, and what will happen to the last one is the certainty that it will go over very quickly." For years to come, that theory would govern the American response to Vietnam.

When the French first enlisted American support in their ongoing struggle with Ho Chi Minh, the U.S. government sent "advisers" into the region. By 1963 the number of "advisers" had escalated to 16,000. In 1964 President Lyndon Johnson ordered bombings of North Vietnam, and in 1965 America committed combat troops to defend the South against communist aggression from the North.

Public support for American involvement in that war soon began to erode for one fundamental reason. The administration feared that an American commitment to total victory might risk a military engagement with the Chinese and the Soviets. As a result, America settled for a more limited objective: to prevent the Communists from winning.

In the meantime, the number of American ground troops committed to the war escalated dramatically, reaching 385,000 in 1966 and 542,000 in 1969. American casualties escalated as well. Each night, the American public learned the official body count for the day on the evening news, and when the war finally concluded in 1973, 51,000 Americans had died. By the mid-1960s, when it became apparent that the government had no strategy to end the war, the mood of a very large segment of the public turned sour.

While America's failure to win the war fueled a broad, general dissatisfaction with the military venture in Vietnam, moral issues related to the war inflamed the counterculture, including religious progressives and America's minorities. In the first place, the government of South Vietnam, which the United States supported, seemed as brutal and oppressive as the Communist government of the North. Critics therefore wondered how America could possibly support such a regime without betraying its noblest ideals. Beyond that consideration, the broad countercultural coalition placed the war squarely in the context of the struggle for equal rights for blacks and other minorities in the United States. Inescapably, the war wrought devastation on the homes, lands, and lives of people of color. Many therefore saw the war as yet another manifestation of American racism and western imperialism.

Muhammad Ali, for example, refused induction into the United States military and gave his reasons for that decision in March of 1967. "Why should they ask me to put on a uniform and go 10,000 miles from home and drop bombs and bullets on Brown people in Vietnam while so-called Negro people in Louisville are treated like dogs and denied simple human rights?" Ali asked. "No, I'm not going 10,000 miles from home to help murder and burn another poor nation simply to continue the domination of white slave masters of the darker people the world over." Ali knew that decision might land him in jail, but he asked, "So what? We've been in jail for 400 years."[63] As it was, he was stripped of his title and barred from the ring.

One month later, on April 4, 1967, Martin Luther King Jr. addressed many of these same issues at a meeting of Clergy and Laity Concerned at the Riverside Church in New York City. Early in that speech, he anticipated the inevitable question, "Why are *you* speaking about war, Dr. King? Why are *you* joining the voices of dissent?" To this question, King affirmed that he was a minister of Jesus Christ, and for that reason, "the path from Dexter Avenue Baptist Church—the church in Montgomery, Alabama, where I began my pastorate—leads clearly to this sanctuary tonight." Because of his Christian convictions, he had to speak.

King argued that the war worked hand in hand with domestic racism to destroy the lives of poor black people. The war, he pointed out, sent the poor "to fight and to die in extraordinarily high proportions to the rest of the population." It took "black young men who had been crippled by our society" and sent "them eight thousand miles away to guarantee liberties in Southeast Asia which they had not found in southwest Georgia and East Harlem." He also lamented the fact that the war diverted money, energy, and attention from the domestic war for civil rights. He recalled that "a few years ago there was a shining moment in [the] struggle [for equal rights]. . . . Then came the buildup in Vietnam and I watched the program broken and eviscerated as if it were some idle political plaything of a society gone mad on war."

For King, the most fundamental issue by far was the massive level of destruction that America had rained on Vietnam. Because of that destruction, King concurred with a man he called "one of the great Buddhist leaders of Vietnam": "The image of America will never again be the image of revolution, freedom and democracy, but the image of violence and militarism." In that context, King spoke of the violence in America's ghettos. When he tried to counsel young blacks to embrace nonviolent protest, they inevitably asked, "What about Vietnam?" "They asked if our own nation wasn't using massive doses of violence to solve its problems, to bring about the changes it wanted. Their questions hit home, and I knew that I could never again raise my voice against the violence of the oppressed in the ghettos without having first spoken clearly to the greatest purveyor of violence in the world today—my own government."

King spoke to these issues, he said, because of his "commitment to the ministry of Jesus Christ." Because of that commitment, he felt "called to speak for the weak, for the voiceless, for victims of our nation and for those it calls enemy, for no document from human hands can make these humans any less our brothers."

The audience at the Riverside Church that night was a sympathetic audience. When King's remarks hit the newspapers the following morning, though, many Americans were puzzled, perplexed, and angry. It was fine to speak on behalf of the weak, the voiceless, and the poor. But to speak on behalf of the nation's enemies? That was going too far. King knew his remarks would prompt that reaction. Perhaps that is why, at one point in his speech, he explained what he called "the true meaning and value of compassion and nonviolence": "It helps us to see the enemy's point of view, to hear his questions, to know his assessment of ourselves. For from his view we may indeed see the basic weaknesses of our own condition, and if we are mature, we may learn and grow and profit from the wisdom of the brothers who are called the opposition."[64]

9/11 and Beyond

The terrorist attacks of September 11, 2001 resurrected the myth of American innocence with a vengeance, and—along with it—the effort to divide the world into a simple grid of right versus wrong, good versus evil. President George W. Bush, for example, wondered out loud why "people would hate us" since "I know how good we are."[65] In his 2002 "State of the Union Address," he identified three nations—North Korea, Iran, and Iraq—as "an axis of evil, arming to threaten the peace of the world."[66] And in an address to a joint session of Congress on September 20, 2001, he gave the world an ultimatum that rested squarely on the good-versus-evil divide: "Every nation in every region now has a decision to make," the president said. "Either you are with us or you are with the terrorists."

This robust sense of American innocence informed the American sense of self during all the years of the "War on Terror" and provided the backdrop for race relations in the early years of the twenty-first century. With that backdrop in place, nothing did more to define race relations during those years than a series of fatal shootings of unarmed blacks, chiefly black males by armed security guards or police. While those killings had transpired under the radar on a regular basis for years, cell phone-camera technology finally brought them into the public consciousness. Now the public could see who did the killings, who was killed, and under what circumstances.

When in 2012 a neighborhood watch volunteer killed Trayvon Martin—a teenager carrying candy and soda as he walked through a gated community in Miami Gardens, Florida—the reality of black lives snuffed out at the hands of police or white vigilantes became national news. The fact that those responsible were seldom convicted became national news as well.

Following Martin's death, scores of other cases emerged. A small sample of those include Eric Garner, suspected of illegally selling cigarettes and choked to death on July 17, 2014, by New York City police; Michael Brown, killed on August 9, 2014, by a white policeman in Ferguson, Missouri, following a petty robbery; Tamir Rice, age 12, killed on November 22, 2014, in Cleveland, Ohio, for holding a toy gun; Freddie Gray who died in a police van on April 19, 2015, in Baltimore, Maryland, while handcuffed and shackled to the floor; Walter Scott, shot by police in North Charleston, North Carolina on April 4, 2015, following a minor traffic violation; and Sandra Bland found hanged in a Waller County, Texas, jail cell on July 13, 2015, also following a minor traffic violation.

I suggested in chapter 4 that these killings, which seldom resulted in convictions, plunged blacks into what would become America's fourth time of trial. The black community responded to that trial with the affirmation that "Black Lives Matter" and with the creation in 2013 of a national organization that wore that name. On the other hand, many in the white community responded with affirmations of innocence. "I didn't do it, I'm not responsible," and "Don't put that guilt trip on me" became a common refrain among whites who seemed to have no sense of the meaning of systemic racism—the fundamental inequalities embedded into social structures and economic systems that I discussed at length in chapter 6.

At the same time, many whites essentially trivialized the affirmation that "black lives matter" by making the obvious point that "all lives matter." Former

New York City mayor, Rudy Giuliani, even demonized the affirmation that "black lives matter." "When you say 'black lives matter,'" Giuliani said, "that's inherently racist. Black lives matter, white lives matter, Asian lives matter, Hispanic lives matter. That's anti-American and it's racist."[67]

Even before the rise of the Black Lives Matter movement, the "average white respondent" to a *Washington Post* survey of 2011 "believed that . . . anti-white bias was an even bigger problem than anti-black bias." Consistent with my argument in chapter 4 that many white conservatives sought for half a century to reverse the cultural and social changes of the 1960s, whites "agreed that anti-white bias was not a problem in the 1950s, but . . . that bias against whites started climbing in the 1960s and 1970s before rising sharply in the past 30 years."[68]

Following the terror attacks of September 11, 2001, and in the context of the racial divide that intensified in subsequent years, three black writers, all of them public intellectuals, wrote important books designed, at least in part, to help the public understand in depth the realities of white supremacy, systemic racism, and the myth of American innocence: Ta-Nehisi Coates's *Between the World and Me*, Molefi Kete Asante's *Erasing Racism: The Survival of the American Nation*, and Michael Eric Dyson's *Tears We Cannot Stop: A Sermon to White America*.

Ta-Nehisi Coates

Coates wrote his book as an intimate letter to his young son. Born in 1975, Coates grew up in Baltimore where his experience of systemic racism and police brutality rendered the Freedom Movement of the 1960s all but incomprehensible. "Every February," he recalled, "my classmates and I were herded into assemblies for a ritual review of the Civil Rights Movement. Our teachers urged us toward the example of freedom marchers, Freedom Riders, and Freedom Summers, and it seemed that the month could not pass without a series of films dedicated to the glories of being beaten on camera. The black people in these films seemed to love the worst things in life. . . . I judged them against the country I knew, which had acquired the land through murder and tamed it under slavery, against the country whose armies fanned out across the world to extend their dominion. The world, the real one, was civilization secured and ruled by savage means."[69]

Indeed, Coates judged the Freedom Movement against the backdrop of his own reality—the routine murder of blacks in America's streets.[70] While lamenting police brutality against black American citizens, Coates made it clear that he did not blame the police so much as he blamed the nation. Speaking of the killing of Howard University student Prince Carmen Jones in

Prince George's County, Virginia, in 2000, Coates wrote that "Prince was not killed by a single officer so much as he was murdered by his country." Indeed, he wrote, "to challenge the police is to challenge the American people."[71]

We introduced in chapter 5 Coates's understanding of white Americans as "the Dreamers"—people whose American Dream glorifies manicured suburbs and picnics and portrays the United States as "exceptional, the greatest and noblest nation ever to exist, a lone champion standing between the white city of democracy and the terrorists, despots, barbarians, and other enemies of civilization." To challenge that dream, Coates wrote, was difficult precisely because of the myth of American innocence. "There exists, all around us," he observed, "an apparatus urging us to accept American innocence at face value and not to inquire too much. And it is easy to look away, to live with the fruits of our history and to ignore the great evil done in all of our names."[72]

Paradoxically, Coates insisted, the myth of American innocence simply assumed the existence of a brutalized, black underclass. "The right to break the black body," he told his son, "is the meaning of their sacred equality. . . . There is no them without you, and without the right to break you they must necessarily fall from the mountain, lose their divinity, and tumble out of the Dream."[73]

Coates understood that the American claim to innocence is deeply rooted in the claim the Dreamers make that the United States transcends the constraints of history—the notion voiced by Ronald Reagan, noted earlier in this chapter, that "the calendar can't measure America because we were meant to be an endless experiment in freedom, with no limit to our reaches, no boundaries to what we can do, no end point to our hopes."[74] For Coates, Americans who embrace that assumption must inevitably look away from the terrors of their history, not to mention the terrors of their own time. "The mettle that it takes to look away from the horror of our prison system, from police forces transformed into armies, from the long war against the black body," Coates wrote, "is not forged overnight. This is the practiced habit of jabbing out one's eyes and forgetting the work of one's hands."[75]

Coates found this habit of forgetting in virtually every nook and corner of American history. The Civil War is but one example. "American reunion was built on a comfortable narrative that made enslavement into benevolence, white knights of body snatchers, and the mass slaughter of the war into a kind of sport in which one could conclude that both sides conducted their affairs with courage, honor, and élan. The lie of the Civil War is the lie of innocence, is the Dream." For that reason, America's national battlefields "had been retrofitted," Coates believed, "as the staging ground for a great deception"—a deception designed to protect the myth of American innocence. He recalled how he and his son had visited the Petersburg Battlefield where "every visitor seemed most interested in flanking maneuvers, hardtack, smoothbore rifles, grapeshot, and ironclads, but virtually no one was interested in what all of this engineering, invention, and design had been marshaled to achieve," namely, the perpetuation of enslavement in the United States.[76]

With that history in mind, Coates placed upon Ground Zero—that area of Manhattan devastated by the attacks of September 11, 2001—an interpretation altogether different from the one that was generally accepted. "I kept thinking about how southern Manhattan had always been Ground Zero for us. They auctioned our bodies down there, in that same devastated, and rightly named, financial district. And there was once a burial ground for the auctioned there." And then he recalled how America had covered up that history and denied that it ever existed. "They built a department store over part of it and then tried to erect a government building over another part. Only a community of right-thinking black people stopped them. . . . Bin Laden was not the first man to bring terror to that section of the city. I never forget that." To his young son he counseled, "Neither should you."[77]

Having to live among Dreamers who consistently deny their own history has placed an almost unbearable burden on blacks, Coates contended, for they tell "you that the Dream is just, noble, and real, and you are crazy for seeing the corruption and smelling the sulfur. For their innocence, they nullify your anger, your fear, until you are coming and going, and you find yourself inveighing against your own humanity and raging against the crime in your ghetto, because you are powerless before the great crime of history that brought the ghettos to be."[78]

Molefi Kete Asante

After graduating from several institutions related to Churches of Christ—one of the two restorationist traditions I explored both in this chapter and in chapter 4—Molefi Kete Asante earned his PhD in communication studies at UCLA and later served as professor and chair in the Department of African American Studies at Temple University. Widely recognized as the father of Afrocentric Studies, Asante authored over 75 books and, with Robert Singleton, cofounded the *Journal of Black Studies*.

In his book, *Erasing Racism*, first published in 2003, Asante offered two metaphors for the racial divide in the United States: the Promised Land and the Wilderness,[79] metaphors that extend Coates's appraisal of "the Dreamers" who live in the land of innocence, completely unaware of the Wilderness that is everywhere in the American nation.

From his own childhood in the American South, Asante knew the Wilderness well. He was born Arthur Lee Smith Jr. in Valdosta, Georgia, "a place where in the early twentieth century a black woman named Mary Turner was violently murdered and her unborn fetus ripped from her womb and stomped to death, because Turner protested the lynching of her husband." Asante "never forgot . . . the uncontrolled hatred against black people [which] was palpable, real, immediate, and violent in my father's, as well as my own, lifetime."

When he was only twelve, he entered a "whites only" barbershop and "asked permission to shine the shoes of the customers for twenty-five cents." While bent over to prepare his supplies, his very first customer spat on his head. Asante recalled that "other whites, including the owner of the shop, began to laugh. Knowing precisely the disdain and hatred the men in the barbershop had for him, he gathered his shoebox with his waxes, cloths, and brushes and, without saying anything, walked out of the shop."[80]

"Growing up in Georgia and Tennessee," he wrote, "my earliest memories are of a society without whites, segregated, self-contained, and filled with the Holy Ghost. Nevertheless, we all knew that distant whites had created the miserable world in which we lived. We knew this because from time to time they entered our world, and their entry was vile, oppressive, arrogant, and brutal. They were bill collectors, police, night riders, and others looking to harass African people."[81]

With no sense of history, Asante wrote, whites have steadfastly maintained their innocence in matters of race. "Quite frankly," he wrote, "we are basically historically illiterate as a nation about the destructive nature of white supremacy as an ideology of dominance pervading every arena of American life. We have come to accept the abnormality as normal, the distortion of racial supremacy as the only American way of life." Their lack of a sense of history helps explain "the surprise some whites feel hearing of the fury felt by many African Americans. They wonder why African Americans seem never to be satisfied. They act as if all debts have been paid and the scores settled."[82]

Asante told one particularly poignant story that illustrates this point—a story of "a white man from the tree-lined and rock-manicured streets of Simi Valley [who] made his way in the late evening toward a section of the American Wilderness in South Central Los Angeles soon after the 1992 uprising. Smoke still lingered in the air, broken glass was everywhere, the bombed-out buildings were the skeletal remains of the rage of Los Angeles . . . [and] this Simi Valley Samaritan was struck dumb by the intensity of the collective fury of the people."

Asante continued:

"Why?" he asked, half muttering to himself as he walked toward a knot of people who were already helping with the cleanup effort. "Why?" he repeated, almost in disbelief. He walked resolutely, as he mentally prepared himself to assist in the rebuilding of the community and do anything he could to create a climate of goodwill.

The perplexed Samaritan from Simi Valley was genuine in his earnestness, but he did not know very much about the bewildering conditions that caused the fury in the American Wilderness. . . . This man, with his Simi Valley consciousness, was like so many other whites—and some African Americans who exist on the fringes of the American Wilderness. . . . To them, the Wilderness represents strangeness, distance, mystery, and alienation like they have never known. . . . Their daily encounters with Wilderness dwellers . . . yield no real understanding of life in the Wilderness.

As David, the Samaritan from Simi Valley, walked deeper into the burned-out war zone, he encountered Kofi, a man whose store had been destroyed. Perhaps Kofi could answer the question, "Why?" But David's questions revealed his innocence and naïveté and frustrated Kofi who responded,

"Man, you're taking my time. You want a lesson, I'll give you a lesson in American history. Our ancestors worked in hot fields and . . . wore burlap to protect their scarred and bleeding feet while building up this country for other people. No, it is not the same. We've worked as hard and longer than anyone, but let me try to get $50,000 or $100,000 to start my business from your bank. Racial prejudice and discrimination are ingrained in the way whites respond to African Americans."

"What do you mean?"

"I mean even the police treat us differently: rudely, almost with hatred," Kofi argued.

"This is America; are you serious?" David said in disbelief.

"Let me tell you something. In the most affluent white suburbs, we're the ones the police follow the most, the ones who must always give an accounting of our presence, the ones who are stalked like prey in department stories. . . ."

"Well, I want to help. What should I do?" David exasperatedly asked.

"Damn, David, you've got to start in your own neighborhood by getting your friends and neighbors to discuss their own prejudices against African Americans. . . . Hell, I don't know what kind of therapy whites need. Anyway, I've got to think about rebuilding my store. Have fun." Kofi turned and walked toward a parked car a half a block away.[83]

Innocence? Innocence, indeed!

Michael Eric Dyson

Police brutality against black lives also prompted Michael Eric Dyson, sociologist at Georgetown University, prolific author, and radio host, to address the realities of white supremacy, systemic racism, and American innocence in his *Sermon to White America*. Dyson wanted whites to understand that "to be black in America is to live in terror"—a terror that intrudes on black lives in a thousand different ways. "That terror is fast," he wrote. "It is glimpsed in cops giving chase to black men and shooting them in their backs without cause. Or the terror is slow. It chips like lead paint on a tenement wall, or flows like contaminated water through corroded pipes that poison black bodies. [Or] it is slow like genocide inside prison walls where folk who should not be there perish."

From the perspective of many blacks, Dyson wrote, the police were the American equivalent of ISIS. "At any moment, without warning, a blue-clad monster will swoop down on us to snatch our lives from us and say that it was because we were selling cigarettes, or compact discs, or breathing too much for his comfort, or speaking too abrasively for his taste. Or running, or standing still, or talking back, or being silent, or doing as you say, or not doing as you say fast enough."[84]

Dyson, like Coates and Asante, argued that most whites did not understand, did not "feel our terror," because the pervasive myth of American innocence blinded their moral vision. And like Coates and Asante, he traced the myth of innocence to the nation's denial of its history or, failing that, to its effort to rewrite history in ways that sustained the myth.

The Civil War was a case in point. "A flood of writing," Dyson lamented, "tells us that the Civil War wasn't really about slavery but about the effort to defend states' rights. . . . The right wing," he noted, promoted the notion that the war "was fought over the ability of individual states to beat back a federal government out to impose its will. From the left wing there's the belief that the Civil War was a conflict between the planter class and the proletariat. In each case, race as the main reason for the war is skillfully rewritten, or, really, written out."[85] Moreover, Dyson writes, in the normative telling of American history, "black lives were excluded from the start."[86]

Dyson also rooted the myth of innocence in another great American myth—the myth of American individualism which allowed whites to reject the argument that systemic racism is real in American life, even as they denied personal responsibility for crimes against blacks. Obviously, no single person was responsible for those crimes. The issue, rather, was complicity in a massive system that no American citizen, black or white, could escape.

But "by sidestepping complicity," Dyson wrote, "you hold fast to innocence. By holding fast to innocence, you maintain power."[87] And that, Dyson wrote, "is why the cry 'Black Lives Matter' angers you so greatly, why it is utterly offensive and effortlessly revolutionary. It takes aim at white innocence and insists on uncovering the lie of its neutrality, its naturalness, its normalcy, its normativity."[88]

Similarly, Dyson argued, that is why so many white Americans were so offended when San Francisco 49ers quarterback Kevin Kaepernick chose to kneel, not stand, during the national anthem. "He did so," Dyson wrote, "to protest injustice against black folk . . ., to offer correction rather than abandon the nation. . . . But innocent whiteness recoils at such instruction. It pushes back against the notion that it could possibly learn anything from a black body kneeling on white sacred territory." Dyson, however, hoped the nation might somehow come to view "Kaepernick's criticism as . . . the tough love that America needs."[89]

Conclusions

I began this chapter with Lawrence Wright who discovered, along with millions of other white youth in the 1960s, that the world does not divide as neatly between good and evil as the myth of the Innocent American Nation might suggest. That realization came as a shock to Wright's generation since, in the aftermath of World War II, the nation had raised its children to believe that the United States always stood on the side of right against wrong and good against evil. Had the nation listened to the voices of African Americans, it would have known better. It would have known what blacks knew all along—that the myth of American innocence is an illusion.

Human innocence is always an illusion in any event. But in the case of the American nation, innocence was grounded in a grand deception—the claim that whites were superior to blacks. So powerful was that deception that it sealed the ears of whites against the truth and their hearts against the massive guilt upon which the nation was founded.

Malcolm X shed abundant light on the myth of American innocence when he claimed that the notion of white supremacy was "deeply rooted . . . in the national white subconsciousness."[90] That phrase—"national white subconsciousness"—helps us understand how it is possible to have "racism without racists" as sociologist Eduardo Bonilla-Silva so memorably put it. During the Obama presidency, for example, many whites mounted the claim that the United States had entered a "post-racial" period. In point of fact, as Bonilla-Silva reminds us, they had substituted for the older, more blatant racism a series of rationalizations that could allow racism to flourish in the midst of denial. Bonilla-Silva labeled that phenomenon "color-blind racism."[91] Tim Wise extended that analysis when he argued that many Americans, even liberal Americans, "carve out acceptable space for individuals such as Obama who strike them as different, as exceptions who are not like the rest . . . [while continuing] to look down upon the larger mass of black and brown America with suspicion, fear, and contempt."[92]

Whatever mechanisms the nation may employ to assert and protect its myth of innocence, that myth is the nation's Achilles's heel. Frederick Buechner once observed that "reality can be harsh and . . . you shut your eyes to it only at your peril because if you do not face up to the enemy . . ., then the enemy will come up from behind . . . and destroy you while you are facing the other way."[93] The myth of American innocence is the enemy of the nation that may yet destroy us. It is that enemy precisely because it encourages the American people to deny the extent to which white supremacy pervades American culture, to shut their eyes, and to face the other way.

Notes

1. Lawrence Wright, *In the New World: Growing Up with America, 1960–1984* (New York: Alfred A. Knopf, 1988), 109–110.

2. Ibid., 109.

3. Ronald Reagan, "Address before a Joint Session of Congress on the State of the Union," January 27, 1987, in *Public Papers of the Presidents of the United States: Ronald Reagan: 1987*, vol. I: *January 1 to July 3, 1987* (Washington: Government Printing Office, 1989), 59–60.

4. Jessica Mitford, *The American Way of Death* (New York: Simon and Schuster, 1963), 13–17.

5. James Baldwin, *The Fire Next Time*, in Toni Morrison, ed., *Baldwin: Collected Essays* (New York: Library Classics of the United States, 1998), 339.

6. Edward T. Linenthal, *The Unfinished Bombing: Oklahoma City in American Memory* (Oxford: Oxford University Press, 2001), 16.

7. Mark Slouka, "A Year Later: Notes on America's Intimations of Mortality," *Harper's Magazine* 305 (September 2002): 36.

8. For a far more expanded discussion of the illusions of innocence in American life, and the way those illusions grow from the attempt to sidestep human history, see Richard T. Hughes and C. Leonard Allen, *Illusions of Innocence: Protestant Primitivism in America, 1630–1875* (Chicago: University of Chicago Press, 1988). In addition, Robert Jewett and John Shelton Lawrence have written perceptively on the myth of American innocence in a variety of texts, though their focus is somewhat different from my own. See, for example, Jewett's *The Captain America Complex* (Philadelphia: Westminster, 1973; rev. ed., Santa Fe: Bear and Company, 1984); Jewett and Lawrence, *The American Monomyth* (Garden City: Doubleday, 1977); and most recently, Jewett

and Lawrence, *The Myth of the American Superhero* (Grand Rapids: Eerdmans, 2002). For a more recent treatment of American innocence, see Suzy Hansen, "Unlearning the Myth of American Innocence," *The Guardian*, August 8, 2017, https://www.theguardian.com/us-news/2017/aug/08/unlearning-the-myth-of-american-innocence, accessed October 1, 2017.

9. On this point, see Richard T. Hughes, "Soaring with the Gods: Early Mormons and the Eclipse of Religious Pluralism" in Eric A. Eliason, ed., *Mormons and Mormonism: An Introduction to an American World Religion* (Urbana: University of Illinois Press, 2001), 23–46.

10. John R. Howard, "A Warning to the Religious Sects and Parties in Christendom," *Bible Advocate* 1 (January 1843): 82.

11. Peter Crawley, "The Passage of Mormon Primitivism," *Dialogue* 13 (Winter 1980): 33; and Introduction to *Key to the Science of Theology/A Voice of Warning* (Salt Lake City: Deseret Book Co., 1978), i–ii.

12. Parley P. Pratt, *A Voice of Warning and Instruction to All People, Containing a Declaration of the Faith and Doctrine of the Church of the Latter Day Saints, Commonly Called Mormons* (New York: W. Sanford, 1837), 140–142. This chapter, which is the pivotal "warning" section of *Voice of Warning*, has been deleted from the modern 1978 edition.

13. Woodrow Wilson, "We Must Accept War," message to the Congress, April 2, 1917, in Woodrow Wilson, *Why We Are at War: Messages to the Congress, January to April, 1917* (New York: Harper and Brothers, 1917), 57.

14. Wilson, "Presenting the Treaty for Ratification" in Conrad Cherry, ed., *God's New Israel: Religious Interpretations of American Destiny* (Chapel Hill: University of North Carolina Press, 1998), 280.

15. Wilson, "Speak, Act and Serve Together," message to the American people, April 15, 1917, in Wilson, *Why We Are at War*, 71.

16. Wilson, "We Must Accept War," message to the Congress, April 2, 1917, in Wilson, *Why We Are at War*, 55.

17. Wilson, "Presenting the Treaty," in Cherry, ed., *God's New Israel*, 280 and 287.

18. Wilson, "A World League for Peace," message to the Senate, January 22, 1917, in Wilson, *Why We Are at War*, 16.

19. Wilson, "We Must Accept War," 55.

20. Wilson, "Request for a Grant of Power," message to the Congress, February 26, 1917, in Wilson, *Why We Are at War*, 31.

21. Cited in Emily Rosenberg, *Spreading the American Dream: American Economic and Cultural Expansion, 1890–1945* (New York: Hill and Wang, 1982), 74.

22. Wilson, "Request for a Grant of Power," in Wilson, *Why We Are at War*, 36–37.

23. Emily Rosenberg explores the "self-evident" qualities of CPI propaganda in *Spreading the American Dream*, 86.

24. Paul Robeson, *Here I Stand* (Boston: Beacon Press, 1958), 10–11.

25. Franklin D. Roosevelt, "Annual Message to Congress," January 6, 1942, in Cherry, ed., *God's New Israel*, 295.

26. Ibid., 295.

27. Ibid., 290 and 295.

28. Ibid., 291.

29. Baldwin, *The Fire Next Time*, 317–318.

30. Toni Morrison, *The Origin of Others* (Cambridge: Harvard University Press, 2017), 59–61.

31. Cited in William G. McLoughlin Jr., *Billy Graham: Revivalist in a Secular Age* (New York: Ronald Press, 1960), 48.

32. All citations from McLoughlin, *Billy Graham*, 139 and 142–143.

33. Ibid., 138–39.

34. All citations from ibid., 117.

35. William Lee Miller, *Piety on the Potomac* (Boston: Houghton Mifflin, 1964), 28.

36. Wright, *In the New World*, 110–111.

37. Martin Luther King Jr., "I Have a Dream," in James Melvin Washington, ed., *A Testament of Hope: The Essential Writings and Speeches of Martin Luther King, Jr.* (San Francisco: HarperSanFrancisco, 1986), 217 and 219.

38. Wright, *In the New World*, 137.

39. James Forman, "The Black Manifesto," in Thomas R. West and James W. Mooney, *To Redeem a Nation: A History and Anthology of the Civil Rights Movement* (St. James, N.Y.: Brandywine Press, 1993), 251.

40. Angela Davis, *Angela Davis: An Autobiography* (New York: Random House, 1974), 83.

41. Ibid., 89–90, 92–93.

42. Ibid., 109.

43. Ibid., 128–131. One of the suspects in this crime died in 1994 without being charged. Three others were convicted, one in 1977, one in 2001, and one in May of 2002, almost forty years after the bomb exploded and the girls were killed.

44. Ibid., 189.

45. Angela Davis, *If They Come in the Morning: Voices of Resistance* (New York: The Third Press, 1971), 20, 31, 32.

46. Davis, *Autobiography*, ix.

47. Baldwin, *The Fire Next Time*, 292–293.

48. Ibid., 294.

49. *Newsweek*, October 25, 1970.

50. Baldwin, "An Open Letter to My Sister, Miss Angela Davis," *New York Review of Books*, January 7, 1971, http://www.nybooks.com/articles/1971/01/07/an-open-letter-to-my-sister-miss-angela-davis/, accessed July 19, 2017.

51. Eldridge Cleaver, *Soul on Ice* (New York: Dell Publishing, 1968), 70.

52. Ibid., 68.

53. Ibid., 76–78.

54. Malcolm X with Alex Haley, *The Autobiography of Malcolm X* (New York: Grove Press, Inc., 1964), 36–37.

55. Ibid., 246.

56. Ibid., 310.

57. Ibid., 374.

58. Ibid., 246.

59. Ibid., 366–367.

60. Malcolm X, "A Declaration of Independence," March 12, 1964, in George Breitman, ed., *Malcolm X Speaks: Selected Speeches and Statements* (New York: Grove Weidenfeld, 1965), 22.

61. Sam Fulwood, "The Rage of the Black Middle Class," *Los Angeles Times Magazine* (November 5, 1991). See also "White and Black Lies," *Newsweek* (November 15, 1993): 52–54.

62. See James H. Cone, *Martin & Malcolm & America: A Dream or a Nightmare* (Maryknoll, N.Y.: Orbis Books, 1991).

63. Muhammed Ali, "Muhammed Ali Refuses to Fight in Vietnam (1967)," "Alpha History," http://alphahistory.com/vietnamwar/muhammed-ali-refuses-to-fight-1967/, accessed March 22, 2017.

64. All citations are from King, "A Time to Break Silence," speech delivered at Riverside Church, New York City, April 4, 1967, in *A Testament of Hope*, 231–243.

65. "This Is a Different Kind of War," *Los Angeles Times*, Oct. 12, 2001, A16.

66. George W. Bush, "State of the Union Address," Jan. 29, 2002.

67. Jason Silverstein, "Rudy Giuliani Says Black Children Have a '99% Chance' of Killing Each Other, Calls Black Lives Matter 'Inherently Racist,'" *New York Daily News*, July 10, 2016, http://www.nydailynews.com/news/national/rudy-giuliani-black-kids-99-chance-killing-article-1.2706349, accessed July 12, 2017.

68. Samuel Sommers and Michael Norton, "White People Think Racism Is Getting Worse. Against White People," *The Washington Post*, July 21, 2016, https://www.washingtonpost.com/posteverything/wp/2016/07/21/white-people-think-racism-is-getting-worse-against-white-people/?utm_term=.6f03ea99a665, accessed July 14, 2017.

69. Ta-Nehisi Coates, *Between the World and Me* (New York: Spiegel and Grau, 2015), 30–32.

70. Ibid., 9.

71. Ibid., 78–79.

72. Ibid., 8–9.

73. Ibid., 104–105.

74. Reagan, "Address before a Joint Session of Congress on the State of the Union," January 27, 1987, 59–60.

75. Coates, *Between the World and Me*, 98.

76. Ibid., 102–103, 106, 99–100.

77. Ibid., 86–87.

78. Ibid., 106.

79. Molefi Kete Asante, *Erasing Racism: The Survival of the American Nation*, second edition (New York: Prometheus Books, 2009), 10.

80. Ibid., 7–8, 227.

81. Ibid., 48.

82. Ibid., 88 and 92.

83. Ibid., 135–138.

84. Michael Eric Dyson, *Tears We Cannot Stop: A Sermon to White America* (New York: St. Martin's Press, 2017), 177–178.

85. Ibid., 87.

86. Ibid., 92.

87. Ibid., 105.

88. Ibid., 104.

89. Ibid., 112, 114.

90. Malcolm X, *The Autobiography of Malcolm X*, 369.

91. Eduardo Bonilla-Silva, *Racism without Racists: Color-Blind Racism and the Persistence of Racial Inequality in America*, 4th edition (New York: Rowman and Littlefield Publishers, Inc., 2014), 73–96 and 301–309.

92. Tim Wise, *Between Barack and a Hard Place: Racism and White Denial in the Age of Obama* (San Francisco: City Light Books, 2009), 23.

93. Frederick Buechner, *The Sacred Journey: A Memoir of Early Days* (New York: HarperOne, 1991), 45.

Conclusion

As I write these final reflections on the Great American Myths, the United States stands potentially on the brink of the unthinkable—nuclear war with North Korea—a prospect that sends my mind spinning back to the horrific fear Richard Wright expressed exactly sixty years ago. "What I dread," he wrote, "is that the Western white man ... will feel that only a vengeful unleashing of atom and hydrogen bombs can make him feel secure. I dread that there will be an attempt at burning up millions of people to make the world safe for the 'white man's' conception of existence."[1]

In the United States, the "white man's conception of existence" is deeply rooted in the Great American Myths—that the United States is a Chosen Nation, Nature's Nation, a Christian Nation, the Millennial Nation, and an Innocent Nation. James Baldwin wrote in 1963 that "the American Negro has the great advantage of having never believed that collection of myths to which white Americans cling."[2] They have rejected them because each is rooted in yet another myth, which on its face is a vicious lie—that white people are superior to people of color. And that myth is rooted in still another—that color, when applied to human beings, means anything at all beyond the pigmentation that one can see with one's eyes.

If the Myth of White Supremacy has defined and shaped the other Great American Myths, we must wonder how those other myths might serve us if stripped of their coloration. In chapter 1, I speculated on that very question:

To argue, for example, that God—or at least some power beyond themselves—chose the American nation for a special mission in the world may be a useful idea if the American people can imagine that God chose this nation in the same way that God whose every other nation—not for power or dominance or might, but for healing and reconciliation and to promote the common good among all people, both within and outside of America's borders.

To argue that the bedrock principles held by this nation conform to the natural order of things may be a useful theme if Americans can discern in the natural order what their Pledge of Allegiance asserts—that this is "one nation, under God, with liberty and justice for all."

And the claim that the United States is a Christian nation can be useful as well if this admittedly pluralistic nation were to embody not only the basic principles of the Christian faith but the basic principles of all the world's great religions—compassion for the oppressed, welcome for strangers, and justice for the poor.

If the United States were to embrace those ideals in those ways, then perhaps the Myth of the Millennial Nation—the claim that the American nation will in some way help promote those same ideals throughout the world—might make some sense.

The problem, of course—the problem that prevents us from reframing our myths apart from coloration—is the problem that W. E. B. Du Bois identified in 1900—"the problem of the color line." [3] The question that confronts us, then, is this—can that problem be solved?

This is the crucial question of our time. Our very survival is at stake. But the problem of the color line can only be solved if all of us—white Americans and black Americans and Americans of every race and ethnicity—are willing to acknowledge "the basic humanness and Americanness of each of us," as Cornel West put it. "We as a people," he said, "are on a slippery slope toward economic strife, social turmoil, and cultural chaos. If we go down, we go down together" for "the paradox of race in America is that our common destiny is more pronounced and imperiled precisely when our divisions are deeper." [4]

Nothing can enhance our embrace of a common "basic humanness" more fully than face-to-face personal relationships that bridge the racial divide. In that context, I share the following story.

Some years ago I served as Senior Fellow in the Ernest L. Boyer Center at Messiah College and was hard at work planning an initiative called "Community Conversations on Race, Education, and Faith." With that project, we hoped to bring blacks and whites and churches and schools from both sides of the Susquehanna River into a larger partnership for the sake of the children in Harrisburg, Pennsylvania. We knew from the start that our success would depend to a great degree on the involvement of people of color who lived in the city.

But I had a problem. We had just moved to the Harrisburg area and I knew almost no blacks there at all. And then I met Reverend Wayne Baxter, one of the two people to whom this book is dedicated.

A few days later we met for breakfast. I told Baxter about our project and how much we needed the involvement of blacks in the city of Harrisburg. And that's when he looked me in the eye and quietly asked, "Richard, may I speak candidly with you?"

"I hope you will," I responded.

"All right," he said. "Then get out a pen and a piece of paper and write what I tell you."

Once I was ready to write, he doled out a simple message, one word at a time.

"First," he said, "write the word, 'It's.'" And I did.

"Now write the word, 'all,'" he continued. And I wrote down that word, too.

"Now write the word, 'about.'" And I scribbled "about" on my note pad.

"Now write the word, 'relationships.'"

And once I had written that word, he made his point. "Relationships!" he said. "That's what you don't have." He paused a moment, as if reflecting on what he was about to say. And then he said those five magical words that launched our friendship: "But I will help you."[5]

And help me he did. He helped me with my project, but even more important, through the medium of personal relationship, he helped me grasp in ways I had never grasped before some of the challenges that face impoverished children of color, the impact of white supremacy on black communities, and the role of white privilege in American life.

Simply put, Baxter helped me grasp at an experiential level the meaning of the words I had read from Cornel West: "If we go down, we go down together" for "the paradox of race in America is that our common destiny is more pronounced and imperiled precisely when our divisions are deeper."

Claiming our common humanity, however, calls for more than relationship. It also calls for determined resistance against the myths of exclusion. Because no one I have read has issued that challenge with greater force than James Baldwin, I turn to Baldwin for the last word in this reflection on the myths America lives by. The problem of the color line, he wrote, is "a fearful and delicate problem, which compromises, when it does not corrupt, all the American efforts to build a better world—here, there, or anywhere." He continued:

It is for this reason that everything white Americans think they believe must now be reexamined. What one would not like to see again is the consolidation of peoples on the basis of their color. But as long as we in the West place on color the value that we do, we make it impossible for the great unwashed to consolidate themselves according to any other principle. . . . And at the center of this dreadful storm, this vast confusion, stand the black people of this nation, who must now share the fate of a nation that has never accepted them, to which they were brought in chains. Well, if this is so, one has no choice but to do all in one's power to change that fate, and at no matter what risk—eviction, imprisonment, torture, death. For the sake of one's children, in order to minimize the bill that they must pay, one must be careful not to take refuge in any delusion—and the value placed on the color of the skin is always and everywhere and forever a delusion. I know that what I am asking is impossible. But in our time, as in every time, the impossible is the least that one can demand.[6]

The Myth of White Supremacy is so deeply embedded in American life and culture that widespread rejection of that myth does seem impossible. Still, the fact that Baldwin called for resistance; that he asked us to resist, even if resistance means torture and death; that he asked us to reject the temptation "to take refuge in any delusion," especially regarding "the value placed on the color of the skin"—that fact alone suggests that, at some level, Baldwin held onto a thin sliver of hope. Perhaps a thin sliver of hope is all that American history can justify. But hope we must, for if we abandon hope, we have also abandoned our future.

Notes

1. Richard Wright, *White Man, Listen* (New York: HarperPerennial, 1957), 42–43.

2. James Baldwin, *The Fire Next Time*, 1963, in Baldwin, *Collected Essays*, ed. by Toni Morrison (New York: The Library of America, 1998), 344.

3. W. E. B. Du Bois first drafted that line in the "Address to the Nations of the World," adopted by the delegates to the First Pan-African Conference, which convened in London in 1900. He used that phrase again in *The Souls of Black Folk* (New York: New American Library, Inc., 1903), 19.

4. Cornel West, *Race Matters* (Boston: Beacon Press, 1993), 4.

5. Some of the language in this narrative is taken from a tribute I paid to Baxter: "Five Words that Made a Difference," *Harrisburg Patriot News*, March 3, 2013, http://www.pennlive.com/opinion/ accessed February 23, 2017.

6. Baldwin, *The Fire Next Time*, 345–346.

Index

"Acres of Diamonds" (Conwell), 168
Adams, James Truslow, 159
Adams, John, 47, 82, 139
African Methodist Episcopal Church, beginnings of, 93
Aguinaldo, Emilio, 145
Alexander, Michelle, 12, 192; and *New Jim Crow*, 193
Alfred P. Murrah Federal Building, Oklahoma City, 201
Ali, Muhammed, 12, 224
Allen, Ethan, 86
Allen, Richard, 93
American Antislavery Society, 90
American Baptist College, 18
American Bible Society, 89
American Colonization Society, 89
American Council of Trustees and Alumni, 25
American Creed, 18, 19, 23, 24, 174, 214; and Martin Luther King Jr., 213
American Dream, 159–61
American Education Society, 89
American Federation of Labor, 176
American individualism, 232
American Peace Society, 89
American Revolution, and millennial expectation, 138–39, 172
American Supremacy (Kitchell), 174
American Temperance Society, 89
The American Way of Death (Mitford), 200
America's Original Sin: Racism, White Privilege, and the Bridge to a New America (Wallis), 120
Amish, 90
Anabaptists, 61, 90–91, 100
Anderson, Carol, 12, 16, 17, 18, 188, 192; *White Rage: The Unspoken Truth of Our Racial Divide*, 1
Anderson, William, 12, 53
Anglo-Saxon people, 20–21, 116, 173
Anne Boleyn, 33
Arbella, 40, 147
Asante, Molefi Kete, 9, 12, 18, 229–31; and *Erasing Racism: The Survival of the American Nation*, 227, 229; and the "Wilderness," 229–30
Atlanta Constitution, 182
Atlanta Exposition Address, 183
Autobiography of Malcolm X (Haley), 54

Baldwin, James, 6, 12, 55, 200, 217–19, 239, 241–42; and *The Fire Next Time*, 217; and "An Open Letter to My Sister, Miss Angela Davis," 218; and rejection of Christian religion, 97; and World War II, 209
Balmer, Randall, 118, 120
Barons of industry, 167
Baruch, Bernard, 205
Battle of Little Big Horn, 158
Baxter, Wayne, 9, 12, 241
The Beast of Berlin (Committee on Public Information), 206
Becker, Carl, 72, 79, 148, 166

Beecher, Henry Ward, 50, 168–69
Beecher, Lyman, 50, 144; and American Colonization Society, 89; and millennial expectations, 140–41
Belcher, Cornell, 12, 191
Bellah, Robert N., 23–24, 110, 114; *The Broken Covenant: American Civil Religion in Time of Trial*, 23, 103
The Benedict Option (Dreher), 102
Benjamin, Rich, 12, 191
Benton, Senator Thomas Hart (Missouri), 151
Berry, Senator James Henderson (Arkansas), 50, 174
Bethel Church, Philadelphia, 158
Between the World and Me (Coates), 227
Beveridge, Senator (Indiana), 50–51, 72–73, 146, 174, 205
Biblical criticism, 111
Big Foot, 155
Billings, David, 45, 48, 78; *Deep Denial: The Persistence of White Supremacy in United States History and Life*, 4; and experience of white supremacy, 4
Bill of Rights, 68
black codes, 15–16
Black Elk, 156
Black Hawk, Chief, 152–53, 156
Black Hawk War, 152–53, 156
Black Lives Matter, 226, 227, 233
Blackmon, Douglas A., 189
Black Muslim movement, 54, 220
black nationalism, 221
Black Panther Party, 219
Black Wall Street, 16
Bland, Sandra, 226
Blow, Charles, 12, 107
The Bluest Eye (Morrison), 5–6
Bonilla-Silva, Eduardo, 233
Booker, Senator Cory (New Jersey), 12, 119
Boyer, Ernest L., 240
Boyle, Robert, 11
Bradford, William, 42
Branham, Robert, 180
The Broken Covenant: American Civil Religion in Time of Trial (Bellah), 23, 103
Brown, Dee, 156
Brown, D. P., 12, 158–59, 184
Brown, H. Rap, 222
Brown, Michael, 106, 226
Brown, William Wells, 7–8, 12
Brownson, Orestes, 176
Brown University, 211

Brown v. Board of Education (1954), 18, 102, 192
Bryan, William Jennings, 112
Bucer, Martin, 36
Buechner, Frederick, 73, 234
Bullinger, Heinrich, 36
Bush, George Herbert Walker, 141
Bush, George W., and "axis of evil," 225; and "State of the Union Address," 2002, 225

Calvin, John, 84
Calvinism, and cultural dominance, 83–84
Cane Ridge Revival (Kentucky), 87
Carleton, General James, 155
Carmichael, Stokely, 222
Carnegie, Andrew, 167, and "Wealth," 170–72, 181, 182
Carnegie Steel strike, 177
Carr, Raymond, 2
Carrie A. Tuggle Elementary School, Birmingham, Alabama, 216
Carson-Newman College, 188
Catherine of Aragon, 33
Central Intelligence Agency, 192
Central Labor Union, 176, 180
Charles I, 39
Cheney, Lynne, 25
Cherokee Nation, and Manifest Destiny, 153–55
Cherokee Phoenix, 153
Christensen, Linda, 16
Christian Coalition, 115
Christianity and the Social Crisis (Rauschenbusch), 178
Christianity as Old as the Creation; or, the Gospel a Republication of the Religion of Nature (Tindal), 64
Christianity Not Mysterious (Toland), 64
Churches of Christ, 107–8, 202–3, 229
Civil Rights Act of 1964, 119
Civil War, 24, 49, 104, 110–11, 122, 165, 166–67, 232
Cleaver, Eldridge, 13, 219–20; and Black Panther Party, 218; and *Soul on Ice*, 219
Clergy and Laity Concerned, 224
Coates, Ta-Nehisi, 13, 46, 227–29; and American Dream, 160–61; and *Between the World and Me*, 227; and Myth of Nature's Nation, 77–78; and police killings of blacks, 105–6; and rejection of Christian religion, 55, 97–98
Collins, Addie Mae, 216

color line (W. E. B. Du Bois), 240
Committee on Public Information, 206
Communism, 210–11, 216–17
Communist Manifesto, 216
Communist Party, 216
Conant, Charles, 166, 175
Cone, James, 13, 21, 77, 112–13, 122; and critique of white Christianity, 98–100; *The Cross and the Lynching Tree*, 2, 98; and description of lynching, 98–99
Congress of Racial Equality, 213
Connor, Sheriff Eugene "Bull," 214
Constantine, Roman Emperor, 61
Constitution of United States, Article I, Section 2, 103; Article I, Section 9, 104; Article IV, Section 2, 48; and creation of secular state, 83; Fifteenth Amendment to, 20; First Amendment to, 68–69, 83, 109; and slavery, 103–4
Conwell, Russell: "Acres of Diamonds," 168
Cooper, Anna J., 13; and critique of white Christianity, 94–95
Cotton, John, 41, 43
The Courage to Be (Tillich), 121
Coy, Ed, lynching victim, 99
Cranmer, Thomas, 33, 36
Creel, George, 206
The Cross and the Lynching Tree (Cone), 2, 98
Cuba, 50, 174
Cushing, John, 48
Custer, Colonel George A., 158

Darrow, Clarence, 112
Darwin, Charles, 111, 173; and *Origin of Species*, 170
Davis, Angela, 13, 215–17, 218
Declaration of Independence, 13, 18, 20, 21, 83; shaped by Deism, 67–68
Declaration of the Rights of Man, 87
Deep Denial: The Persistence of White Supremacy in United States History and Life (Billings), 4
Deism, 63; and America's Founders, 64; and Benjamin Franklin, 66; and Christianity, 83; and Declaration of Independence, 67–68; and Thomas Jefferson, 64–65
Democratic Review, 143, 152
De Veritate (Herbert of Cherbury), 62
DeVos, Betsy, 119
Dexter Avenue Baptist Church, 212, 224
De Zurara, Gomes, 11
Disciples/Churches of Christ, 107–8, 202–3

domino theory, 223
double-consciousness, 6
Douglas, Kelly Brown, 13; and myth of Anglo-Saxon exceptionalism, 20–21; *Stand Your Ground: Black Bodies and the Justice of God*, 30n53
Douglas, Stephen A., 20
Douglass, Frederick, 13, 75, 122, 157, 181; rejection of American Christianity, 22, 93–94; rejection of patriotism, 8; and sharecropping, 190; and *Why Is the Negro Lynched?*, 26
Dreher, Rod: *The Benedict Option*, 102
Du Bois, W. E. B., 6, 13, 15, 180, 240; and American Communist Party, 183; and Booker T. Washington, 183; and capitalist South, 182; and role of blacks in American life, 12
Duke, David, 117
Dwight, Timothy, 87–88
Dyson, Michael Eric, 13, 21, 46, 187–88; 232–33; and *Tears We Cannot Stop: A Sermon to White America*, 227

Edict of Milan, 61
Edwards, Jonathan, and millennial predictions, 136–37
Edward VI, 36
Eisenhower, President Dwight D., 211, 223; and "domino theory," 223
Eliade, Mircea, 121
Elizabeth I, 38–39
Emancipation Proclamation, 15
The End of White Christian America (Jones), 100
Engel v. Vitale (1962), 114
Enlightenment: as backdrop for postmillennial thinking, 133; as backdrop to Myth of Nature's Nation, 61–64
Episcopal Church, 101
Erasing Racism: The Survival of the American Nation (Asante), 227, 229
Ernest L. Boyer Center, Messiah College, 240
Espionage Act of 1917, 207
Evangelicalism: and complicity in racism, 99; and cultural dominance, 101; and decline of, 121; and restoration of golden age, 114–16; and silence on Civil Rights Movement, 104–5; and support for Donald J. Trump, 102, 118, 120
Evers, Medgar, 95

Falwell, Jerry, 102; and birth of Moral Majority, 115; and "Ministers and Marchers" sermon, 105
Farmer, James, 213
Federal Bureau of Investigation, 107, 218
Federal Housing Administration, 191
Ferguson, Missouri, 226
Fifteenth Amendment. *See* Constitution of United States, Fifteenth Amendment to
Finney, Charles, 88
First Amendment. *See* Constitution of United States, First Amendment to
First Indochina War, 223
Folsom Prison, California, 219
Foner, Eric, 2
Foner, Philip, 180
Ford, Henry, 200
Forman, James, 215
Fortune, Thomas, 13, 180–81
founding of America, as restoration, 109–10
Franklin, Benjamin, and opinion of blacks, 75; and seal for United States, 47
freedom riders, 119, 213, 227
freedom summers, 227
Freeman (Fortune), 181
Frelinghuysen, Theodore, 135
French and Indian War, 137, 171
French Revolution, 86–87
Freud, Sigmund, 111
Fulwood, Sam, 13, 222
Fundamentalism, 199; birth of, 112; and restoration of golden age, 114–16

Gabriel (enslaved man), 52
Gandhi, Mahatma, 214
Gardner, Eric, 226
Garrison, William Lloyd, 24
George, David Lloyd, 205
German War Practices (Committee on Public Information), 206
Ghost Dance, 155
Gibbons, James Cardinal, 178
Gilded Age, 111, 167, 183, 184, 187, 189
Giuliana, Rudy, 227
Gladden, Washington, 178
Globe (Fortune), 181
Gospel of Wealth, 111, 167–70, 181, 182, 183, 184, 193
Grady, Henry, and *Atlanta Constitution*, 182
Graham, Billy, and Communist threat, 210–11
Gray, Fred, 13, 192

Gray, Freddie, 226
Great American Myths, 18, 19, 20, 23; absolutized, 1, 113, 116
Great Awakening, 135–37, 171
Great Depression, 17, 185, 191, 198
Great Recession, 17
Great Seal of the United States, 138–39, 144, 199
Greeley, Horace, 151
Green, Steven K., 110–11
Greenwood, Oklahoma, 16
Gregory, D. S., 166
Ground Zero, 228

Haley, Alex: *Autobiography of Malcolm X*, 54
Hamite myth, 44, 97; rejection of by William Anderson, 53
Harris, Forrest E., Jr., 13, 18
Harrison, William Henry, 151
Haymarket Square, 176, 177, 180
Hebrew Bible, as backdrop for Myth of the Chosen Nation, 32
Henry VIII, 33, 34
Herbert of Cherbury, 62–62; and book of nature, 62; *De Veritate* (1624), 62
history, American rejection of, 200
History of the American People (Wilson), 14
The History of White People (Painter), 45
Ho Chi Minh, 223
Hollinger, David, 100
Homestead Act of 1862, 190
Hooker, Thomas, 40
Howard, John R., 202
Howard University, 227
Hughes, Langston, 13; and "Let America Be America Again," 185–86
Huntington, Henry, 167
Hurley, Edward N., 205
Hutterites, 90

incarceration of people of color, 192–93, 201
Indian Removal Act of 1830, 152, 155
individualism, 232
Industrial Workers of the World, 177, 180
In His Steps (Sheldon), 179
Interstate Commerce Commission, 213

Jackson, President Andrew, and Native Americans, 151–55
Jacobson, Matthew Frye, 13
James I, 39
Jefferson Bible, 65

Jefferson, Thomas, 11; and blacks, 21, 48, 74–75; and Deism, 64–66, 85; and election of 1800, 85; and Israel as model for American nation, 48; and Native Americans, 150; and *Notes on the State of Virginia*, 21; and seal for United States, 47; and "self-evident truths," 70; as slave owner, 13
Jim Crow, 116, 174, 192, 207–8; and new Jim Crow, 192–93
Johnson, Andrew, and a "country for white men," 14
Johnson, President Lyndon, 119, 223
Johnson, Robert, 165
Johnson, Senator H. V. (Georgia), 145
Jones, Prince Carmen, 78, 227
Jones, Robert: *The End of White Christian America*, 100, 104, 118
Jordan, Winthrop, 49

Kaepernick, Kevin, 233
Kendi, Ibram X., 13; *Stamped from the Beginning: The Definitive History of Racist Ideas in America*, 11
Kennedy, President John F., 119
Kennedy, Robert, 119
Keteltas, Abraham, 47–48
King, Coretta Scott, 13, 119
King, Martin Luther, Jr., 13, 104, 116, 192, 212–13; and American Dream, 160; and Christian heritage, 214; and critique of white Christianity, 95–96; and identification with Moses and Promised Land, 53; and "I Have a Dream" speech, 213; and Mahatma Gandhi, 214; and Malcolm X, 221; and Vietnam War, 224–25
King, Miles, and letter from Thomas Jefferson, 65
Kitchell, J. G., and *American Supremacy*, 174
Knights of Labor, 178
Ku Klux Klan, 117

Land Ordinance Act of 1785, 190
Langston, John Mercer, 7, 13
Latter-day Saints (Mormons), 107–8, 202–3
law of competition, 171, 177
Lawrence, William, 166, 168, 173, 182
"Let America Be America Again" (Hughes), 185–86
Leyden pilgrims, 41
Limbaugh, Rush, 16
Lincoln, Abraham, and Declaration of Independence, 20; and Dred Scott Decision, 14; and slavery, 14
Linenthal, Edward T., 201
Locke, Hubert, 11, 13
Locke, John: *Second Treatise on Government*, 138
Luther, Martin, 33
Lynchburg Christian Academy, 102
lynching of blacks, 98–100, 184–85

Madison, James, and Bill of Rights, 69; and "Memorial and Remonstrance (1785), 69
mainline Protestantism, cultural dominance of, 100; and loss of cultural dominance, 101
Malcolm X, 13, 220–22; attempting to be white, 5; and Martin Luther King Jr., 221; and Mr. Ostrowski, 187; and national white subconsciousness, 233; and rejection of Christian religion, 96; and rejection of patriotism, 8–9; and Yacub's History, 54
Manifest Destiny, and the Chosen Nation, 146–47; and the Millennial Nation, 144–46; and Native Americans, 148ff; and Nature's Nation, 148–51
Mansfield, Stephen, 115
March in Birmingham, 1963, 214
March on Washington, 1963, 213
Marian Exiles, 37
Marin County, California jail, 217
Marshall, Chief Justice John, 154
Martin, Trayvon, 21, 56, 226
Mary Tudor, 36–37
Mason, Reverend John M., 85
Massachusetts Bay Colony (1630), 39, 56
Mather, Cotton, 11, 41, 44
McCormick Harvester Works, 176, 177
McKinley, President William, 145, 146
McLoughlin, William G., 82, 211
McNair, Denise, 216
Mead, Sidney E., 168
Meeks, Catherine, 6, 13
Melville, Herman: *White Jacket* (1850), 49
Memphis Free Speech, 99, 184
Mencken, H. L., 112
Mennonites, 90
Meredith, James, 119
Messiah College, 129n84, 240
Mexican War, 145
Militia Acts, First and Second (1792), 49
millennial interpretations: premillennialism, 132–33; postmillennialism, 133

millennium, and American Revolution, 138–41; and French and Indian War, 137; and Great Awakening, 136–37; and Revelation 20:1–3, 131–32
Miller, Kathy, 187
Miller, William, 211
Mitford, Jessica, and *The American Way of Death*, 200
Montgomery Bus Boycott, 104, 113, 192, 212, 213
Moody, Anne, 13; and critique of white Christianity, 95
Mooney, James, 154
Moore, Reverend Clement Clarke, 85
Moore, Russell, 120
Moral Majority, 115, 123
Moral Man and Immoral Society (Niebuhr), 214
Morgan, J. Pierpont, 167
Morgan v. Virginia (1946), 213
Morrison, Toni, 13, 105, 209; *The Bluest Eye*, 5–6; *Song of Solomon*, 77
Mundus Novus (Vespucci), 148
myth, meaning of, 10–11

Nashville Republican, 150
National Association of Evangelicals, 101
National Housing Act of 1934, 191
Nation of Islam, 54, 220
Native Americans, and Andrew Jackson, 151–55; and critique of Manifest Destiny, 156–57; and doctrine of Manifest Destiny, 148–51; and effects of Manifest Destiny, 151–56
Naturalization Act (1790), 48
New Deal, 191
The New Jim Crow (Alexander), 192–94
New South, 182
Newsweek, 218
The New World Order (Robertson), 115
New York Age (Fortune), 181
The New York Morning News, 143, 151, 152
Nicaragua, 192
Niebuhr, H. Richard, 51
Niebuhr, Reinhold, 27; and *Moral Man and Immoral Society*, 214
nineteen-sixties, 104, 113–17, 198, 211–12
Ninety-Five Theses, 33
Noel, James, 2–3, 10, 13
North American Review, 170
North Korea, 239
Notes on the State of Virginia (Jefferson), 21;

and David Walker, 73–77; and Reverend Clement Clarke Moore, 85; and Reverend John M. Mason, 85
Novak, Michael, 64, 68, 83

Obama, Barack Hussein, 3, 233; and America's fourth time of trial, 106; and Donald Trump, 17; as symbol for cultural change, 117; and vilification of, 16–17, 21, 106
Obergefell v. Hodges (2015), 102
"Open Letter to My Sister, Miss Angela Davis" (Baldwin), 218
O'Sullivan, John L., 143–44, 146–47, 151, 152, 153, 173
Our Country (Strong), 172–73

Paine, Thomas, 70, 86
Painter, Nell Irvin, 13; *The History of White People*, 45
Palmer, Benjamin, 50
Palmer, Elihu, 86
Parks, Rosa, 192, 212
Parsons, Albert, 176, 180
Parsons, Lucy, 13, 180
Pearl Harbor, 208
Philippines, 50, 174
Pierce, Yolanda, 13, 121–22
Platt, Senator Orville (CT), 50
Plessy v. Ferguson (1896), 184
Plymouth Plantation (1620), 39, 42
police killings of blacks, 105–6, 226, 232
Powderly, Terrence, 178
Pratt, Parley, and *A Voice of Warning*, 202–3
Princeton University, 207
prisons, function of, 192–93, 201
private property, sacredness of, 171, 177–78
Pullman Palace Car Company strike, 177
Puritan Revolution, 62
Puritans, 47; birth of, 37; and idea of chosenness, 146–47; ideological revolution of, 38; migration to America, motivation for, 39–40; and Reforming Synod of 1679, 133–34; and religious decline in New England, 133–35

Quinney, John, 157

Randolph, A. Philip, 213
Rauschenbusch, Walter, 178–79; and *Christianity and the Social Crisis*, 178; and *A Theology for the Social Gospel*, 178
Reagan, Governor Ronald, 216–17

Reagan, President Ronald, 192, 200
Reconstruction, 15, 189, 192
redlining, 191
Reformed Christianity, and founding period of Christian faith, 71
Remond, Charles Lenox, 7–8, 13
Republican Party, 16–17
residential security maps, 191
restoration vision, 107–8
Rice, Tamir, 226
Riverside Church, New York City, 224–25
Robertson, Carole, 216
Robertson, Pat, 115; *The New World Order*, 115
Robeson, Paul, 207–8
Robinson, John, 41
Robinson, Randall, 49
Rockefeller, John D., 167, 182
Rocky IV as reflection of "Nature's Nation," 70–71
Roe v. Wade (1973), 114
Roosevelt, President Franklin, 191; and World War II, 208–9
Rosenberg, Emily, 175–76

San Quentin Prison, 217
Scopes, John, 112
Scopes "Monkey Trial," 112
Scott, General Winfield, 154
Scott, Walter, 226
Second Great Awakening, 86–90, 104; and abolition of slavery, 89, 90; and Calvinist social order, 85; and Cane Ridge Revival, 87; and Charles G. Finney, 88–90; and Christianizing the American nation, 90; and Deism, 85; and Harriet Beecher Stowe, 89; and humanitarian crusade, 88–90; and Timothy Dwight, 87–88
Second Treatise on Government (Locke), 138
Sedition Act of 1918, 207
segregationist academies, 116
Selma (Alabama) march, 192
Separatists (Puritans), 38
September 11, 2001, 25, 200, 201, 225–27, 229
Sessions, Senator Jefferson Beauregard (Alabama), 119
Shaffer, Peter, *Equus*, 10
Shakespeare, William, 11
sharecropping, 189–90
Sheldon, Charles, and *In His Steps*, 179
Sixteenth Street Baptist Church, Birmingham, Alabama, 216

Slouka, Mark, 201
Smith, Arthur Lee (Molefi Kete Asante), 230
Smith, Henry, lynching victim, 99
Smith, James, and letter from Thomas Jefferson, 68
Social Darwinism, 170–72
Social Gospel, 178–79
Social Security Act of 1935, 191
Sojourners magazine, 120
Song of Solomon (Morrison), 77
Soul on Ice (Cleaver), 219
Spanish-American War, 50, 174
Sparks, Jared, and letter from Thomas Jefferson, 65
Speckled Snake, 152
Spencer, Herbert, 170, 173
Spies, August, 176
spirituals, 53
Stamped from the Beginning: The Definitive History of Racist Ideas in America (Kendi), 11
Stand Your Ground: Black Bodies and the Justice of God (Douglas), 30n53
Stanford, Leland, 167
Stanley, Sara G., 7, 13
Stannard, David E., 152, 154
Stevens, Uriah, 178
Stewart, Maria W., 13, 52
St. George's Methodist Episcopal Church, Philadelphia, 92
Stiles, Ezra, 139
Stowe, Harriet Beecher: *Uncle Tom's Cabin*, 50, 89
Street, Nicholas, 48
Strong, Josiah, 145, and *Our Country*, 172–73
Supreme Court of United States: *Brown v. Board of Education* (1954), 17–18, 192; *Engel v. Vitale* (1962), 114; *Morgan v. Virginia* (1946), 213; *Obergefell v. Hodges* (2015), 102; *Plessy v. Ferguson* (1896), 184; *Roe v. Wade* (1973), 114; *United States v. Macintosh* (1931), 90; Voting Rights Act of 1965, 119
survival of the fittest, 171
Sutherland, Justice George, 90
systemic racism, 187, 189–91

Taney, Roger B., and Dred Scott Decision, 13, 14
Tanner, B. T., 13, 158
Tears We Cannot Stop: A Sermon to White America (Dyson), 227

Temple University, 229

Tennent, Gilbert, 135

Theodosius, Roman Emperor, 61

A Theology for the Social Gospel (Rauschenbusch), 178

Thirty Years War, 62, 63

Till, Emmett, 104, 113, 116

Tillich, Paul: *The Courage to Be*, 121

Tindal, Mathew: *Christianity as Old as the Creation; or, the Gospel a Republication of the Religion of Nature* (1730), 64

Toland, John: *Christianity Not Mysterious* (1696), 64

Trail of Tears, 154

Trimble, Representative (Kentucky), 150

Truman, President Harry, 223

Trump, Donald J., 117–20, 187; and America's fourth time of trial, 106; and election of, 17; and evangelical support for, 102; and Federal Bureau of Investigation, 107; and Muslim ban, 107, 120; and support for Evangelicals, 117–18; and white supremacy, 118–19, 120

Tubman, Harriet, 52

Turner, Mary, 230

Turner, Nat, 52

Tuskegee Institute, 182

Tyndale, William, 33–36, 210; as biblical translator, 34–35; covenant theology of, 35, 40

Uncle Tom's Cabin (Stowe), 50

Underground Railroad, 52, 53

Unitarian Church, 63; and Jefferson's expectations for America, 68

United Nations Human Rights Committee, 193

United States Shipping Board, 205

United States v. Macintosh, 1931, 90

University of California at Los Angeles, 217, 229

University of Mississippi, 119

vagrancy, charge of, 189

Vanderbilt, Cornelius, 167

Vesey, Denmark, 52

Vespucci, Amerigo: *Mundus Novus*, 148

Vietnam War, 113, 212, 222–25; and Martin Luther King Jr., 224–25

A Voice of Warning (Pratt), 202–3

voter suppression, 20

Voting Rights Act of 1965, 20, 119

Walker, David, 13, 73–77; and attack on Thomas Jefferson, 73–77; murder of, 77; and *Walker's Appeal . . . to the Colored Citizens of the World* (1829), 73; and white Christianity, 93

Walker, Lesley, 5

Walker's Appeal . . . to the Colored Citizens of the World (Walker), 73

Wallis, Jim: *America's Original Sin: Racism, White Privilege, and the Bridge to a New America*, 120

War Industries Board, 205

War on Drugs, 116, 192

War on Terror, 226

Washington, Booker T., 13; and "Atlanta Exposition Address," 183; and northern capitalism, 182; and role of blacks in American life, 12; and Tuskegee Institute, 182

Washington, George, 47; "Farewell Address," 120; slave owner, 13

Waterhouse, Benjamin, and letter from Thomas Jefferson, 64

"Wealth" (Carnegie), 170

Wells, Ida B., 13; and description of lynching, 99; and *Memphis Free Speech*, 99, 184

Wesley, Cynthia, 216

West, Cornel, 13, 240, 241

Westerhoff, John H., III, 10–11, 24

White, Jack, 177–78

Whitefield, George, 135–36

White Jacket (Melville), 49

white privilege, 189, 191

White Rage: The Unspoken Truth of Our Racial Divide (Anderson), 1

Whitfield, James M., 7, 13

Whitman, Albery A., 13

Why Is the Negro Lynched? (Douglass), 26

Wigglesworth, Michael, and "God's Controversy with New England," 42–43

wilderness, people of the, 9

Willard, Samuel, 44

Wilmore, Gayraud, 13, 184

Wilson, Woodrow, and "Birth of a Nation," 15; and *History of the American People*, 14; and Ku Klux Klan, 15; and racism of, 14–15, 207; and re-segregating federal civil service, 15; and World War I, 204–5, 207

Winthrop, John, 40–41, 51, 52, 56, 147

Wise, Rabbi Isaac Mayer, 47

Wise, Tim, 234

Wobblies, 177, 180

Woodard, Isaac, 209–10
World War I, 198, 204–8
World War II, 198, 208–10
Wounded Knee, South Dakota, 155–56
Wovoka, 155
Wright, Jeremiah, 13, 189
Wright, Lawrence, 198, 199, 212, 214, 233

Wright, Richard, 9, 77; and fear of racial
    holocaust, 159–60, 161, 239; and rejection
    of Christian religion, 55, 96

Yacub's History, 54

Zinn, Howard, 152

Richard T. Hughes is Distinguished Professor
Emeritus at both Pepperdine University and Messiah
College. He is the author, coauthor, or editor of more
than a dozen books including *Illusions of Innocence:
Protestant Primitivism in America, 1630–1875* and
Christian America and the Kingdom of God.

The University of Illinois Press
is a founding member of the
Association of American University Presses.

University of Illinois Press
1325 South Oak Street
Champaign, IL 61820-6903
www.press.uillinois.edu